Teaching Food Technology in Secondary Schools

David Fulton Publishers
London

Published in association with the Roehampton Institute London

David Fulton Publishers Ltd
The Chiswick Centre, 414 Chiswick High Road, London W4 5TF
www.fultonpublishers.co.uk

First published in Great Britain in 1997 by David Fulton Publishers

Note: The right of Marion Rutland to be identified as the author of this work
has been asserted by her in accordance with the Copyright, Designs and Patents
Act 1988.

David Fulton Publishers is a division of Granada Learning Limited, part of
Granada plc.

Copyright © Marion Rutland

British Library Cataloguing in Publication Data
A catalogue record for this book is available from the British Library.

ISBN 1-85346-426-0

Typeset by FSH Ltd, London
Printed and bound in Great Britain

Contents

Section 5 Food Technology and IT

Preface

This book focuses on the teaching of food technology in secondary schools. It aims to provide students, lecturers and teachers with an understanding of the context within which changes to the teaching of food curriculum are required, to evaluate recent developments and to give guidance for future practice.

The book originated in research carried out into the historical background of the teaching of food in secondary schools in England and Wales and a conference run at Roehampton Institute London for teachers of food technology, following the publication of the revised Orders for National Curriculum Design and Technology (D&T) in 1995. Many of the contributors in the book were speakers at the conference and agreed, alongside very busy work commitments, to contribute to the book. We were very pleased that day to see such a large audience, which is a recognition of the commitment of food teachers, and we were very fortunate to have Flo Hadley, HMI and long-term supporter for the teaching of food, as a speaker to help us make sense of the new Orders. I saw writing the book as an opportunity to draw together and present a process of thoughts and ideas that has spanned my teaching career in schools and my role in teacher education.

The teaching of food is fascinating and demanding, and it is a subject that children relate to and thoroughly enjoy in the classroom. If I did not truly believe this, I would not still be so involved. It is a subject we all know something about and, as a result, many people have very strong, personal views which they are not slow to express! Over the years, because the teaching of food is so closely linked to human needs and society's changing life style, it has seen many changes. The ability to change can be seen to be a strength, but it can also be a weakness in that we have lacked the stability and assurance of the more traditional subjects of the curriculum.

Recent developments have been quite traumatic. As I go around schools, I have been very concerned with the low morale and confused feelings of some food teachers. This book is my attempt:

- to stand back and put the present situation into perspective
- to look back and trace the roots of the subject up to the present day, as I believe the past can help us understand the present
- to look at the situation today in schools with the National Curriculum
- to provide some guidelines for the future.

Section 1 provides an overview of the historical development of the teaching of food in schools. It specifically identifies concerns related to gender, status, and an association with less able pupils – issues that have affected the subject in the past and need to be understood for us to make the necessary changes and move forward. The book explores the introduction of National Curriculum Design and Technology, the confusion that followed, and the proposed swing in emphasis away from the teaching of food in the traditional context of the home, towards developing food products and commercial food technology within Design and Technology.

Section 2 moves to the classroom and looks at the place of food technology within D&T by examining the philosophy underpinning the teaching of the curriculum area. Issues related to curriculum planning are explored and illustrated by first-hand examples of curriculum planning and cases studies from classroom practice.

Section 3 examines the range of new teaching materials, including the Nuffield Design and Technology Project, the RCA Technology Project and the Science with Technology Project, that are being written and published to support the teaching of food technology.

Section 4 considers practices in food product development through the eyes of industry, and includes an example of a school-based vocational GNVQ course in Manufacturing. The Nuffield Design and Technology and RCA Technology materials are examined to see how they support and provide guidance for teachers and pupils following the new GCSE D&T course with their increased emphasis on the need for knowledge and understanding of industrial practices.

Section 5 looks at the present and also looks into the future. The use of IT in teaching food technology has considerable potential which, it is acknowledged, is not yet fully developed. Realistic opportunities for the use of IT in food technology are suggested and advice given for its development in our teaching, with glimpses of what we could do in the future.

The book is aimed at students and lecturers involved in initial training courses in D&T, including undergraduate and postgraduate secondary courses for food technology specialists and D&T students with other subject specialisms. Food specialists, with the knowledge and skills related to food technology, will gain an understanding of its application to teaching and learning in the classroom. Other D&T students will gain an overview and understanding of the background and concept of food technology and a basic understanding of how it can be taught in the classroom. The book is intended to support teachers in schools and those attending INSET who wish to gain an understanding of the recent developments in the teaching of food technology.

Marion Rutland
Roehampton Institute London
January 1997

Contributors

Sheena Archer
Sheena Archer attended Leicester College in the early 1960s before taking a teaching post in Essex. She has taught the full age range from infants to adults in a variety of educational establishments, before her present position as Head of Food and Textiles at Calthorpe Park School, Fleet, Hampshire. During this time she gained an Open University Degree in educational studies. Sheena has experience of writing food and textile CSE and GCSE examination syllabuses and published the teaching resource 'Orders into Practice' for the Hampshire Inspection Advisory Support Service. Sheena remains a fully involved classroom teacher and participates in in-service courses for teachers.

Anne Constable
Anne Constable is a Teacher Fellow of the Royal College of Art School Technology Project and currently teaching at Beauchamp College, Leicestershire.

Roy Ballam
Roy Ballam completed a honours degree in home economics and resource management with a concurrent Certificate in Education and became a teacher in the charge of food technology at Kemnal Technology College in Bromley. His present position is Education Liaison Officer for the British Nutrition Foundation. Roy has been involved extensively with curriculum development projects and has published a number of articles on the use of information technology in food technology.

Louise Davies
Louise Davies started her career as a teacher for home economics in London schools, rising to head of department and then senior teacher in charge of the Key Stage 3 curriculum. She has an MA in social policy and is currently following an EdD at London University. Before her present post as Deputy Project Director for the Royal College of Art School Technology Project, Louise was a senior lecturer at South Bank University and co-authored a range of books in food and textiles.

Judy Hallet
Judy Hallet is currently head of design and technology at Berkhamstead Collegiate School with a specialism in food. She has worked closely with the Nuffield Design and Technology Project, has been involved in trialing Key Stage 3 materials and contributing as a writer to the Key Stage 4 materials. As a Nuffield Field Officer, Judith has kept abreast of changes and developments in design and technology, meeting the demands of the National Curriculum and ensuring a creative approach to the subject by using the Nuffield approach for her own and her department's classroom activities.

Brenda Jamieson

Brenda Jamieson, a home economist by profession and a Fellow of the Institute of Home Economics, has spent her professional life working in the food industry in a variety of senior positions, initially in manufacturing and subsequently in marketing. Currently she is The Food Centre Manger for J. Sainbury plc, managing a team responsible for the innovation and quality of own brand products. Brenda holds an MPhil, has been involved in diverse research and evaluation, is the author of several published papers and has a range of experience in education–industry partnerships.

Jenny Jupe

Jenny Jupe is currently Head of Technology and INSET Co-ordinator at Selly Park Technology College, an 11–16, LEA maintained comprehensive school in Birmingham. She has worked in food education for 18 years as a teacher, head of department and advisory teacher, the latter being combined with information technology. Jenny is actively involved with national schemes to raise standards in design and technology, most notably the Technology Enhancement Programme (TEP), the Royal College of Arts Technology Project (RCASTP) and Nuffield Design and Technology.

Jenny has taken an active role in national design and technology exhibitions. Her work and school featured in HMI publications on good practice in design and technology and food technology. A recent project aims to develop teaching materials based on industrial pilot plant food technology equipment.

Pat Moore

Pat Moore has taught at Bodmin Community College in Cornwall for many years and her present role is Director of Assessment and Vocational Studies. General National Vocational Qualifications (GNVQ) is now established in five subject areas at the college and involves more than twenty staff. Currently Pat is preparing case studies of good practice for Cornwall Education Business Partnership and she is a member of the Manufacturing Advisory Committee the National Council for Vocational Education (NCVQ). Pat is engaged in research focusing on GNVQ Manufacturing and the influence of students and employers on the education for students aged 16–19.

Mary Moran

Mary Moran is a Teacher Fellow of the Royal College of Art School Technology Project and currently teaching at Kingsway School, Cheshire.

Barbara Mottershead

Barbara Mottershead is a Teacher Fellow of the Royal College of Art School Technology Project and currently teaching at Shevington High School, Wigan.

David Perry

David Perry is a former teacher and head of a design faculty in Leicestershire and senior lecturer at King's College Winchester. David was involved in a range of research in the curriculum area of design and technology, before taking his present position as Project Director for the Royal College of Art Schools Technology Project.

Marion Rutland

Marion Rutland attended Leicester College in the late 1950s and early 1960s. She has over 25 years' school and advisory experience as teacher and head of department in Stoke-on-Trent, Manchester, Leicester, Sydney Australia, Surrey and ILEA. This was followed by a period as an advisory teacher for information technology in ILEA and Wandsworth and training as an Ofsted inspector. Marion is a Senior Vice President of the National Association of Teachers of Home Economics and Technology (NATHE) and a member of the Design and Technology Association (DATA) initial teacher education (ITE) group. Her principal areas of research interests include food technology, ITE and curriculum development.

Currently she is Senior Lecturer in Education (Technology) at Roehampton Institute London, Co-ordinator of Design and Technology and Tutor for the PGCE Secondary Design and Technology. She also teaches on masters and professional development programme.

Jim Sage

Jim Sage taught science and technology in secondary schools for 18 years, the last 8 as head of a science and technology faculty in a large comprehensive school, before working on curriculum and professional development with the County of Avon. During this time Jim Sage was involved in a range of local and national projects such as the Secondary Science Curriculum Review and TVEI. He then became the director of the joint ASE/DATA Science with Technology Project which published a wide range of curriculum materials developing strategies for linking work in these two key subject areas.

Currently he is Assistant Director of the Royal College of Art Schools Technology Project as well as carrying out advisory work in science for Shropshire LEA, co-ordinating the Science Bursary Scheme for the Nuffield Foundation and working as a freelance writer and educational consultant. Jim Sage has written extensively in the fields of science and technology education.

Christine Thompson

Christine Thompson has over 25 years' teaching experience in a variety of schools including secondary modern, primary and comprehensive, for pupils ranging from 5 to 18. She taught for 8 years in primary school before being appointed head of department in a large comprehensive, where she remained for 11 years. She has educational experience as a teacher adviser before holding her current post as Inspector for Design and Technology for Hampshire with a county responsibility for food and textiles and an Ofsted team inspector.

Section 1

Food in the School Curriculum

Chapter 1 traces the development of the teaching of food in the school curriculum from its original aims in the eighteenth century to raise basic living standards and train for future employment, up to the introduction of the National Curriculum in 1990. Factors which have influenced the study of food in schools are examined, including changing attitudes and values in society regarding gender, the status of food, an association with the teaching of the less able and the use of traditional teaching styles.

Chapter 2 examines the effects of the introduction of the Orders *Technology in the National Curriculum* (DES, 1990), with specific reference to the implications for the study of food within home economics. The document *Technology for Ages 5 to 16 (1992)* (DfE, 1992) is examined with special reference to the requirement for a change of emphasis from domestic to commercial production and the implications of this for the teaching of food. References are noted to the teaching of food in further documents including those published by the National Curriculum Council (NCC) in 1993, the Dearing Interim and Final Report (1993) and the School Curriculum and Assessment Authority (SCAA) in 1994. The chapter concludes with a dissemination of the revised Orders for *Design and Technology* (DfE, 1995a) and considers the implications of these changes for the teaching of food in secondary schools.

Chapter 1

An Historical Perspective

Marion Rutland

The introduction of food into the school curriculum

The British Museum contains a record of a cookery school in London dated 1740, indicating that the study of food was originally available for ladies with private means from the upper classes. A number of eighteenth century educational writers referred to the importance of girls or young ladies from wealthy families learning how to cook (Yoxall, 1965), and throughout the nineteenth century specialist high class private cookery schools provided for the upper classes. These developments were given added impetus by the very successful Great Exhibition of 1851, which was followed by smaller international exhibitions in later decades. Considerable public interest was aroused by the introduction of cookery lectures into these exhibitions in the 1870s (Gibbs-Smith, 1981). In 1873 Sir Henry Cole, a member of the Commission responsible for organising the exhibitions that year, decided to include the subject of food and he appointed Buckmaster, a well-known lecturer on technical subjects, as lecturer-demonstrator (Stone, 1976).

However, the origins of food in the school curriculum were more philanthropic or utilitarian and linked to providing training for low paid employment. The origins can be traced directly to the elementary state system for the lower working classes of the 1840s when domestic economy was introduced to improve basic living standards (DES, 1978). The emphasis in the elementary schools was not on high class cookery skills, but on teaching girls the skills of plain cookery which they could use to feed their families. This was considered to be necessary because of the break-up of the domestic-based system of industry and the movement of people to the overcrowded, poor living conditions of the new centres of factory industry in towns (Sillitoe, 1966). Dr James Kay-Shuttleworth, Assistant Poor Law Commissioner and Secretary of the Committee of the Privy Council on Education formed in 1839, noted the poor conditions of pauper children and introduced domestic training, including plain cooking for girls, at his school for pauper children in Norwood, London. This resulted in improved living standards for the poor, but it was also noted that the girls were more able to find employment on leaving school (Smith, 1923). Similar slum conditions were noted in Liverpool in 1874 and a need was voiced for the teaching of the preparation of wholesome food to help fight disease (Scott, 1967). Unfortunately, the Hadow Report on *The Education of the Adolescents* (Board of Education, 1926) noted the initiative had little influence on the majority of primary schools. It was suggested that this was due to economic reasons, as successful, effective practical instruction cost more than the teaching of the three R's.

Similarly, Matthew Arnold, a nineteenth century HMI, linked the welfare of people with the teaching of domestic economy, as he believed that lessons in domestic economy would help pupils develop an understanding of nutrition and the management of their resources (Arnold, 1908). Grants were first made available for the teaching of domestic economy through the National Society and the British and Foreign School Society in 1833, but few elementary schools set up courses and the grant was withdrawn in 1860. In the 1870s, the medical profession drew the government's attention to the importance of food education by linking poor diet with rickets, scurvy and chlorosis, factors that led to the inclusion of cookery in Schedule 1V of the New Code of 1875 for Specific Subjects. This was followed in 1892 by the establishment of practical cookery as a subject of instruction in the code of Regulations for Public Elementary School, along with the appropriate grant provision (Geen *et al.*, 1988).

The link between the teaching of food and health reccurred during the Boer War, where the government noted that the vast majority of the men who volunteered were physically unfit as a result, it was suggested,of incorrect or insufficient food. Though domestic subjects had been taught in schools for many years the emphasis, until the changes in the grants system in the 1880s and 1890s, had been on needlework (Brennan, 1986). It was recommended that instruction in domestic economy, including food, should be, as far as possible, compulsory for older girls at school and an HMI was appointed to carry out inspections throughout the country.

The Hadow Report (Board of Education, 1926) reiterated the theme, justifying the teaching of food in terms of its value in promoting good health and efficient management to raise basic standard living standards. The Report said the general aim should be to provide practical instruction in the choice and preparation of the food required for a simple wholesome diet. Later, in the *Handbook of Suggestions for Teachers* (Board of Education, 1937) the emphasis moved to setting high standards of home life. The study of food should be part of domestic subjects and taught to girls to make them aware of the main household duties they would be expected to do in adult life. After the Second World War the teaching of the food to girls was emphasised because it was felt that there was a need to restore the health of a nation after a period of austerity and to rebuild family life.

As has been already noted, a second reason for the original introduction of food into the elementary state school system had been to train for low paid employment, for example servants (Dyhouse, 1977). The teaching of food and textiles has a long history of links with industry, though it can be argued (Whyld, 1983) that this has been limited to preparing the working classes for menial, low paid employment. In the eighteenth century Charity Schools provided training in crafts for future employment and the 'Schools of Industry' opened 1799 in Kendal taught knitting, lace making, spinning, sewing and bakery for a this reason. An increased emphasis on vocational training in state education in the nineteenth century resulted in the creation of schools with a technical bias in the early years of the twentieth century.

As a result, the Hadow Report of 1926 gave qualified approval to the suggestion that modern schools and senior classes should give a practical bias to their curriculum, though it was emphasised that this should not prejudice general education. Geen *et al.* (1988) has argued that in the post-war era secondary modern schools offered a curriculum with a practical bias for the same reason, and it was the Newsom Report (DES, 1963) which suggested that practical subjects for girls should have a vocational slant towards catering and the food trades as a preparation for adult life. However, both these occupations were relatively low paid. Creese (1965) has described two main divisions in careers following a course in domestic science: a commercial path based on household management or catering in a large institution and another leading to teaching or advising girls how to run their own homes efficiently.

Gender

Food preparation, as with other household duties, has a long association with females, and it can be argued that this factor has had a strong influence on the way in which food has been taught in the school system. Cockburn (1991) has argued that it was females who first invented tools to select, sow, grow, reap and cook food so they could care for themselves and their young. In the Middle Ages rural women prepared food, looked after the children, prepared textiles and gardened. According to Geen *et al.* (1988), sexual division of labour is a characteristic of human society as first described by the Greek historian Xenophon (c.430–354 BC). Xenophon argued that 'God adapted women to work indoors and man to do outdoor tasks' because of man's ability to endure cold heat and military campaigns, and he concluded that 'man has courage to defend the home and women has affection to care for children'. Later in the Middle Ages St Thomas Aquinas (1225–1274) stated that the allocation of roles was based on the assumption that 'the male was the thinker and the woman the doer': women were irrational creatures and only able to do practical and procreative activities. Geen *et al.* contend that home management as the primary concern of females has survived over the centuries, and that this is why nineteenth century educational planners introduced domestic economy into elementary schools for girls and not for both sexes.

Educationalists at that time considered that boys required a different kind of education to girls, and domestic subjects for girls and technical instruction or craft design technology (CDT) for boys both owe their introduction into the school curriculum to that philosophy. It was thought that girls should be taught how to feed and look after their families and boys how to earn their living outside the home. Geen *et al.* (1988) have argued that a common belief was that certain forms of knowledge were appropriate for the education of each of the sexes. Domestic subjects were considered essential to prepare girls to be wives and mothers; and, as Eggleston (1989) has described, 1885 saw the beginning of technical instruction or manual training in the playground shed of a Paddington School to prepare boys for the world of work outside the home. The introduction of technical instruction for boys into the school curriculum resulted from the Royal Commission on Technical Instruction, which highlighted the need for a skilled workforce (Penfold, 1988). Boys, but not girls needed to be taught workshop subjects as preparation for life. Generally girls' future life was considered to be in the home and so a different education was needed. Any preparation for the world of work was of a secondary nature, except in the case of those girls, who for family financial reasons, needed to earn their living as servants before marriage. After marriage it was expected that the male would be main wage earner.

Attar (1990) describes an extract from a domestic economy textbook published in 1874, in which it was emphasised that a woman's domestic duty was to make a comfortable home for her man and this was inseparable from her moral and religious duty. Similarly, Newton (1990) has noted that the Code of 1880 required girls to be taught plain needlework and introduced cookery as a grant-earning subject, while the Education Code of 1897–98 stated that it was responsive to the idea of modifying the curriculum to fit girls for their future domestic life.

In the early part of the twentieth century discussion returned to the link between food and health. There had been considerable anxiety outside educational circles regarding the health of the nation and high infant mortality. This led to the Report of Inter-Departmental Committee of 1904, which blamed women for these factors because of their ignorance of household affairs, hygiene and nutrition. It was decided that that there was a need to raise the standard of domestic competency among the young girls who were to be the future wives and mothers, and this was to be achieved through an increased emphasis on domestic training in elementary schools and its introduction into secondary education for girls. It was even suggested that girls should drop certain other subjects in the curriculum to make room for household management. According to Dyhouse (1977), an academic of that time thought too much time was wasted teaching pure physics and chemistry to girls who were not interested and lacked logic. It was argued that scientific principles were best taught to girls through applied science related to the home.

When the new state secondary schools were created following the 1902 Education Act, the Board of Education Regulations (1904) applied a similar philosophy and stated that there should be different forms of manual instruction offered to boys and girls. Girls should take cookery, laundry work, dairy work, needlework or housewifery and boys manual instruction. This theme was repeated in a circular, *Advanced Courses in Secondary Schools* (Board of Education, 1919) which suggested that the curriculum in girls' schools was too closely modelled on that of boys' and that the educational requirements of boys and girl were different, as their capacities were not identical.

Post 1914–18

The range of roles undertaken by women during the 1914–18 War, when the men were away fighting, had little effect on attitudes. The Hadow Report of 1926 stated that girls should be made aware of their role in the running of the home for the well-being of its members. In the Spens Report (Board of Education, 1938) *Secondary Education with Special Reference to Grammar and Technical Schools*, the study of domestic subjects was again recommended for girls and manual instruction for boys. During the Second World War the Norwood Report (Board of Education, 1943) argued that proficiency in domestic subjects courses was necessary for girls as potential makers of homes.

The sexist attitudes and values outlined above, which formed the basis for the introduction of domestic economy into the school curriculum, were increasingly challenged by educationalists and feminists in the post-war era. It was the Crowther Report (DES, 1959) *15 to 18 year olds* which first noted that radical changes in the structure and life style of the population had, and would continue to have, many repercussions on the education system. Women would no longer spend all their life bringing up the increasingly common smaller family, women now had a longer life expectancy, better health with earlier marriage and child birth. It suggested that child birth and not marriage would be the cause of a break from employment, but noted that the education provided in secondary schools for girls did not accommodate these changes. Domestic science was still based on outdated sexist thinking and as a consequence was failing to provide pupils with a relevant contemporary education.

However, despite these observations, the Newsom Report (DES, 1963) *Half Our Future* on the education of pupils aged 13–16 of average or less than average ability still referred to the provision of workshop crafts for boys and domestic crafts for girls, on the grounds that girls did not need the same form of education as their role in life was fundamentally different with an ultimate responsibility for making and running a home. The emphasis in the report was on *management*, as 'real' housewives had to balance their own recreation with looking after children, keeping appointments, cooking, sewing and cleaning.

The Sex Discrimination Act (1975) was a landmark in the provision of a common education for girls and boys as it made sexual discrimination unlawful in schools admission, the appointment of teachers and access to the curriculum. The Equal Opportunities Commission (EOC) (1980) commented that it was no longer possible to exclude pupils from courses of study in schools on the grounds of sex, though it acknowledged that the influence of tradition, custom and prejudice could not be removed from society overnight and that legislation alone was not enough. The Commission considered that it had a responsibility to raise the issue in peoples' minds to ensure both sexes received equal treatment and opportunities.

The EOC published a document, *Equal Opportunities in Home Economics* (1983), where it observed that in a DES report of 1975, *Curricular Differences for Boys and Girls*, the greatest division by subject between boys and girls at that time was in the areas of home economics and CDT. Concern was expressed and curricular changes were recommended to remedy the situation. The EOC observed critically that 'the prevailing picture is of traditional assumptions were being worked out through the curricular patterns of secondary schools, with the support and acceptance of the majority of teachers, parents and pupils'. It was suggested that this was a waste of talent and skills and any differences should be based on genuine choice after real equality of access and not on traditional assumptions about the 'proper' spheres of interest and influence of men and women.

Since that time there have been attempts to encourage a gender-free approach to home economics and make courses more attractive to males. Brown (1985) has described his experiences gaining a Bachelor of Science Honours degree in Home Economics, included remarks from fellow school pupils regarding 'woman's' work.

He felt it would be difficult for a man to become a teacher of home economics because of the traditional view that it should be taught to girls by females. After graduation, it took him some time to find employment as he felt that he was confronting both female and male stereotyping in a female dominated sector of society (Brown, 1988).

Wadsworth (1986) has outlined the introduction of home economics into boys schools in the Inner London Educational Authority (ILEA), where she noted that in secondary schools nationally in 1977 only one per cent of home economics teachers were men. However, when a London male art teacher retrained into home economics under a special scheme, he found the subject to be very popular in his school, and he aimed to present alternative images and role models to pupils to show that caring for the home and family was a vital part of all people's lives. Despite such initiatives, boys were still under-represented at examination level in home economics in schools (Equal Opportunities Commission, 1983).

These radical changes in attitudes led to considerable debate over the rationale for teaching the subject of home economics. Wynn (1983) went as far as to suggest that the subject of home economics encouraged girls to think only of marriage and motherhood, reinforcing outdated social and traditional values. She pointed out that sixty-nine per cent of households were not married couples living with dependent children and that women were now spending far less time bringing up children. This trend has continued into the 1990s with the British Household Survey, the government's Labour Force Survey, and other research showing that in one in five two-adult households, women earn more than their husbands or male partners, up from one in fifteen a decade ago. In addition, in seven per cent of households the woman is working while the husband or partner is unemployed (Smith and Thomas, 1996). Attar (1990) has argued that if, because of social changes, it is now accepted that boys and girls should have the same education, there is no valid reason to teach a subject that was created as a girls' subject to prepare girls for preconceived traditional female roles in the home.

This argument has been developed by Lawson (1993) who considers that home economists should no longer ignore the tide of social and economic events. He argues that from its conception home economics has been regarded as women's work. Despite the family focus of the founders, the field has been populated largely by women and has directed its message to a female audience. He suggests that home economists are generally politically weak and naive, far too 'nice' and afraid to offend. They are resistant to change and avoid the political arena of the school staffroom. There is a pre-occupation with trivia and an unwillingness to take a public stance on critical issues. They rigidly adhere to traditional ways that demand larger than usual time blocks on the time-table. However, Lawson does not argue for the abolition of home economics but rather a need to identify the key areas to retain and develop. He calls for increased flexibility to find a new direction for the teaching of the subject, suggesting that it is technology that may provide home economics in schools with its best opportunities in the future, an approach that would accommodate changes in society and improve the status or image of the subject.

Status in the curriculum

Concern regarding the status or relative standing of home economics in the curriculum is not new phenomena. Cockburn (1991) notes that the skills of tool-making gave early man a higher status than women's traditional skills of nurturing children, weaving cloth and ploughing land. Riggs (1992) argues that even today there is still an underlying belief that home economics is a low status area of knowledge. Whyte (1980) suggests three reasons for this: that it was seen as a 'feminine' subject, a 'craft' subject particularly suitable for the less able and and of low-level vocational relevance. Edwards (1981) notes that home economics was rarely taught to boys or to the most able girls after the age of 13, while Buttle (1982) confirms that the subject was usually considered for the less able or academically second rate. There does seem to be a tendency in our culture to give a lower status to skills-based subjects in general (Brennan, 1986).

Practical subjects, such as domestic subjects and CDT, have since the last century been considered of a lower status than the more academic subjects in the school curriculum, and home economics has not traditionally been regarded as a 'legitimate' discipline on a par with the academic areas of the curriculum (Geen *et al.*, 1988). Penfold (1988) points out that initial attempts to introduce manual instruction into schools was met with hostility, partly because the working class associated it with pauper training and corrective institutions. Similarly, domestic subjects in elementary schools were associated with raising the standard of living of the poor (Scott, 1967). In Wynn's (1983) view one of the most outstanding features of domestic subjects teaching in the nineteenth century and early twentieth century was the highly differentiated approach to girls from different social backgrounds. Teachers were trained to teach girls 'plain' cookery for the working class, 'household cookery' for the middle class and 'superior cookery' for the upper classes.

In the view of Geen *et al.* (1988), the main reason for the low status of home economics is a deep-rooted educational philosophy that only verbal or propositional knowledge, that is 'knowing *that* something is the case', is of any real importance. Practical, procedural knowledge or process, that is 'knowing *how* to do something', is considered to be of secondary importance. This he argues, can be traced back to theory of education outlined by Plato who, in *The Republic*, saw two distinct groups of people in society – the intellectual abstract thinkers or 'philosopher kings' who were highly *educated* through a theoretical, not practical, process, and the second-class workers or artisans who were given a very different inferior *training* to do everyday practical craft and skill-based activities. Similarly, Aristotle (384–322 BC) saw a ruling citizen freemen class with authentic knowledge and the working class with practical skills. Both Roman and medieval education was based on this philosophy.

In this country during the last century a similar pattern of two distinct education systems can be seen. Gordon (1978) has described the public or independent schools containing secondary education for fee-paying pupils of the upper classes, and the elementary or state system for the workers. The independent or private fee paying sector of education was based on the ancient languages and the humanities and aimed to produce gentleman of character and future leaders. On the other hand, the aims of the elementary state education were to provide the lower classes with a basic education, instil mechanical obedience and an acceptance of their status in society. Geen *et al.* (1988) observe that practical subjects were not a high priority in the independent schools, and he highlights a report by the Education Department in 1896–97, describing girls' public day schools where the more able missed needlework to study Latin, while lessons in hygiene were given once a week to pupils not learning Latin.

The secondary schools in the state system, which were created following the Education Act of 1902, were based on the traditional academic curriculum taught in the private grammar and independent sector. In an HMI report of 1906, Mrs Pillow summed up the situation by stating that domestic subjects, except needlework, were outside the ordinary curriculum and not considered important enough to be included in general education (Sillitoe, 1966).

Association with the less able and attempts to change this perception

The Board of Education showed disapproval of too much theoretical teaching in elementary schools related to food preparation and nutrition. Domestic science was to be as *un*scientific as possible with the teaching adapted to the practical requirements of working-class homes (Dyhouse, 1977). In 1908 it was suggested that, in secondary education, girls over 15 should follow a course in domestic subjects instead of science, on the grounds that scientific principles were best taught to girls through the vehicle of Applied Science in the Household. Between 1909 and 1913 there was considerable educational controversy and debate over attempts to teach science through housecraft. Some teachers in secondary girls' schools thought that housecraft was a suitable subject for the least intelligent, who could not be interested in more academic work.

During the 1970s the aims and objectives of the subject area were broadened in an attempt to improve the academic status of the subject to appeal to pupils of all abilities. Home economics, as the subject was now known, was to include five overlapping areas of content: people and their environment, home, food, fabric and consumer education (Schools Council, 1973). A number of writers at the time discussed attempts to redefine the subject. Whyte (1980) thought that the subject was undergoing an identity crisis trying to improve its status by attempting to become a traditional academic subject, and she suggested a number of strategies to address the crisis. Home economics could join with science and technical crafts' departments, or adopt a rationale for providing children with 'life-skills' and join with non-examined subjects such as health education and personal and social education. A third suggestion was that craft departments, including home economics and technical drawing, would address the issue of the gender divide within these subjects.

Discussion at that time was wide and reflected differing views. Bennett (1978) argued that the subject area was multidisciplinary and reflected the lives of families and individuals in a world where rapid social change and technological advances were taking place. Mathieson (1979) agreed that the subject was multidisciplinary but argued that it was also closely related to changes in lifestyles and society. He suggested that these changes would inevitably affect the content, presentation, strength and appeal of the subject to different groups of people. In relation to the study of food, he commented on the increased use of convenience foods and argued that this could lead to a decreased need to teach the skills related to domestic cookery. He indicated there might be a need to focus on food science and nutrition with an increased scientific emphasis rather than on traditional cooking skills. He warned there were dangers for home economics becoming a multidisciplinary subject concerned with the home and family and using skills and knowledge from different disciplines. Home economics could cease to exist because it was unable to compete with specialist departments, with its prime aim to improve the condition of home life obscured in the process of social and economic change.

Discussion and debate were not confined to this country. In the USA Firebaugh (1980) noted the need for frequent explanations to people regarding to the nature of the subject following the change of name to home economics. She commented on the increasing range of specialisms, a need for cohesion and an ability to attract more men into home economics. Davies (1981) investigating the interest of home economics teachers in the new contributory areas of the subject, commented that the subject was a complex field of study demanding a high level of conceptual thinking to integrate and synthesise the varied contributory disciplines into a whole. She also noted that the *scientific* aspect of the subject was the least liked by home economics teachers, irrespective of their age.

In this country, Thorne (1979) agreed that home economics was undergoing an identity crisis. Like Mathieson, she thought there was a danger in becoming too closely involved with recognised, traditional academic areas to improve the subject's status and that in the final analysis this could lead to its demise. Thorne added to the discussion regarding the definition and content of the subject by describing a 'Janus-headed' situation. She suggested that home economics was trying to accommodate two incompatible worlds, *social* and *commercial*, based on critically contrasting philosophies. The aims of home economics teaching in the educational context were noticeably different from the aims of the subject area in an industrial or commercial setting. At the educational level the subject had been traditionally concerned with the concept of the 'home' and improving family life, by considering the social aspects of family life and developing practical skills to improve physical conditions and fight poverty. In the context of home economics, preparation for the demands of the commercial or industrial world were thought to be of secondary importance.

Two years later Thorne (1981) argued that home economics was fundamentally concerned with developing the human competencies necessary to cope with the personal and immediate environment of health and home. This theme was developed by HMI (DES, 1985), who stated that the primary aim of the teaching of home economics was to help prepare boys and girls for some important aspects of everyday living and the adult responsibility of family life. A previous HMI document had defined the subject as 'studies of the needs of the individual in the community, and the best uses of human and physical resources in the context of home and family life' (DES, 1978).

Traditional teaching style

Other factors affecting the status of home economics in the field of education have been a cause for concern. Since the early days of domestic economy the traditional teaching strategies adopted can be directly related to the development of routine and mechanistic skills or 'training' as described by Corson (1991). Training, it can be argued, is distinct from 'education', which involves a body of knowledge and the development of concepts. Geen *et al.* (1988) have described the main teaching method used in the late nineteenth century as *instruction* in the form of demonstration, with an emphasis on a narrow range of craft skills. Thinking was not required as it was based on rote learning and copying taught skills.

Not until the 1970s was it recognised that, although manipulative dexterity and the ability to use tools safely and efficiently were important, other skills such as experiential work, organisation and management skills and ability to communicate should be included (DES, 1978). In the past both home economics and CDT teaching had focused on the mechanical drill of useful practical skills (Newton, 1990; Eggleston, 1996). The Nuffield Home Economics project of the late seventies and early eighties introduced a more scientific, investigative approach to practical activities, aiming to providing pupils with a sound knowledge of the major concepts of home economics and the underlying scientific knowledge and principles (Faulkner and Mansell, 1982).

Working towards these new aims, Townsend (1983) outlined a problem-solving approach with an emphasis on developing intellectual skills that could be applied to a variety of situations rather than a specific body of practical skills. Likewise, the GCSE National Criteria for Home Economics (SEC, 1986) introduced investigations and problem solving to emphasise the *process* of learning as well as the final *product*. Two distinct but overlapping approaches, design and scientific method, were described. In the design approach the context of the investigation was given and an appropriate solution evolved, whereas in the scientific method approach questions were posed and an hypothesis put forward, which was investigated to arrive at a solution and conclusions.

Summary

- The teaching of food had first been introduced into the elementary school curriculum in the mid to late 1800s as a practical subject to raise the living standards of girls from the working classes and to prepare them for low paid employment.

- It was seen as a subject for girls, it had a low status in the school curriculum and was associated with less able pupils.

- Despite many social and economic changes these attitudes had been slow to alter.

- Prior to the introduction of the National Curriculum Technology in 1990, some people had recognised that the knowledge, skills and processes used in home economics were common to other technological areas (Wadsworth, 1986). However, this was not a common perception, and as recently as 1985 official guidance (DES, 1985) put the emphasis for home economics on the domestic scene and preparing for everyday and family life with all pupils gaining competence and make informed choices in matters of hygiene, safety, health and diet.

- The importance of practical and investigative work as processes were noted but the emphasis was on the content of home and family, nutrition and food and textiles.

● On the other hand, when 2 years later the HMI published guidance for CDT (DES, 1987) the emphasis had shifted to designing practical solutions and creative problem-solving activities for boys and girls, a philosophy that was reflected in National Curriculum Technology. Indeed, Newton (1990) was able to argue that CDT teachers were more able to relate to the central philosophy of the *design process* in the National Curriculum Technology document when it arrived, because the CDT HMI paper was closer to its requirements.

Chapter 2

Food in the National Curriculum

Marion Rutland

Before the National Curriculum

Prior to the introduction of the National Curriculum there was a marked lack of direct reference to home economics in official documents. Two publications in 1981 which were concerned with the whole school curriculum and the current debate about its content and structure at that time did have relevance to the position of food in the school curriculum. It is interesting to note, however, that of the two craft-based practical subjects traditionally taught to boys and girls, home economics, unlike craft design technology (CDT), was not mentioned in either document. *The Practical Curriculum* (DES, 1981a) simply discussed 'learning through experience' and noted that 'cooking' allowed children to acquire from an early age scientific and mathematical experience through 'making things'. *The School Curriculum* (DES, 1981b) referred to CDT as part of the preparation for living and working in modern industrial society and microelectronics but made no mention of home economics in a similar context.

The potential role of home economics, including food, did not appear to have any relevance as preparation for future careers, though attention had been repeatedly drawn to the continuing sex differentiation in subject choice for pupils after the age of 14 in the secondary school (DES, 1975, 1979, 1980). Girls, as in the past, were still studying home economics, but its potential as preparation for adult life outside the home was not recognised in career guidance given in schools (Rutland, 1984). Even though The School Curriculum made some references to obstacles in equality of employment opportunities for women, no connection was made to the situation regarding home economics. Indicating that attitudes had not changed and that many people still perceived the main purposes of the subject as preparing girls for their future roles within the home and/or for low-level employment rather than a sound career.

It has been argued that these obstacles were rooted in attitudes found in the home and in society. Whyld (1983) pointed out that, despite the Equal Pay Act 1975, the average earnings for women in full-time work had fallen from around

75% of men's in 1976 to 65% of men's in 1982. Over half of all females manual workers were employed in catering, cleaning, hairdressing or other personal services, with half of the female non-manual workers in clerical and related occupations – all low-paid jobs. As Riggs (1992) more recently has commented men are under-represented in routine jobs on production lines in the food and textiles industry and the majority of workers operating sewing machines and packing food are female.

Its early place in the National Curriculum

It was the introduction of technology as a foundation subject in the National Curriculum (Table 2.1) that signalled radical changes for the teaching of home economics.

RE	MATHS ENGLISH SCIENCE	TECHNOLOGY HISTORY GEOGRAPHY MUSIC ART PE A FOREIGN LANGUAGE	OTHER SUBJECTS: DRAMA DANCE 2ND LANGUAGE
CROSS-CURRICULAR COMPETENCES: IT, LITERACY, NUMERACY. CAREERS EDUCATION AND GUIDANCE HEALTH EDUCATION PERSONAL AND SOCIAL EDUCATION GENDER AND MULTICULTURAL ISSUES			

Table 2.1 Subjects in the National Curriculum

Kenneth Baker, as Secretary of State for Education in 1988 stated that he was concerned with shortage of skills, and he therefore wanted to ensure that boys and girls would not be able to opt out of National Curriculum Technology: 'Even those who are academically gifted will have to roll up their sleeves and learn some craft'. In the publication *Design and Technology for ages 5 to 16* (DES, 1989), home economics was listed as one of the subjects contributing to the development of design and technology capability, though many senior managers in schools frequently read the title 'design and technology' and immediately sent the document to the CDT department. This mistake could be forgiven when the suggested programmes of study were almost entirely concerned with resistant materials, the traditional materials used in CDT. The intention, according to the introduction in the document, was to co-ordinate the knowledge, skills and values from a range of subjects, including home economics; even so, there were few detailed references to food and textiles. The danger of perpetuating a narrow interpretation of technology as the sum of civil, electrical and mechanical engineering, with the technology of food and textiles brought in only in relation to girls, with all this implies in terms of the resulting image presented to boys and girls, had been noted by Black and Harrison (1985, 1990). They argue that approaches to technology should be comprehensive and identical for boys and girls. Although the early National Curriculum documents for technology played lip service to this notion, they failed to provide evidence to back the intention.

Another problem was that the terminology 'design and technology capability' and the 'design process', as described in the document, were new terms to many home economists with a specialism in food. Although in the past staff had been used to working to the design process in textiles or a design brief when planning and making food dishes, many teachers, including the senior management in schools, found it difficult to recognise the connection between food and textiles as materials that could be used to 'design and make' in design and technology (D&T). This was despite the work done by the Assessment and Performance Unit (SEAC, 1991), which identified 'the interaction of mind and hand – inside and outside the head' as the essence of design and technology (see Figure 3.3, page 26). Their document emphasised that the design process – that is the processes or capacity to think, investigate, design, make and appraise – are as important as the acquisition of knowledge, and they defined design and technology capability as the ability 'to operate effectively and creatively in the made world'. In the *Non-Statutory Guidance for Design and Technology* (NCC, 1990), the importance of the design process was further highlighted and clarified. D&T was about identifying needs, generating ideas, planning, making and testing to find the best solution – an activity that is as relevant to working with food and textiles as it is with other materials.

Unfortunately, many home economics teachers were confused and alienated by the terminology used in the National Curriculum documents. True they could find some examples related to home economics in the programmes of study, but the knowledge, understanding and skills related to home economics were not be clearly identified. Though home economics was named as part of the framework, the programmes of study cited few examples directly related to food or textiles. Typical terms used – for example systems, structures, and mechanisms (DES, 1989) – were unfamiliar to home economists. As Atherton (1990) commented, many home economics teachers felt ill prepared and 'de-skilled' when they considered the implications for them in schools of the document *Design and Technology for Ages 5 to 16* (DES, 1989).

Despite these problems attempts were made to relate home economics to the National Curriculum Technology document. Fisher (1989) examined the work currently being carried out in home economics and emphasised that the subject had developed considerably since the days of rock buns and sewing, though many people still viewed it in this way and were unaware of its educational potential. Similarly, Newton (1990) discussed the place of home economics in National Curriculum Technology and saw a role for home economics, but thought that the role would require teachers to develop new skills. Technology was a new subject area, which in itself could create fear of the unknown, but on the positive side it offered a real opportunity, long overdue, to change the way people viewed the area of the curriculum and those who taught it.

Some home economics teachers did begin to establish their place in technology. The National Association of Teachers of Home Economics (NATHE) (1988) thought that the subject had a special role to play in the teaching of technology because it provided broad, balanced and relevant situations for technological activities, including ones based on energy, clothing and food. However, there were still differences of opinion regarding the place of home economics in the school curriculum. The Inner London Education Authority (ILEA, 1989) discussed a number of options for the delivery of the subject area and suggested that home economics could be delivered in a number of ways. It could be a discrete subject in the optional curriculum outside the core or foundation areas of the National Curriculum; or it could be a component of D&T as the foundation subject technology; or it could be part of the cross curricular non-examined themes of Personal and Social Education (PSE) and Health Education.

It was acknowledged that incorporating home economics into D&T, and the resulting need to develop a closer relationship with CDT, could cause problems (Fisher, 1989). The National Curriculum Technology Orders required teachers from the traditional specialist areas to collaborate and co-ordinate their activities so that pupils were able to develop D&T capability (DES, 1989). This integrated approach posed no problem for primary school teachers who were used to working in this way, but it was a new concept for the traditional separate subject specialist found in secondary schools.

A number of suggestions to deal with this problem were put forward. Murray (1991) described a 'federated' approach, where a group of teachers worked together to gain a greater understanding of D&T, develop ideas, and build a framework for planning and managing the curriculum. Similarly, Eggleston (1996) outlined three main forms of organisation:

- 'Federalisation', where teachers work alongside each other offering a general range of technology teaching to their class throughout the year.
- 'Collaboration', where teachers offer their specialist expertise for a period of weeks to a range of classes over the year.
- 'Integration', where teachers work as a team allowing children to call on the expertise of a range of teachers when necessary.

Research has been carried out to identify the problems and concerns of home economics teachers attempting to work within this framework. Ridgewell (1992) discovered from a survey of state and independent schools in England and Wales that 60% of the heads of technology were CDT specialists, whereas only 18% were home economists. This helped to confirm fears expressed in the survey that home economics teachers might become the junior partners in a technology faculty, which was led and dominated by CDT teachers with little knowledge or understanding of the changes that had already taken place in the teaching of home economics. Other issues of concern were identified by Atherton (1990) who described a technology and home economics project for pupils aged 5–16 in Sheffield. It was found that the project teachers were uncertain about their role within the D&T curriculum and how the curriculum would be delivered. They were particularly concerned about the additional skills they would need to acquire and they were unhappy about the place of other valuable aspects of home economics that did not appear to have a place in D&T but deserved a place in the school curriculum.

Despite these areas of concern, food technology thrived in part of the country following the introduction of the National Curriculum Technology in 1990. Shannon (1991) described the remodelling of a traditional home economics room into a multi-purpose area with two food preparation areas, a carpeted section and space for design and computer activities. Baker (1991), when writing about future development, was convinced that home economics had a very bright future with a unique contribution to make to the area of National Curriculum Technology. However, he clarified this by advocating multi-disciplinary areas for investigative work in both textiles and food but adding that the additional areas of study other than food and textiles introduced into home economics in the 1970s would not be included.

Difficulties concerned with the implementation of D&T within the National Curriculum Orders for Technology were not restricted to food technology. HMI (DES, 1992) noted in their report of the first year of National Curriculum Technology that only 50% of lessons in all respects of D&T were satisfactory or better and 33% of lessons were unsatisfactory. This, they felt, was disappointing and highlighted difficulties experienced by teachers trying to implement the Orders in the classroom. Similarly, Smithers and Robinson (1992), writing on behalf of the Engineering Council, said 'Technology in the National Curriculum is a mess' and described the character of technology in schools as being 'generalised problem solving without a specified knowledge base' rather than being essentially about design and making'. They observed a lack of structure in delivery, difficulties in organisation and poor quality outcomes for pupils. In their view, teaching children to cook was not technology and this should have its own slot on the curriculum outside technology. This comment unfortunately reflected a lack of understanding of the concepts of food technology and food product development as distinct from 'cookery'.

These views were added to by the National Curriculum Council (NCC) (1992), which advised John Patten, the Secretary of State for Education at the time, that though the Council supported the concept of technology, there was a case for the revision of the technology Order. The principal objectives of the review was to improve clarity and intelligibility, introduce more precision in both the basic concepts and practical skills, introduce more flexibility and choice, particularly at secondary level, and strengthen links with the other subject Orders of the National Curriculum. It was also recommended that the introduction of GCSE Key Stage 4 syllabuses for technology should be postponed from September 1993 to September 1994 to enable changes to the Orders to be introduced, advice that was not taken by the Government.

More recent developments

As a result of these concerns statutory proposals, developed by HMI and others, were published (DfE, 1992). They included textiles as a 'construction material' and food as a material alongside other materials to be used to '*design and make good* quality products fit for their intended purpose'. Considerable work was done by HMI in the publication to specify the extensive and rigorous knowledge, understanding and skills that pupils would need to design and make food products, rather than simply 'learn how to cook'. Food had a separate programme of study because it was considered that, when using food as a material to design and make food products, pupils would be required to understand and use physical, chemical and nutritional properties unique to food and different to those used when working with construction materials. The practical skills related to food technology contained in the *making* programmes of study were intended to help teachers plan and implement appropriate schemes of work, clearly identifying progression and using increasingly complex knowledge and skills developed through the levels of attainment. Examples were the use of hygienic practices (level 3), knowledge of the presence of micro-organisms in food that are affected by critical temperatures (level 5) and the ability to operate within the requisite legal standards for hygiene in food production (level 9).

The food technology knowledge that was needed related to hygienic practices, basic food characteristics, food choice, evaluation of food products using difference and attitudinal sensory tests, and preservation and storage to retain organoleptic qualities of foods. In addition, the nutritional needs of people – for example special diet for clinical, cultural, social, economic or ethic reasons – were suggested for inclusion. The skills listed covered the management of working areas, selection of appropriate tools and equipment, cutting and mixing foods, using tools that allow a degree of precision and control, selecting and combining raw and processed foods to create products of different sensory characteristics, and experimenting with ways of combining foods to create or modify products to improve sensory characteristics. Test procedures to improve products and the functional properties of food were highlighted, as were the sequencing of steps in food production. It was emphasised that food products should be tested, modified and evaluated against specific criteria to ensure quality and fitting their intended purpose, taking into account moral, social, economic and environmental values.

For the first time there was a move away and change of emphasis from 'domestic cookery' or cooking meals for the home, an image that had for so long influenced the image of the subject in schools, to food product development. This required specialist knowledge and its application in nutrition and food science with the analytical sensory food evaluation needed for commercial production. HMI's reference to food production could arguably be interpreted as catering. However, the requirements in the document were broader and very different to the traditional catering courses of the past which had emphasised manual skills and presentation. A book (Cracknell and Kaufmann, 1981) written for professional chefs, teachers of catering, catering students, apprentices, assistant cooks and housewives can be used to illustrate this point since it emphasises *set* classical recipes in logical sequences. In contrast, in National Curriculum Technology, food is a *material* that can be used *to design and make food products*. Basic concepts, knowledge and skills are required together with an understanding how a range of foods can be used in a creative, original manner to produce high quality food products for specified, targeted groups of consumers. These food products comply with identified criteria and address the needs of the consumers, taking into account a range of social, economic and health-related issues.

Following the publication of the proposed statutory proposals in December 1992, the Secretary of State asked the NCC to seek views on the proposals and address a number of general issues including clarity, manageability, flexibility and progression and in particular, along with other points, the proposed place of food but not home economics. The objective of the statutory consultation was to assist in producing clear recommendations for the draft Orders. The initial response in May of the NCC (1993) was disappointing for many supporters of food technology, as it considered that 'all pupils should be given opportunities to work with food but had not yet been able to resolve whether it was appropriate for this work to take place in technology'. It was suggested that the increased flexibility in the curriculum as result of the slim-down of the core and foundation subjects of the National Curriculum under consideration by Dearing (1993a) would enable *life skills such as cooking*, along with aspects of home economics to be taught alongside National Curriculum subjects.This again indicated that there were still groups of people whose view of food technology was based on outdated ideas and past practice.

In September of that year the NCC (1993b) admitted that there had been considerable debate about the place of food in the technology curriculum. Arguments against its inclusion centred around the view that technology is essentially about making structures and artefacts, and that broadening the range of acceptable materials would reduce rigour and diminish the status of the subject. Arguments in favour of food as part of technology included the suggestion that 'as technology is concerned with meeting human needs, food should be central to the subject'. Others argued that there should be additional curriculum time for home economics to ensure that all pupils understand about nutrition and healthy eating, implying that they thought these aspects would not be covered in food technology. The NCC noted that respondents to consultation thought that the proposals 'gave a clear analysis of the contribution of food technology in developing pupils' technological knowledge and skills and for gaining practical experience of quality assurance procedures'.

Fortunately for the food lobby, the NCC concluded that the proposals did present a convincing case for the inclusion of *food technology*, described as 'the study of food as a material for designing and making with the study of the preparation, preservation and packaging processes used by the food industry'. The NCC suggested that food technology should be retained as a compulsory area of study in their revised programmes of study for Key Stages 1 and 2 and as an optional specialism at Key Stage 3. However, the view was that pupils should be allowed to do additional work in compliant materials as an alternative to food technology. At Key Stage 4, under the core and extension framework, pupils would be able to choose further specialist courses focusing on food.

The original intention had been to implement the revised Orders for Technology for Key Stages 1, 2 and 3 in Autumn 1994 and Key Stage 4 in Autumn 1995. However, the review of the whole National Curriculum by Dearing (1993b) delayed the move to produce to a new draft Order for almost a year. When the Draft Orders for Design and Technology were published in May by SCAA (1994) it was based on the recommendations of the NCC (1993b). However, although food was present as a material in the programmes of study for Key Stage 3, it was included as an alternative to compliant materials. It would be possible to study food technology as a full or half course GCSE course at Key Stage 4.

Two fundamental changes had been made that were to have considerable effect on the teaching of food in schools. The first was that the two aspects of Technology were now to be considered as separate curriculum areas. There was to be a much clearer division between *design and technology*, that is designing and making with a range of materials, and cross-curricular *information technology*, with guidance on the two curriculum areas produced in separate booklets.

The other interesting development was at GCSE. It had been suggested by the NCC in May 1992 that the introduction of the original GCSE syllabuses for technology should be postponed a year from September 1993 to September 1994 to enable the changes to the Order to be incorporated into the syllabuses. But, as noted above, this did not happen, and the new technology GCSE examination syllabuses were introduced in September 1993. This created considerable problems for schools as the D&T GCSE examinations had a core part of the course based on resistant materials, requiring staff expertise and resources that many schools found it difficult to provide. Half of the content of the courses related to resistant materials and the other half to a range of other, often unrelated, options, including food, textiles and business studies. Fortunately for schools, the Dearing Report (1993b) recognised these problems and recommended that, pending the introduction of the revised Order for technology for Key Stage 4 in 1996, technology should not be compulsory for pupils entering Key Stage 4 in 1994 and 1995. As a result of this, many schools quickly reverted to the old pre-National Curriculum GCSE examinations to reduce the problems they were experiencing. In the Draft Proposals for Design and Technology (1994) it was intended that new GCSE examinations would moved away from a core based on resistant materials to, as had been originally intended in the Technology Orders (1990), a core about designing and making skills based on the design process. GCSE courses would now enable pupils to specialise in one or more focus areas, including food technology.

The future?

Many of the controversies discussed so far in this chapter were resolved in the new Orders for Design and Technology (DfE, 1995a). Resistant materials are now compulsory at Key Stage 3 and there is an 'and/or' situation between compliant materials and food. This allows schools to choose whether they will teach food at Key Stage 3, or do additional work in compliant materials, which may be textiles or plastics, and not cover food. As a result boys' schools, for example, are not required to teach food or textiles at Key Stage 3 and may instead concentrate on resistant materials and control. There are a number of implications of such a decision, including the traditional lack of equal curriculum access commented on in the 1980s by the Equal Opportunities Commission (1983) and the reinforcement of attitudes and values of the past. It will be interesting to see whether these dangers are realised and hear the views of pupils and parents in the schools which choose not to include food and textiles at Key Stage 3.

In England, but not Wales where Welsh is compulsory, National Curriculum Design and Technology at Key Stage 4 is statutory and pupils have to follow either a full,or at least a half, course written to the design and technology criteria based on the new Orders. This course may be D&T: Food. There are Home Economics: Food GCSE courses, but they are written to different criteria and cannot be taken by pupils as part of their statutory D&T course. It is an interesting issue whether Home Economics: Food and Textiles will survive outside the National Curriculum within option columns, or whether schools will decide to offer a D&T option as either a long or short course of Design and Technology: Food or Textiles to fulfil the statutory D&T requirement. If schools choose the former, food could be restricted to optional home economics courses and all pupils could follow a compulsory Design and Technology GCSE course based on resistant and complaint materials.

Farrell (1996) argues that the debate about home economics versus technology had been decided for everyone, whether all of us agree with the outcome or not. At the present time we have food and textiles technology alongside home economics in England and Wales at Key Stage 4 and 'A' Level, though the curriculum for pupils aged 14–19 is under review to be revised. She sees the important issue to be that food at Key Stages 1, 2 and 3 is now taught as part of D&T in the majority of the state schools, who are required by law to teach the National Curriculum Design and Technology programmes of study.

Farrell argues that the option of teaching of food and textiles as part of the National Curriculum gives increased status. However, she notes that teachers vary in their attitude here; some argue that they value the aspects of home economics not covered by D&T or they just do not like or want change. This, she thinks may be due to real conviction, but it could also be because they lack confidence and perhaps the knowledge and skills to teach food or textiles technology. If so, the decision may be made by senior management that, unless food and textiles are taught in D&T, it will not be taught at all at Key Stage 3, because the schools recognise the place of food and textiles technology, but are not willing, or able, to support home economics at Key Stage 3. The break in progression across the key stages could result in no food technology at Key Stage 4. On the other hand, if food technology is taught in Key Stage 3, teachers and pupils may find it difficult to revert to home economics in the option column at Key Stage 4.

Summary

- There have been many changes in education and society since food was first introduced into the school curriculum. Originally it was taught as part of home economics by females to girls to prepare them to be good wives and mothers and as an option for older pupils.
- Today it is has a place as food technology in National Curriculum as D&T, a compulsory subject for all pupils up to the age of 16 (DfE, 1995a).
- The curriculum in food technology focuses on the physical, chemical, nutritional, biological and sensory properties of food and the ways in which these properties can be exploited when designing and making food products to specified criteria.
- This differs from home economics where the focus on food is on immediate consumption and the nutritional, social, economic, cultural and aesthetic requirements of the people who eat them.
- Food technology centres on understanding the properties of the materials used and the effects of processing on these properties. Developing and drawing on scientific knowledge, understanding the natural and technological processing of food and engaging in practical activities where this knowledge of ingredients and processes are brought together in the designing and making of food products (DfE, 1995b).
- Teachers of food technology should not be complacent, as HMI (Ofsted, 1993) have commented that the technological content of food lessons at Key Stage 3 is often minimal.
- The new GCSE Design and Technology examinations offer opportunities for food technology, in both full and half specialist food technology syllabuses based on the D&T criteria. There are also home economics examinations, based on the home economics criteria, where pupils can specialise in food.

Section 2

The Classroom

This section moves to the classroom and looks at food technology within National Curriculum Design and Technology (D&T).

Chapter 3 examines the philosophy and thinking underpinning the teaching of food technology within the D&T curriculum area and explores issues related to curriculum planning.

Chapter 4 provides detailed first-hand examples of food technology curriculum planning for the classroom.

Chapter 5 uses a case study of food product development to illustrate curriculum planning in food technology.

Chapter 3

Planning to Teach Food Technology

Christine Thompson and Marion Rutland

Introduction

It can be argued that if we, as teachers, fail to acknowledge that food technology can be successfully taught as part of Design and Technology (D&T) and that it is essentially a practical subject (DfE, 1995b), we could be in danger of losing the very essence of the teaching of food and eventually the subject area from the school curriculum.

Although the name 'technology' had not appeared previously on most school timetables before the introduction of the National Curriculum, it was not a new subject. The document *The Curriculum from 5–16* (DES, 1985) included technology as an area of experience and learning and a particular form of *problem solving* concerned with bringing about change, of designing to effect control. Black and Harrison (1985) thought technology was not mere academic study. Rather it was concerned with the human capacity for action, and was used when practical solutions to problems were needed. More recently, Ritchie (1995) has emphasised that humans have from earliest times tried to control the world around them in order to survive and enhance the quality of their existence. They have done this by imagining new possibilities, putting their ideas into action and evaluating the outcomes. He sees the process of problem solving as the essence of D&T in the school curriculum.

The Revised National Curriculum Orders

The introduction of National Curriculum Technology in 1990 was a landmark in that a non-compulsory subject was now compulsory, centred around the design process of designing and making and the traditional practical subjects, for all pupils aged 5–16. In 1992, following the decision to rewrite the Technology Orders, there was period of discussion, confusion and delay, and it was not until 1995 that the Revised Orders for Design and Technology (DfE, 1995a) were finally published along with the decision that the cross-curricular subject of information technology should have its own separate Orders. The Design and Technology Orders are now slimmer and generally they have been welcomed by schools and teachers, though many D&T teachers have a low morale and enthusiasm from having to adapt and cope with a Technology curriculum that has changed around them. Those who joined the profession in 1990 have not seen any continuity in either examination courses or lower school planning, and have been expected to rewrite schemes of work for their pupils on a regular basis. The 1995 Orders, however, are expected to govern curriculum planning until at least the end of the century.

The new Orders for Design and Technology (DfE, 1995a) and advice for HMI (DfE, 1995b) both emphasise the practical nature of the subject. It is expected that pupils will develop their D&T capability through combining their designing and making skills with knowledge and understanding to design and make products. Three types of activity are set out through which pupils should develop D&T capability. They are:

- designing and making assignments in which the pupils use their D&T capability to develop products that meet real needs;
- focused practical tasks in which pupils develop and practise particular skills and knowledge;
- products and applications tasks in which pupils explore existing products, and use what they find out to increase and strengthen their knowledge, understanding and skills in D&T.

D&T has its own distinctive knowledge, understanding and skills, but it is made clear that pupils are required to apply the skills, knowledge and understanding from other subjects, especially art, mathematics and science. It is also stressed that D&T has a capacity to motivate and stimulate pupils to develop their creativity and inventiveness when they develop products to meet precise specifications. Solutions to initial problems may succeed in different ways: some may function well yet lack aesthetic appeal and some will be pleasing to the eye, yet not function as they were intended. The need for balance between function and aesthetic appeal, combined with the ability to design for themselves or a range of other people, presents pupils with many opportunities to improve and develop their products.

Food technology capability

If we accept that food technology is part of D&T, how do pupils learn in this subject area? Banks (1995) sees D&T as 'an active study, involving the purposeful pursuit of a task to some form of resolution that results in improvement (for someone) in the made world'. Kimbell *et al.* (1996) see an essential difference between technological understanding and technology capability. They consider that *capability is more complex than understanding*, as it is the combination of ability and motivation that enable creative development. Capability 'bridges the gap between what is and what might be', taking into account human desires, dissatisfaction with technical constraints and possible outcomes.

If we accept the idea that understanding is necessary, but capability is a more complex activity or process then we might arrive at the following definitions:

- **Food technology** is knowledge and understanding of the properties of foods, and *involves the ability to select and use the appropriate tools and materials to explore these properties for developing food products.*

● **Food technology capability** is demonstrated by using the designing skills, many of which are generic to other materials such as textiles, wood, plastic and metal, with the appropriate knowledge and understanding, and selecting the making skills needed to follow the creative design process to develop food products.

● **Food product design and development** occurs when pupils select ingredients, modify recipes, combine foods to design food products.

Figure 3.1 shows the main areas that pupils need to know, understand and be able to do in food product design in food technology.

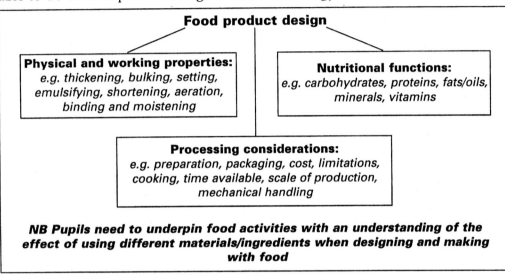

Figure 3.1 Food product design

Food product design as with product design in any materials (Figure 3.2), is a process consisting of the following elements:

● The consumer market, consumer awareness, retailing.
● Principles of food manufacture, raw materials, recipes, formulas, mixing, process centred.
● Nutritional aspects.
● Devising product specifications, research development.
● Test procedures – sensory, evaluation, consumer acceptability.
● Large-scale manufacture, pilot, batch, continuous production, packaging, transport.

Problem solving and the design process

A not uncommon question is 'How does an understanding of the concepts of problem solving and the design process help us when developing food products?' Fisher (1989) sees problem solving as involving critical or analytical thinking and creative thinking, which generates possible solutions, together with doing or acting for some purpose. The development of a food product is problem solving in that it does require critical and creative thinking about what could be made to fit the brief before an idea is explored, extended and refined.

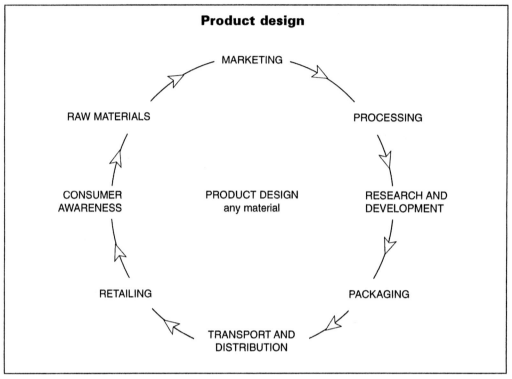

Figure 3.2 Product design

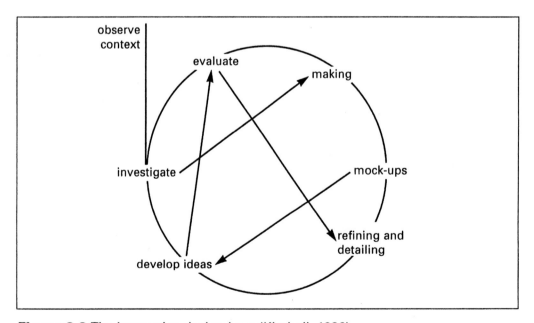

Figure 3.3 The interactive design loop (Kimbell, 1986)

Reproduced from The Assessment of Performance in D&T – Final Report (SEAC,1991) by permission of the School Curriculum and Assessment Authority.

Early models of D&T activity and the Orders for Technology in 1990 provided a linear model of the design process, starting with a problem and progressing through linear steps to a final solution which is then evaluated. In practice, this model proved to need refinement as it was felt that evaluation is not carried out just at the end of the process but is part of a continual process of refinement and modification. The linear process thus becomes a 'loop' or circle as shown in Figure 3.3.

In food technology, for example, when developing a low-cost, high-energy product to sell at a student union bar, a range of dishes using different foods would be developed, made and evaluated for their cost, energy value and appeal, before one dish is chosen for further development as a prototype and taken through to the manufacturing stage. It is a constant process of investigation, developing a prototype, evaluation and modification.

It is also important to remember that a *creative* practical activity requires the interaction of mind and hand. The Assessment and Performance Unit (APU, 1989) devised a way of looking at D&T, where the interactive process between mind and hand was central. The Unit concentrated on the *thinking* and *decision-making* processes that took place and were more interested in *why* and *how* pupils choose to do things rather than what it is they choose to do. The APU saw the essence of D&T as the interaction of hand and mind inside and outside the head, with conceptual understanding and practical skills both needed and dependent on each other, so ideas conceived in the mind can be expressed in a concrete form that can be evaluated and further modified, as shown in Figure 3.4.

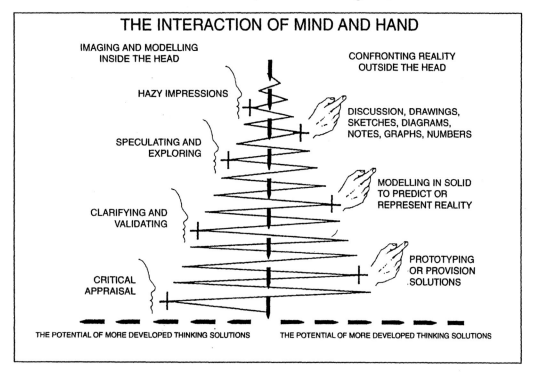

Figure 3.4 The APU model of interaction between mind and hand

Reproduced from The Assessment of Performance in D&T – Final Report (SEAC, 1991) by permission of the School Curriculum and Assessment Authority.

For example, when pupils follow a recipe out of a book and just copy what other people have designed and made with no thoughts of their own, they are engaged in rote, mechanistic learning without any understanding of the concepts and knowledge underpinning the activity. Such pupils are not designing, being creative, thinking and *making* decisions: they are only making. The process is not one of problem solving, as it does not involve actionable knowledge, the interaction between thinking and doing or the intermeshing of thought and action (Watts, 1994). Food technology requires pupils to be creative, to design and make their own food products based on a sound knowledge of the working properties of foods.

Problem solving and its relationship to D&T

The use of general problem solving to deliver D&T does raise a number of issues for teachers which are not restricted to food technology. These are some of them:

Pupils may:
- Lack the knowledge, understanding and skills to carry through an activity.
- Only centre on their past knowledge and experience.
- Not be able to move forward to new experiences.
- Lack ownership of the activity if working in groups.

Teachers may:
- Find there is no time or place to teach knowledge and skills.
- Find there is not enough time, as open-ended problem solving can be a long process.
- Be unsure of their role as a teacher (when do they structure, intervene, facilitate?).
- Be unsure of the optimum number of children that can be taught effectively by this approach.
- Ask how resources can be managed effectively.
- Ask how the teacher accommodates all the pupils needs.
- Feel de-skilled and unable to cope with the need for a range of knowledge/expertise.
- Not be able to think in a technological way if they are working in isolation at a general problem solving level.

The messages are that:
- There is a need for a balance between problem solving and the acquisition of knowledge and skills.
- The activity needs to be broken into manageable pieces for teaching and learning purposes.

Characteristics of good teaching and learning in D&T

Ofsted (DfE, 1995b) has advice for teachers on good quality teaching and learning in D&T, including food technology. The inspectors observe that standards of teaching are high in the following circumstances:

Personal qualities of teachers. Teachers are:
- enthusiastic about their subject
- confident in own subject knowledge.

Lesson organisation. The lesson:
- is well planned
- has clear objectives which are shared with pupils
- involves teachers observing pupils at work
- reflects teachers' knowledge of their pupils
- includes ideas suggested by teachers to stimulate pupils
- sets realistic deadlines
- provides opportunities for pupils to reflect
- encourages pupil to review and refine their work.

Teaching skills. The teacher:
- encourages pupils to try out ideas
- gives clear and carefully timed demonstration of practical skills.

Knowledge and understanding. The teacher:
- builds on past experiences
- takes opportunities to extend pupils' subject knowledge.

Monitoring. The teacher:
- carries out monitoring year by year, with an analysis of the rate of progress to aid future planning
- uses assessment to identify strengths and weaknesses of teaching to inform future planning.

Teaching strategies

It is important that there is variety to suit the needs of all the pupils and the situation. For example, in a lesson the more formal teaching style of demonstration successfully teaches knowledge, understanding or particular skills. The same lesson may include some pupil coping very well using more independent learning, whilst other pupils need help, support and confidence from a more structured approach. Ofsted (DfE, 1995b) suggests good teachers select teaching strategies according to the knowledge, understanding and skills that they wish the pupils to develop.

In good food technology (D&T) lessons a range of activities can be included: talking, writing, listening, drawing, looking, making and thinking. More specifically lessons might include:

- Presentations by the teacher to teach specific facts, give explanations and supply instructions.
- Demonstrations by the teacher/pupil to show particular skills/methods or working.
- Supervised practical tasks to do with designing/making.
- Question-and-answer sessions where ideas are challenged.

- Paired group activities allowing time to discuss, think, solve problems, plan future work and present ideas.
- Out-of-school visits to see and hear about contexts for work.
- Quick problem-solving tasks which might be competitive.
- Role play to held pupils understand the views of others.
- Comparison tasks to explore and compare existing products to increase pupils' own knowledge/understanding.

Continuity and progression

The *Non-Statutory Guidance for D&T* (DES, 1990) suggested some characteristics of progression. They were:
- increased knowledge, skills and understanding
- moving from the familiar to unfamiliar context
- meeting needs that need more complex or difficult solutions.

Davies (1995) suggests a more detailed range of factors that provide evidence of progression in food technology (D&T), as follows:

Process skills
Autonomy:
- to work independently
- to apply knowledge
- to identify clear targets
- to balance active and reflective practices.

Understanding others:
- to work increasingly in unfamiliar contexts
- to address other people's needs.

Designerly thinking:
- to select and use an increasingly sophisticated range of materials, equipment, processes, skills
- to use knowledge to inform designing/making
- to produce a detailed specification and deal with a number of variables
- to take responsibility for resource demands
- to carry out in-depth research
- to judge the value of gathered data.

Judgement:
- to try less familiar solutions to problems
- to use evaluation techniques effectively.

Propositional knowledge
1. To acquire propositional knowledge:
- by increased knowledge about materials/processes
- by more understanding of industrial practices
- by distinguishing between a single product/prototype and bulk production
- by using information from other cultures.

2. To use propositional knowledge:
- by gathering information to make judgements
- by applying knowledge and understanding of everyday products
- by moving from a simple awareness to the application food technology (D&T) knowledge/skills and of other subjects.

Practical skills
- to increased competency in skills, manual dexterity
- to increased application of new processes and skills
- to record and communicate idea using more technical and specialist terms
- to improved quality of the final product.

If capability in food technology is a creative activity, where pupils operate in a thinking or reflective and an active or doing mode, then a young child at Key Stage 1 will already be operating in a very capable manner in this active, reflective or procedural way. Children of this age should be able to design and make a sandwich for themselves in a safe and hygienic manner with sufficient teaching and guidance. They are demonstrating food technology capability using simple concepts and skills within their experience and at an appropriate level for their age range.

However, whether this level of food technology capability is appropriate for Key Stages 2, 3 and 4 pupils is another question. There is a need for teachers to plan a programme of work to ensure that a childs' learning develops in progressive manner. High-quality food technology capability at the age of 6, restricted by limitations of knowledge, skills and understanding, is not acceptable for pupils aged 13 with the additional experiences and expectation for that age range. Bentley and Watts (1994) advocate that progression is advancement by successive steps which relate to the childs' ability to change.

An example of progression across the key stages in food technology in the knowledge, understanding and skills associated with flour-based products is illustrated as follows:

- Year 2 in 'The beach': a simple sandwich
- Year 6 in 'Food around the World': variation on a sandwich
- Year 8 in 'Eating healthy: making bread
- Year 10 in 'The bakery': a new flour-based product

At each stage, pupils will need to have more sophisticated knowledge, understanding and skills. These may be taught through open-ended assignments, but it is likely at Key Stages 2, 3 and 4 that short, focused tasks or investigations are used to teach the knowledge, understanding and skills, which are then used by the pupils in less structured design briefs. The key issue is to match the classroom activity to the needs of the pupils to ensure they develop and extend their food technology capability.

A framework of knowledge, understanding and skills in food technology, first produced in 1993 and now refined, is outlined in Table 3.1. It provides a framework for progression built around the physical, chemical, sensory and nutritional properties of food.

	Physical/chemical properties	Sensory properties	Nutritional properties
Key Stage 1 (ages 5–7)	Personal safety and hygiene when handling food Measuring foods – simple weighing Using tools to cut, chop, peel, mix	Assessing their products drawing on the opinions of others, using appropriate sensory descriptors Serving food attractively	Sources of fruit and vegetables Why we need them
Key Stage 2 (ages 7–11)	Safety and hygiene factors related to their working environment and the storage of foods Properties of foods for energy and growth Measuring and combining starchy, sugar and dairy foods Energy sources that cook food	Evaluating consumer acceptability of their products using tests with verbal and/or pictorial scales	Sources and functions of foods for energy and growth Foods that are needed for healthy eating
Key Stage 3 (ages 11–14)	Safety and hygiene factors related to product development The use of attribute analysis in food product development The selection, modification and use of a range of recipes when making a food product Controlling the quality and shelf life of a food product through knowledge of the physical and chemical properties of foods Batch production and quality control	Setting up and conducting sensory tests which produce valid and reproducible results e.g. attitudinal and difference tests – triangle, ranking, hedonic Understanding the need to control portion size, temperature of samples, number of people on the taste panel to standardise results	Goals for healthy eating Sources and nutritional functions of fats, proteins, carbohydrates. The use of dietary analysis to 'model' with food Links between food intake and energy expenditure
Key Stage 4 (ages 14–16)	The safety, hygiene and environmental legal standards required for food production and distribution. Food packaging and storage Causes and control of food spoilage Controlling the shelf life, organoleptic and nutritional qualities of foods using physical and chemical preservatives. The product development process Marketing and retailing	The use of statistical data derived from different sensory tests to evaluate key characteristics of products The use of tests on key characteristics of products to specify criteria for consumer acceptability The use of tests to produce a product specification	The sources and functions of fibre, water, fats, carbohydrates, proteins, vitamins, minerals for different population groups Knowledge of simple/complex sugars, low and high biological value proteins, saturated/polyunsaturated fats, vitamins A/B/C/D/E Effects of processing freezing/heating/mechanical manipulation on nutrient content The use of food analysis in writing a food product specification

Table 3.1 Food technology

Differentiation

When planning the curriculum teachers have to satisfy two contrary require-ments.First of all there are the broad aims of education for all pupils and secondly differences in ability of pupils, even within the same age range (DES, 1980b). The Warnock Report (DES, 1989) stresses that the purpose of education is the same, but the help that individual pupils will need to progress will be different.

Differentiation starts from the assumption that pupils learn effectively at different rates and by different methods, it is a planned process of intervention in the classroom to maximise potential based on individual needs. It is not a single event but a process which recognises the variety of needs in a class and plans to meet those needs by providing appropriate delivery and by constantly evaluating the progress made. The **content** of the curriculum is defined by statute, but **differentiation** takes place because:

- a range of **resources** are used
- different **tasks** have to be designed
- teachers provide **support and guidance** for pupils
- **outcomes** of the students will vary (very common in food technology)
- **responses of teachers** to these outcomes will vary.

Hutchinson (1995) makes the following suggestions for planning and writing worksheets for different abilities.

For the less able:
- use graphics and pictures to explain key terms/ideas
- highlight key words – spell them clearly
- use idea balloons to get pupils started
- limit information on each page, use a simple layout
- use a simple reading level with short sentences
- vary capital and lower case lettering for effect
- include charts with blank spaces to be filled in by the pupil
- make the worksheet interactive to involve pupils/teacher
- ensure progression of difficulty for pupils by providing extension activities.

A range of activities might include:

- complete these sentences
- which is the odd-one out?
- fill in the blanks
- describe what you see in the picture
- think of anther word.

More able pupils:
- use a more difficult reading level and longer sentences
- provide less help with ideas and more information
- use more sophisticated graphics
- challenge the learner by expecting application of knowledge, not simply re-present it
- use a variety of contexts, e.g. industry, business
- use a range of activities to challenge their thinking

- encourage pupils to produce a wide range of outcomes
- expect the use of a wider range of sophisticated textbooks
- encourage pupils to use more primary reference materials
- expect pupils to explain and give reasons and evaluate
- allow learning to be more pupil led
- use competitions to motivate/encourage.

Activities could include:

- design a chart to show the class
- present graphics, pie charts, simple statistics
- rewrite in own words
- summarise main points
- make a list of the key factors
- debate
- conduct market research
- take on another role.

Assessing pupils' progress

Assessment in food technology should directly relate to pupils' learning and progression. According to Farrell and Patterson (1993), it should:

- determine whether pupils are learning and making progress
- identify a pupil's strengths and weaknesses to recognise positive achievement and support learning difficulties
- measure the success of the teaching programme against the aims
- identify modifications for future planning.

Food technology capability can be assessed using a variety of evidence:

- *Outcomes* – food products, packaging, understanding and use of control systems.
- *Documentation* – design project folder, research, report of an investigation or survey.
- *Graphics* – free-hand sketch of food product, graphs and charts from analysis of nutritional and sensory factors.
- *Photographs* – sample ideas, stages in the design process, production, finished prototype.
- *Teacher's perception and knowledge of how pupils do things* – the level of teacher intervention, review of a presentation.

Issues in assessment of food technology

- Pupils should understand the purpose of what they are doing (*curriculum led*) rather than simply doing things to gather evidence (*assessment driven*).
- A balance between reflective and active food technology capability (*research and making activities*).
- A balance between acquiring knowledge and understanding and developing *procedural* capability (*focused task and full design and make assignments*).

- Recording evidence (*design folders, using the same generic skills of presentation and format as other D&T areas*).
- Quality (*concise analysis and presentation skills*) is important not quantity.
- Objective performance criteria (*clear project, task criteria*).
- Evidence of food technology programmes of study (*knowledge, understanding and skills*).
- Food technology activities which enable pupils to extend and show their capability (*progression*).

Types of assessment

The following notes are based on Ofsted (DfE, 1995b):
Formative assessment has two main purposes:

1. It helps the teacher evaluate how well the pupils have learnt, the progress they have made and indicates to the teacher future modifications.
2. It gives the pupils regular encouragement and feedback on how well they are doing and areas they need to strengthen.

A range of strategies can be used in food technology to assess pupil progress, including:

- Use whole class question and answer sessions.
- Observe pupils working in food area.
- Discussions with individual pupils about their work.
- Pupil presentations.
- Review of completed homework.
- Mark design and practical work.
- Set short written and practical tests.

Summative assessment is usually longer tasks to enable teachers to judge or verify the level of attainment achieved by pupils. It takes place at the end of a unit or project or is part of the school examination programme. Its main purposes are to:

- Help teachers prepare reports for parents.
- Measure progress of individual pupils.
- Group pupils for food technology lessons so teachers can match work to pupils' ability.
- Enable analyse progress of different classes and carry out moderation.
- Provide information for the school.

The outcomes of assessment activities are often recorded in some way, for example in a mark book or on a record sheet. Different assignments will provide differing information on what pupils know, understand and can do, so allowing teachers to build up a profile of pupils' capability in food technology.

Assessment should be throughout a key stage, but not all pieces of work need to be formally assessed and recorded. Too frequent assessment overloads both teacher and pupils. There needs to be regular and planned formative assessment, particularly when working on longer projects, with helpful written comment and/or oral feedback from the teacher.

A framework for planning to teach food technology

In food technology pupils should be taught:

- To consider the physical/chemical/sensory properties of food as a material and relate them to handling and use.
- The working characteristics/properties of food and shown how they affect their use.
- The use of equipment and resources.
- The use of sensory tests to evaluate products against specified criteria.

Overall effective D&T school team curriculum planning is important because it helps ensure that:

- Pupils experience a well-structured and cohesive D&T programme, including food technology.
- Pupils are given a broad range of experiences and activities are well balanced across each key stage.
- Teachers can plan for the different interests and abilities of pupils and help them make progress in their learning.
- Teachers understand and appreciate the similarities and differences of the D&T experiences pupils meet in the different subject specialist areas.

Planning schemes of work

When planning a module or unit of work for the teaching of food technology, as with planning for other subject in the curriculum, there should be long-, medium- and short-term plans to ensure a sound basis for progression and continuity.

Long-term plans
- Provide an overview of progression across the key stages and within year groups. They should include learning objectives, teaching intentions and aims, and take into account the skills, knowledge, activities and programmes of study (see Table 3.2).

Medium-term plans
- Identify the main learning objectives or intended learning outcomes and assessment priorities for a unit of work (see Figure 3.5).

Short-term plans
- Weekly and daily plans interpret the medium-term plan for the class, group and individuals.

Check-list for planning schemes of work:
- *Continuity* – children's learning should build on previous experiences.
- *Resources* – planning must reflect available facilities/resources.
- *Aims* – decide what you want the pupils to learn about.
- *National Curriculum programmes of study* – cover the relevant knowledge, understanding and skills.

DEPT: D & T		MATERIAL		KS3
	TERM 1	TERM 2	TERM3	
YR 7				
YR 8				
YR 9				

Table3.2 Long-term plans

DESIGN & TECHNOLOGY – PLANNING SHEET

MODULE	FOOD HYGIENE								
	TERM: AUTUMN				YEAR GROUP: 7			AIMS & OBJECTIVES — To instil good practice in practical food work.	
WEEK	1	2	3/4	5	6	7	8	9/10/11	12
PoS	10a	4a, b, d	1b, 2a, 4abd, 10ac		1a 3b	1c 3a 3c	3e 3c	4a, 4b, 4d 4g, 4j	3l, 4j
ACTIVITY	Introduction to course / Micro-organisms	Dem stir fry / Compare modern hygiene and safety	Group practical / Investigation work	TEST	Introduction to DMA / Practice modelling techniques using paper	Research investigate evaluate	Computer graphics in IT room	Make the designed product	Class evaluation of final product
OUTCOME	Written work	Note taking	Food item		Pop-up models	3D graphics		Quality product	
ASSESSMENT	NONE	Mark for Homework	How well organised and precision with knives	Marks out of 10	None			Self-assessment	Agreed mark set against agreed criteria
HOMEWORK	Pages 3 & 4	Share H/W no, between 2 from P.6–7	P. 11 & 12 or Revise for test	Research the DMA	Survey and Conclusion	Design ideas	Final Design Specifications	Work on product	
RESOURCES	Worksheet	Equipment for cutting chopping frying	Knives boards Wok Worksheets	Leaflets etc.			Computers		
CHANGES TO BE MADE									

Figure 3.5 Medium-term plans

- *Intended learning outcomes/objectives* – plan the activities the pupils will do.
- *Differentiation* – specify minimum learning intended in each lesson and provide for the full ability range and pupils' individual needs.
- *Teaching resources* – develop a range of resources to enhance teaching and learning.
- *Assessment* – use formative and summative assessment to monitor pupils' learning.
- *Teaching strategies* – use a variety to stimulate and promote learning.

Chapter 5 will look at a case study and a plan for a scheme of work for a food product development project in greater detail.

Summary

- The revised Design and Technology National Curriculum Orders provide a realistic opportunity for food technology to be taught to all pupils aged 5–16, emphasising, as for other materials, the practical nature of food technology.
- The design process provides a common D&T base for pupils to develop their food technology capability.
- Knowledge, understanding and skills will vary for each of the range of materials, including food, used in D&T.
- There is a need to establish generic skills, especially in designing, and terminology across the specialist areas of D&T.
- Care needs to be taken with open-ended problem solving to ensure pupils are able to progress with their D&T knowledge, understanding and skills.
- Pupils should be given the opportunity to develop their food technology capability through a range of design-and-make assignments, focused practical tasks and investigative activities.
- Teaching strategies used in food technology will vary according to the pupil's needs, with formal teaching styles, such as demonstration, being an effective method for teaching knowledge and understanding or particular skills.
- Both formative and summative assessment is important to ensure feedback and support to pupils.
- Assessment should provide evidence for future curriculum planning in food technology.
- A structure or framework is needed in planning a programme of food technology to ensure progression and differentiation. It should include long-, medium- and short-term plans.

Chapter 4

Developing a Food Technology Curriculum

Jenny Jupe

Introduction

Since 1990, teachers of food education have been charged with the responsibility of delivering a course relating to food technology. However, many teachers, myself included, lacked clarity for some considerable time as to what the food technology curriculum should include. Subsequently the curriculum in my own school has been evolutionary, developing as the department has gained in knowledge and understanding and in response to many outside influences. Such influences have inevitably included GCSE syllabuses, SCAA non-mandatory tasks and tests, national projects and post-16 developments. As a department we feel that we have moved on considerably, but at the same time we recognise that there is continually room for improvement on our previous best.

The following cameos attempt to sketch out ways in which the department has developed. In so doing it is hoped that the exemplification provided will help other teachers move forward with confidence.

The food technology facility

It is my firm belief that the teaching facility (Figure 4.1) must reflect the practice for which it is to be used. The room must allow access to a variety of resources in an attempt to help pupils become discerning, independent learners. The room must demonstrate and demand high standards and expectations. Above all else, it must also excite and motivate the pupils towards learning. To achieve this I continually adapt the food technology area, so that it is never static. The pupils notice; frequently they comment or question my motives. Displays are regularly changed, added to or up-dated so that they become a valuable teaching resource. They are also a valuable means of communicating with individuals and groups. Results of tests and examinations are posted up; overview plans displayed where older pupils commit themselves for a series of lessons; information made available to help pupils complete homework assignments. The cameo 'A Room in Action' (see p.42) illustrates how such a food technology room can be used effectively.

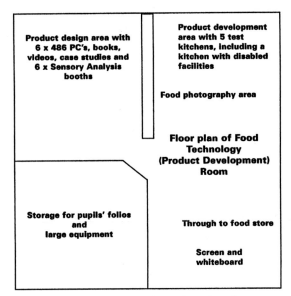

Figure 4.1 Floor plan of food technology room

Planning the food technology curriculum

If food technology is to be viewed with the same respect as other materials used in D&T, then it is vital that a rigorous, well developed and increasingly progressive curriculum is developed. The DATA Guidance Materials (1995), endorsed by the DfEE, present a model of curriculum delivery. This model (Table 4.1), based on specialist teaching, allows pupils a 6-month experience in each of four focus areas, with other aspects servicing the whole D&T curriculum.

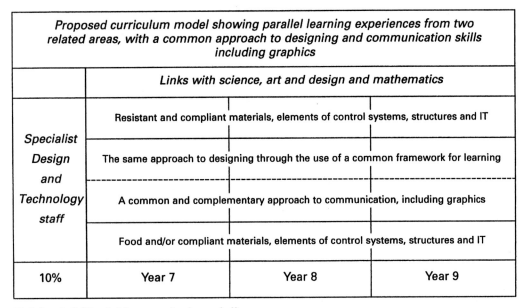

Proposed curriculum model showing parallel learning experiences from two related areas, with a common approach to designing and communication skills including graphics		
Links with science, art and design and mathematics		
Specialist Design and Technology staff	Resistant and compliant materials, elements of control systems, structures and IT		
	The same approach to designing through the use of a common framework for learning		
	A common and complementary approach to communication, including graphics		
	Food and/or compliant materials, elements of control systems, structures and IT		
10%	Year 7	Year 8	Year 9

Table 4.1 Model for curriculum delivery

A Room In Action

Curriculum Planning | **Classroom Practice**

A group of 22 Year 9 pupils enter the food technology room (Figure 4.1) ready to continue work on a design and make task (DMA) set some 5 weeks ago. Coats are hung up immediately outside and bags taken to the resource end of the room, where they are stored under the work benches. Pupils retrieve any necessary folders, pens, crayons and pencils. **Application of HACCP procedures**

4i ————— On the pupil notice board each pupil has signed up the work that she intends doing on the half-termly overview plan. Those who are engaged in developing prototypes start with personal preparation, before collecting ingredients from the food store. Each pupil works in one of five test kitchens, each **Use of all facilities**

4b ————— fully equipped with electronic scales, a microwave cooker, conventional oven, small hand tools and larger equipment. Electronic equipment, knife blocks and overalls are stored on a trolley, wheeled into the room at the start of each day. **Move away from domestic to industrial practice**

Some pupils had developed prototypes the previous week and froze them. These are collected from the technician, regenerated and set up ready for sensory analysis using all 10 sensory booths to speed up the process. The pupils collect the **Appropriate use of technician**

sensory equipment from a cupboard housing spoons, paper

4j ————— towels, plastic cups, jugs, lime juice and recording sheets. However, immediately prior to testing they place some samples on the photography table so that they can make a permanent record of their work to keep in their portfolios. Various pupils are then invited to a sensory booth where they can privately test the prototypes. **Equipment accessible to pupils**

IT available as needed

Three pupils ask to continue using the computers to model recipes that they have developed. They collect a pupil guide entitled 'How to get started with the Food Program' to remind themselves of procedures and quickly code the recipes, using code books kept in a magazine box beside the machines. Having entered and saved the data, they begin to analyse and modify their initial ideas. By the end of the lesson each of the three pupils has printed out information that she needs and refilled the printer paper ready for another class. **Previous teaching used**

Correct use of IT

Open access promotes

3c————— A final group of pupils is at various stages of **independent** researching, sketching ideas and planning to make prototypes, **learning** They sit in the centre of the resource area from where they are able to collect reference books, planning sheets and design **Exemplifica-** work equipment. Close by is a display of Year 11 GCSE **tion of** project work, setting the standard for presentation and **standards** providing ideas about what to include. The pupils move freely to collect the resources they need.

As the lesson draws to a close the pupils are asked to **Good work** tidy their workspace, return all used equipment and fill in the **routines** overview plan for the next two weeks at least. **practised**

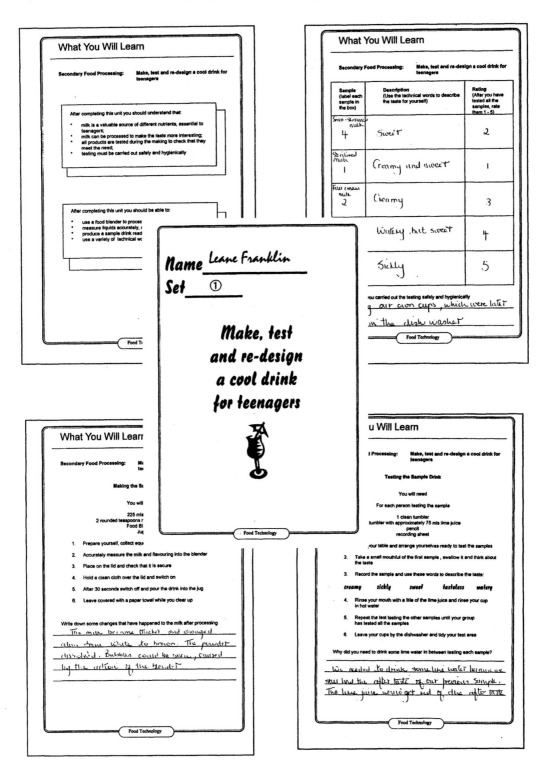

Figure 4.2 Food technology assignment – Pupil workbook

I have yet to find a more appropriate model through which to teach the current Orders. The 6-month experience that each pupil receives allows for the following:

- Opportunities to engage in focus practical tasks (FPT) /IDEAS/ design and make assignments (DMA).
- Opportunities for group and individual activity.
- Time for teachers to get to know individual pupils, thereby helping to develop D&T capability.
- Annual teachers assessments based on classwork and an end of module test.
- Opportunity for pupils to become familiar with teaching staff and a specialist mode of working.
- The development of a known curriculum model from which to build progression in knowledge, skills and understanding.
- Established and progressive resourcing from year to year.
- The progressive development of appropriate pupil learning support materials.
- Thus within my own department I have worked with the D&T team to put in place a process of curriculum development based on the DATA model and annually reviewed (Table 4.2).

When	What	Who
March/April	Department development plan	Whole team
May/June	Curriculum overview: Introductory course Commonality of curriculum design and approach	Whole team
July	Material specific curriculum (Programme of learning)	Specialist teachers
July/August	Teacher planning	Individuals
September	Teaching/learning and assessment	Individuals
Jan/February	Specialist curriculum revision	Specialist teachers
March/April	Department development plan	Whole team

Table 4.2 Cycle of curriculum development

This approach to curriculum development is underpinned by a series of strategies commonly adopted by all members of the design and technology team. The strategies include:

- the use of identical language to describe the design and make process;
- health and safety rules applicable to all areas;
- a common format to modular tests;
- shared use of pupils workbooks, glossaries and storage folios;

- common format to design sheet presentation;
- identical assessment criteria and recording procedures.

The food technology curriculum Year 7 to Year 9

Key Stage Overview – Year 7

Knowledge and understanding
Simple food hygiene, linked to:
- Risk assessment in food handling and serving
- Name and function of a range of hand tools
- Food groupings and daily portion allowances
- Concept of nutritional balance
- Fruit and vegetables
- Vitamins – A, B, C, D
- Mineral elements – iron and calcium ⎫ linked to the teenage diet
- Fibre ⎭
- Use of sensory language to describe food
- Food product specifications
- Conventions used in simple food graphics.

Skills and processes
- Correct use of sharp knives
- Coding of chopping boards
- Safe handling and preparation of raw fruit and vegetables to assemble food products
- Accurate weighing of solids
- Accurate measuring of liquids
- Use of blender
- Use of food database
- Taste testing using hedonic rating
- Graphic presentation of food designs
- Sequencing food production.

Tasks (in hours)
- 'Healthy Bytes' computer program   10.5
- Cool shakes for teenagers   4.5
- Simple food manufacture   6.0
- Soup it up!   7.5

  Total 28.5

Key Stage Overview – Year 8

Knowledge and understanding
Safe food storage linked to:
- Risk assessment: food packaging and storage
- Minimum durability of ambient, chilled and preserved food products
- Food labelling

- Name and function of a range of electronic tools
- Food production – prototypes, batch, core recipes
- Physical, chemical and nutritional properties of:
  - carbohydrates (starch and fibre)
  - proteins (particularly pulses)
- Flow chart for production
- Food graphics – sizing and scaling
- Star profiling for specification
- Methods of preserving food products:
  - canning
  - freezing, chilling
  - addition of chemicals, e.g. sugar.

Skills and processes
- Safe and correct use of electronic preparation equipment
- Oven management and use of timers for quality control
- Food decoration
- Use of spreadsheets for costings
- Graphic presentation of food designs
- Sensory testing using star profiles
- Using heat to combine foods and change their physical properties.

Tasks (in hours)
What has Science got to do with food?	6.0
Jazz Cakes	7.5
It's a Gift	7.5
Preserving Time	7.5
Total	28.5

Key Stage Overview – Year 9

Knowledge and understanding
Risk assessment:
- HACCP procedures for safe food production and quality assurance
- Dietary analysis, DRV's, EAR's
- Physical, chemical and nutritional properties of:
  - Starches
  - Sugars and sweeteners
  - Fats
- Product specification
- Consumer testing
- Time planning for production
- Food graphics – conventions for annotation
- Cost of large-scale production
- Use of microwave energy to heat food and change physical properties
- Bread and the bakery industry
- Control recipes.

Cool shakes for teenagers

Curriculum Planning Practice   **Classroom**

Twenty two pupils arrive knowing that they are beginning a new, but inter-linked project called cool shakes. Coats are hung up outside, bags placed in the resource area and pupils invited to sit in their 'healthy byte' teams.   **Working in teams**

Each pupil has her own workbook for the activity, planned to last 3 weeks. The teacher introduces the activity   **Clear learning objectives shared with pupils**

5a ——— and together they read the first page containing

'What you should know by the end of this activity'
'What you should be able to do by the end of this activity'

Throughout the activity the teacher reminds the pupils of these
4i ——— learning objectives.

The class then focus on the activity for the next 50 minutes – the production of cool shakes using five varieties of milk. A period of quiet reading then follows as the pupils study the instructions. At this stage the teacher is able to help those youngsters whom she perceives may have some difficulty.   **Appropriate differentiation by resources & support**

As each group is ready they prepare themselves, collect the necessary ingredients and equipment and begin production. When the first group are ready to use the blender the   **Sets high standards**
10c ——— teacher stops the class and gives a short, high-quality demonstration – points of safety and correct usage are emphasised.

The samples are left in a covered jug in each test kitchen   **Hygienic practices promoted**
and pupils are directed to use their work books in the resource area until all the samples are ready for testing. At this point each pupils collects two plastic beakers – one for the samples   **Teach technical vocabulary**
and one for plain water – and in groups they move to the test kitchens. Using the 'tasting words' prompt in their work books they test and record their opinion of each sample. Finally they rank the samples in order of preference.

5b ——— The lesson draws to a conclusion and the class briefly discuss and record their preferences using a simple tally chart, drawn by two pupils on the white board.

As homework the class are asked to turn the tally chart   **Explicit teacher expectations**
into a bar graph, using the squared paper at the back of the work book. It is an expectation of the pupils that they will return the completed work the following morning so that it can be marked and returned for the following week. Personalised homework trays are provided in the D&T foyer for this   **Celebrate success**
purpose.

Before leaving the room the teacher mentions that next week they will be designing their own shakes based on the results of preference tests. They are praised for their hard work and reminded about their homework. Figure 4.2 shows pages from a completed pupil workbook.

Skills and processes

- Safe and correct use of microwave cookers
- Consumer testing using paired and triangle tests
- Consolidation of sensory testing
- Shaping food by hand and with prepared moulds/formers
- Use of food database for:
  - dietary analysis
  - nutritional labelling
- Graphic presentation of food designs.

Tasks (in hours)

Chocaholics	6.0
Loafing around	8.5
Wrapping it all up!	10.0
(End of key stage assessment task)	
Total	28.5

Cameos of classroom practice

Year 7 – Building on from Key Stage 2 ('Cool shakes for teenagers')

In previous lessons the pupils have spent time engaged in these activities:

- Using 'Healthy Bytes', a food database, to help them capture, analyse and print out information abut their own dietary needs.
- Developing their skills of sketching and annotating design ideas for new products.
- Preparing food production schedules, which include simple HACCP regulations.
- Working in groups to batch produce cold snacks (healthy bytes!) for a take away snack store.

Year 8 – Developing the concept of manufacturing ('Manufacturing in miniature')

A series of Year 8 lessons take place, focusing on manufacturing technology. In food technology the pupils will be developing a new baked bean product, together with the associated labelling. Complementary to this pupils will be manufacturing small promotional items in resistant materials, using injection moulding and 3-D graphics. Both modules of learning have been developed from an original idea in the TEP 14–16 manufacturing book (TEP, 1995) and the teachers have collaboratively planned the whole module to last 4 weeks (12 hours including homework). The idea for the baked bean product had first been used by the food technology teacher earlier in her career when using the Nuffield Home Economic course, being based on the chapter entitled 'What has Science got to do with Food' in the Basic Course (Faulkner and Mansell, 1982).

Two displays in the room support the activity. One is a very tactile display of dried beans from around the world, together with other ingredients needed to manufacture baked beans. The other is concerned with labelling and includes legal requirements, details of nutritional labelling and sample labels, some of which

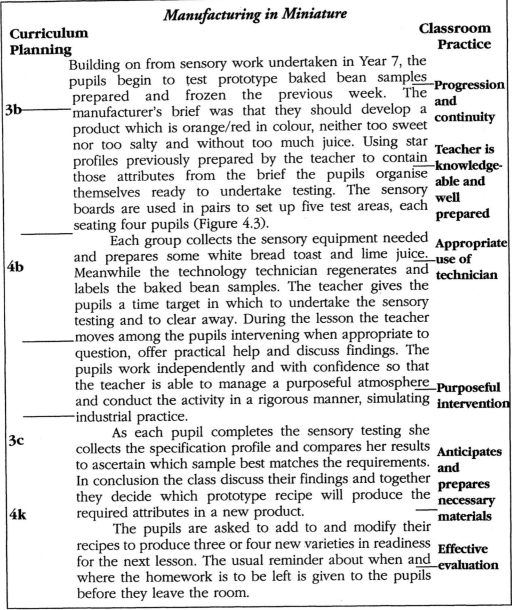

Manufacturing in Miniature

Curriculum Planning

Classroom Practice

Building on from sensory work undertaken in Year 7, the pupils begin to test prototype baked bean samples prepared and frozen the previous week. The **3b** manufacturer's brief was that they should develop a product which is orange/red in colour, neither too sweet nor too salty and without too much juice. Using star profiles previously prepared by the teacher to contain those attributes from the brief the pupils organise themselves ready to undertake testing. The sensory boards are used in pairs to set up five test areas, each seating four pupils (Figure 4.3).

— Progression and continuity

Teacher is knowledgeable and well prepared

4b Each group collects the sensory equipment needed and prepares some white bread toast and lime juice. Meanwhile the technology technician regenerates and labels the baked bean samples. The teacher gives the pupils a time target in which to undertake the sensory testing and to clear away. During the lesson the teacher moves among the pupils intervening when appropriate to question, offer practical help and discuss findings. The pupils work independently and with confidence so that the teacher is able to manage a purposeful atmosphere and conduct the activity in a rigorous manner, simulating industrial practice.

Appropriate use of technician

Purposeful intervention

3c As each pupil completes the sensory testing she collects the specification profile and compares her results to ascertain which sample best matches the requirements. In conclusion the class discuss their findings and together they decide which prototype recipe will produce the required attributes in a new product.

Anticipates and prepares necessary materials

4k The pupils are asked to add to and modify their recipes to produce three or four new varieties in readiness for the next lesson. The usual reminder about when and where the homework is to be left is given to the pupils before they leave the room.

Effective evaluation

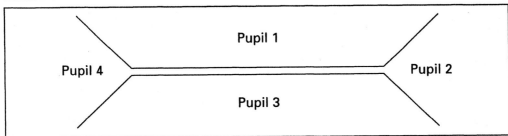

Figure 4.3 Using sensory boards

have been computer generated by last year's Year 8 pupils.

We join the food technology lesson as the pupils are undertaking attribute analysis using star profiling.

Year 9 – Consolidation and Practice

By the time pupils reach Year 9 I believe that they should be well resourced so that they can tackle a more open, longer DMA. I have gradually developed, adapted and refined the Year 9 programme of learning, but the structure, outlined in Table 4.3, has remained the same.

6 weeks Resource tasks (6 hours in school 3 hours homework	12 weeks Capability task DMA (11 hours in school 5.5 hours homework)	End of DMA Test (1 hour)
Total curriculum time 28.5 hours		

Table 4.3 Year 9 Food Technology course 'Chocaholics'

The DMAs have been based on SEAC (1993) non-mandatory tasks *vis-à-vis* the 'Meal Replacement bar' and the 'Toppings and Fillings' product (1994). Latterly (1995–96) the DMA has be to trial the SCAA 'Edible Containers' activity (SCAA, 1996b). Within the planning framework (Figure 4.4) the pupils have followed a series of resource tasks to provide them with the necessary skills in readiness for the DMA. The tasks are generic to developing a new product and aim to build on work in Year 7 and Year 8.

I refer to the programme described in the previous pages as the foundation course and perceive it as a curriculum entitlement for all children within Key Stage 3. However, the purpose of the programme must also be seen in the context of the key stages between which it sits. Just as the programme needs to develop knowledge, skills and understanding taught in Key Stage 2, so it needs to prepare pupils for the rigors of GCSE at Key Stage 4. It is at this key stage that pupils are certainly expected to apply the knowledge previously gained and to work more independently, as an individual to design and make food products of a high quality.

To help pupils achieve such independence a repertoire of knowledge and skills are taught, matching the content within the GCSE syllabus and following the design process in the assessment criteria. Early tasks may only focus on a limited aspect of the design and make process, for example on developing a food product specification from which to undertake testing and evaluation. However, over the 2 years the tasks will gradually become more complex. This is usually achieved by placing work in a less familiar context or by increasing the number of demands upon the product. At whatever level the pupils are studying food technology they are always given sufficient teacher support in order to help them achieve their full capability.

The following task provides a scenario which has been used with successive groups to achieve some excellent results. Following on from the task is a typical cameo ('Chocaholics') from the activity.

Y9 Resource Tasks	Marked weekly. Contributes towards the Y9 portfolio for end of key stage assessment
Control recipes Packaging materials Production schedules and HACCP Food handling skills bread/pastry Consumer testing – triangle test Production costs IT for recipe modelling	
Y9 Capability Task **DMA** Pupils can use and apply knowledge, skills and understanding taught in resource tasks	Monitored weekly. Marked and used to help form end of key stage assessment judgement Level recorded on the department database
Y9 End of Module Test 1 hour paper testing knowledge and understanding	Marked out of 100. Recorded on a database and reported to parents
Y9 Report to Parents Level capability reported once only	Level, Examination percentage and comments sent to parents

Figure 4.4 Planning framework, Year 9

Year 10 – Structured DMA for inclusion in the GCSE portfolio
('Developing a product specification')

Task Frame

A leading fast food chain has recently been criticised for only serving meat or fish based burgers. As a food technologist, you have been approached to develop alternative prototype ideas for initial consumer testing in the Midland region.

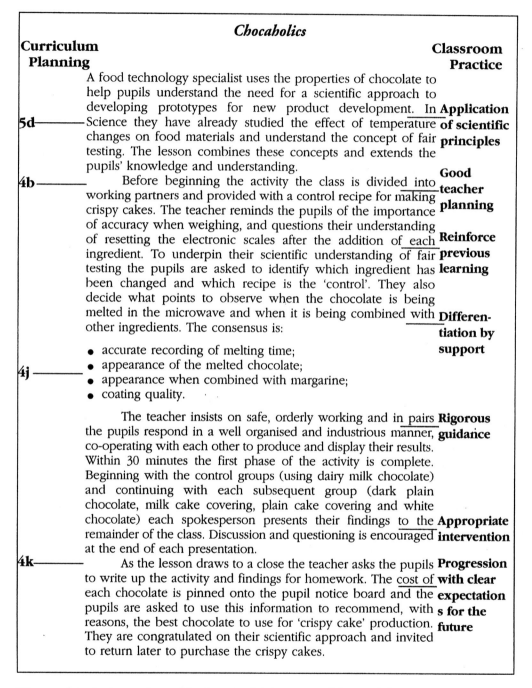

Chocaholics

Curriculum Planning

Classroom Practice

A food technology specialist uses the properties of chocolate to help pupils understand the need for a scientific approach to developing prototypes for new product development. In **Application of scientific principles**

5d — Science they have already studied the effect of temperature changes on food materials and understand the concept of fair testing. The lesson combines these concepts and extends the pupils' knowledge and understanding.

Good teacher planning

4b — Before beginning the activity the class is divided into working partners and provided with a control recipe for making crispy cakes. The teacher reminds the pupils of the importance of accuracy when weighing, and questions their understanding of resetting the electronic scales after the addition of each **Reinforce previous learning** ingredient. To underpin their scientific understanding of fair testing the pupils are asked to identify which ingredient has been changed and which recipe is the 'control'. They also decide what points to observe when the chocolate is being melted in the microwave and when it is being combined with **Differen-tiation by support** other ingredients. The consensus is:

4j —
- accurate recording of melting time;
- appearance of the melted chocolate;
- appearance when combined with margarine;
- coating quality.

The teacher insists on safe, orderly working and in pairs **Rigorous** the pupils respond in a well organised and industrious manner, **guidance** co-operating with each other to produce and display their results. Within 30 minutes the first phase of the activity is complete. Beginning with the control groups (using dairy milk chocolate) and continuing with each subsequent group (dark plain chocolate, milk cake covering, plain cake covering and white chocolate) each spokesperson presents their findings to the **Appropriate** remainder of the class. Discussion and questioning is encouraged **intervention** at the end of each presentation.

4k — As the lesson draws to a close the teacher asks the pupils **Progression** to write up the activity and findings for homework. The cost of **with clear** each chocolate is pinned onto the pupil notice board and the **expectation** pupils are asked to use this information to recommend, with **s for the** reasons, the best chocolate to use for 'crispy cake' production. **future** They are congratulated on their scientific approach and invited to return later to purchase the crispy cakes.

Tips and techniques for achieving the highest possible grade!

- *Brainstorm –*   Identify a range of needs and design opportunities for burger development.
- *Notes and reports –*   Gather a range of research material which could include:

(i)   current dietary advice
(ii) dietary needs of vegetarians
(iii) food suitable for making non-meat burgers
(iv) questionnaire to indicate some consumer preference

Present the research in a logical and relevant manner:

- *Report –*   Analyse your research to decide what to develop.
- *Chart –*   Produce a detailed specification which takes into account the original brief and your research.
- *Graphic techniques*   Use a range of media (pens/crayons/pencils) and specialist (shading/rendering) to communicate three or four design ideas clearly and attractively. Designs should show: size/good or bad points/texture components with reasons/weight/main cooking method;
- *Report –*   Show how your designs have taken into account relevant aspects of:
  – cost (economic issues)
  – dietary advice (moral issues)
  – cultural beliefs (social issues)
  – health & safety (environmental issues)
- *Production schedule –* Plan the correct sequence of activities to produce no more than two prototypes.
- *Realisation –*   Demonstrate well organised making skills which clearly show an understanding of the equipment, tools and materials. Include at least one photograph of each prototype.
- *Charts and analysis –* Develop and carry out a consumer preference test on appearance/texture/flavour and analyse the results.
- *Notes –*   Evaluate the prototypes by referring to the specification
and consumer testing and include comments on:
  – modifications;
  – possible large-scale production;
  – methods of storage and transportation.

To be handed in immediately after Easter, before Year 10 examinations.

Developing a product specification:

Curriculum Planning		**Classroom Practice**

3c — In a previous lesson some Year 10 pupils have conducted market research through questionnaires that they developed. From their work they have found out what consumers want, what already exists that they prefer and how much they are prepared to may for a new burger product. They have analysed their results and each pupil has identified their own market niche for the type of burger.

The pupils have completed the concept development **Teach** phase and have written an outline specification that they **appro-** are working towards. Some pupils are testing out specific **priate** types of ingredients, for example suitable foods with which **techniques** to bind vegetables while others are using the computer to model suitable vegetarian burger recipes. After all this work

3e — is completed the pupils will be able to develop detailed **Use of IT** specifications, i.e. the nutritional, sensory and processing **to model** considerations and finished product standards. **ideas**

The lesson begins with the pupils sharing what they have been considering and what they hope to achieve. Each pupil then works individually at her own specification, seeking assistance from the teacher as and when necessary.

3j — To help support the learning the teacher has provided **Flexible** sample specifications from another product and blank **approach** specifications forms with appropriate headings. However, the **to teaching** pupils are free to use their own specification format.

At the end of the lesson the teacher reminds to pupils to update the overview planning sheets with their work for the next lesson and sets the target of at least two annotated **Good** design ideas which would meet the requirements of their **long-term** specification (Figure 4.5). **planning**

Summary

This chapter clarifies what should be included in the food technology curriculum:

- Food technology teaching facilities must reflect the practice for which it is to be used.
- The room should demonstrate and demand high standards and expectations and excite and motivate the pupils.
- The food technology curriculum must be rigorous, well developed and increasingly progressive.
- It should be based on specialist food technology teaching.
- It should contain strategies and terminologies that are common to all members of the design and technology team.

New Product Specification

Description of Product: _____

User group: _____

Food outlet: _____

Nutritional content: Manufacturing processes:

_____   _____

_____   _____

_____   _____

_____   _____

Sensory attributes: _____

_____   Storage/Shelf life:

_____   _____

_____   _____

Sensory and/or consumer testing procedures:

_____

_____

Production/retail cost:

_____

_____

Signed: _____

Date: _____

Figure 4.5 New product specification

- The use of IT should be incorporated into the schemes of work.
- Manufacturing technology should be included.
- By Year 9 pupil should be able to tackle more open, longer design and make assignments.
- The Key Stage 3 programme should develop pupils' knowledge, skills and understanding for the rigors of Key Stage 4 GCSE courses.
- In Years 10 and 11 the tasks should gradually become more complex by either working in less familiar contexts or by increasing the number of demands upon food product.

Chapter 5

Food Product Development: A Case Study

Sheena Archer

Introduction

The case study for Year 9 pupils contains a design brief based on the development of cakes, always a popular project with both parents and pupils alike!

It is a development from my Key Stage 3 food and textiles pack *Orders into Practice* published by Hampshire Inspection and Advisory Support Service (HIASS, 1993).

The project is in two sections. The first teaches the required *knowledge and skills* and is followed by an assessed design and make activity. The *knowledge and skills* section encompasses a wider selection of work than the pupils will need for their cake development task, providing them with traditional baking skills and the methodology for product development.

Section 1: Teaching knowledge and skills

The pupils use the work sheets on pastry and a *making sponge mixture using the creaming method* (Figure 5.1). These are from their school *Knowledge and Skills* booklet called *Designing with Basic Recipes* (Archer, 1995) used in Year 8.

These worksheets will be the basis of their 'Design and Make Activity' called *The Baker Develops New Cakes* (Figure 5.2). The teaching strategies used relate to the National Curriculum for D&T (DfE,1995a) as they include:

- A structured approach or *focused practical task* in which the pupils develop and practise particular skills and knowledge that they will need later.
- An assessed design and make activity or *assignment* in which pupils design and make food based products.
- Activities in which pupils *investigate, disassemble and evaluate.*

RECIPE DEVELOPMENT WORK SHEET
Based on CREAMING METHOD (Yr. 8)

Unpack ingredients and put bags, jumpers and coats right out of the way. Tie hair back, take jumper off, roll sleeves up. Wash your hands (no rings) and put apron on.

Switch oven on – 180 deg. C or Gas 5. Do not use the floor of the oven.

Collect equipment – Mixing bowl, mixing spoon, (or mixer or food processor), jug or small bowl, fork, appropriate baking tins.

Oven gloves, teatowel, dishcloth, scourer, washing up liquid.

INGREDIENTS FOR BASIC FORMULA
For each size 4 egg add:
50g self raising flour (white or wholemeal)
50g castor sugar
50g polyunsaturated margarine from a plastic carton (**not** hard, block margarine or butter or low fat spread).

BASIC MIXING METHOD
1. Break the eggs into a jug and beat them with a fork.
2. Put all the ingredients in a mixing bowl. Stand the bowl on a damp dishcloth to stop it slipping. Mix and beat until it is all light and fluffy. (Or put it in a mixer or processor and mix on full power.)

USING AND COOKING THE BASIC MIXTURE
This mixture makes sandwich cakes, small cakes in paper cases or small tins and baked, steamed or microwaved puddings.

Sandwich cakes – 2 egg mixture for 2 x 25cm. tins. Line tins with circles of grease-proof paper in the base. Oil the tins and paper. Bake for about 25 mins. before testing. Looks golden. Press the middle lightly with finger. If it bounces back, it's cooked.

Small cakes – Heaped teasp. of mixture into the paper case or oiled tins. Same test as above.

Steamed pudding – 2 egg mixture for a 2 pint oiled basin. Put syrup or fruit etc. in the base with mixture over it. Cover with grease-proof paper and foil. Steam for 1½ hrs.

Baked pudding – 1.5 pint pie dish size for 2 egg mixture or one 15cm. lined, sandwich tin for 1 egg size. Put 2 sliced apples, pineapple and glace cherries, tinned pears etc. in the base of an oiled pie dish/tin. Put mixture on top. It looks cooked before it is. Cook for 40 mins. before testing with a skewer. You can turn it out to make an upside-down cake or pudding.

Microwaved puddings – Add 1 tablesp. milk per egg to the mixture. Use pyrex, china or plastic dish (**not metal**). Prepare like steamed (**but no foil**) or baked pudding. Cook it on full power for 6–8 mins. Test with skewer.

IDEAS FOR DESIGNING WITH FOOD USING DISHES – THE BASIC MIXTURE
Flavourings – To each egg you can add – 25g glace cherries, sultanas, chocolate chips, coconut, 1 tablespoon cocoa, 0.5 teasp. vanilla or other essences.

Sandwich cakes – When cool. Sandwich with chocolate spread, jam, lemon curd, etc.

Topping – When cold. Look for glace icing or butter icing recipe. Or melted *cooking* chocolate.

Figure 5.1 Creaming method sheet

DESIGN AND TECHNOLOGY CAPABILITY

Knowledge & Understanding

Skills Designing & Making

Range of Activities

Design and Make Activity – The Baker Develops New Cakes

Combine materials to create useful properties and aesthetic effects – Basic recipes made into a variety of new products.	**Strategies for generating design ideas** – New basic cookery methods.	**Materials – Food.**
Select materials appropriate to the task – Choosing additional ingredients to create new products.	**Wider range of Information** – New methods.	**Apply designing and making skills.**
	Develop manual dexterity – Using hand tools and new techniques.	**Apply knowledge and understanding.**
Joining, construction and finishing techniques to the characteristics of the ingredients – Shaping and forming food products in pastry etc.	**Become proficient, skilful and accurate with a range of materials, tools and equipment** – Whole course.	**Focused tasks.**
Products for their intended purpose to fill a clear need.	**Assemble, join and combine materials, accurately** – Whole course.	
The effects of food processing on the physical and nutritional properties of food products and that heating, freezing and chemical additives alter the properties and prolong the shelf life of foods.	**Apply finishing techniques** – Decoration, glaze and garnish.	
To select and combine different ingredients to create products which have different sensory characteristics and perform different functions.		
To experiment with ways of combining food to create and modify products in order to improve their sensory characteristics.		
Safety and Hygiene – Use equipment safely.		

Figure 5.2 Design brief

An example of pupil's development of a basic recipe during the "Knowledge and Skills" section of the course:

DESIGN SHEET FOR CREAMED MIXTURE

Draw a picture of what you hope your product will look like.

Name of dish **Ruby Gem Pudding**

Size of cake tins, pie dish or pudding basin:
A pudding basin which takes 2 pts. of water. It must not be metal.

Quantity of basic mixture needed:
A 2 egg quantity.

Amounts of additional ingredients needed:
50 glace cherries. 4 tablespoons red jam. 2 tablespoons of milk.

Method of cooking:
Microwave.

Temperature and time:
Full power for 8 mins.

METHOD OF MIXING AND COOKING
Make the basic creamed mixture as shown in the basic method, but stir in the milk and cherries.
Oil the pudding basin and put the jam in the bottom.
Put the mixture on top of the jam.
Cook it in the microwave for 7 mins. Check whether it is cooked by pressing the top gently to see if it is bouncy.
Cook for a further minute if necessary.
Turn it out onto a serving plate and serve immediately.

EVALUATION

Did the dish turn out as I intended?
It was quite good but most of the cherries sunk. However, that gave quite a good effect when it was turned out!

Were the instructions above correct? Could there be improvements?
Yes, except for the cherries. I could have cut them up to make them lighter, then maybe they would not have sunk.

Did my family enjoy it?
Yes. My dad said it was a long time since he had had a steamed pudding, so I did not tell him it was microwaved! He said it needed some custard.

Figure 5.3 Design sheet for creamed mixture

RECIPE DEVELOPMENT WORK SHEET
Based on CREAMING METHOD
(Yr. 9 extending Yr. 8 work)

**This is an exercise in designing with a recipe as professionals do.
You do not necessarily have to cook it.**

INGREDIENTS FOR BASIC FORMULA

50g self raising flour (white or wholemeal)
50g castor sugar
50g polyunsaturated margarine
50g (one size 4) egg.

RATIO

**1 part flour: 1 part sugar: 1 part fat:
1 part egg**

BASIC MIXING METHOD

1. Break the eggs into a jug and beat them with a fork.
2. Put all the ingredients in a mixing bowl. Stand the bowl on a damp dishcloth to stop it slipping. Mix and beat until it is all light and fluffy. (Or put it in a mixer or processor and mix on full power.)

DESIGNING WITH THE BASIC MIXTURE

This is a basic "creaming method" sponge mixture, with no flavourings.
The formula has a very easy ratio – equal parts of everything (assuming the egg weighs 50g). If the recipe above makes 8 small cakes, write the recipe a baker would use to make 80 cakes.

[____] g   Self raising flour

[____] g   Castor sugar

[____] g   Polyunsaturated margarine

[____] g   Egg

The Baker wishes to make four batches, each with different flavours and textures. Suggest what he could add.

1. _____
2. _____
3. _____
4. _____

THE BAKER WISHES TO DEVELOP NEW PRODUCTS

Bulking ingredient – Flour (and aerating if self-raising flour is used)
The Baker could substitute some flour for another bulking ingredient, such as wholemeal flour, oats, coconut or semolina.
Sweetening, moistening, aerating and shelf life ingredient – castor sugar
The Baker could substitute brown sugar, honey, syrup or dried fruit.
Binding ingredient – egg
Egg coagulates (sets) in the heat of the oven and binds the other ingredients together. He had better keep that!
Texturing, moistening, browning, aerating and shelf life ingredient – margarine
The Baker could substitute butter, white vegetable fat, lard or he could try oil.

Figure 5.4 Recipe development sheet

Pupils complete a design sheet (Figure 5.3) for their basic mixture in which they evaluate and analyse their learning during the focused task.

The recipe development work sheet (Figure 5.4), is intended to extend the work on the basic recipe of a sponge cake and is an exercise in designing a recipe in a more professional manner. It introduces new concepts and new terminology, for example a 'basic formula', a 'basic mixing method', 'ratio' and 'batches', 'bulking ingredients' and 'shelf life'.

The next activity is a focused mini design brief – '*Be a Baker!*' (Figure 5.5). Pupils are asked to design a new cake with a short crust pastry base, with a filling based on the creaming sponge mixture. They learn that that some ingredients are better

---

The Baker will find that some ingredients will do a job better than others:
He can beat or whisk air into margarine and sugar.
It will hold the air and make a light mixture, as well as moistening and browning the product.
If he substitutes oil and honey, the mixture will certainly be moist and brown, but it will not hold much air.
Maybe he had better try making that mixture into biscuit bars or cookies rather than small cakes.
Coating   He could coat his new products with chocolate, icing, jam and coconut, chocolate spread and chopped nuts, etc.
Sandwiching He could sandwich together two different mixtures, either before or after cooking if he uses a gooey ingredient such as peanut butter, jam, lemon curd, chocolate spread, egg, etc.

MINI DESIGN BRIEF – BE A BAKER!

Design a new cake which is based on a short crust pastry tartlet base, with a filling based on creaming method sponge mixture.

First choose your ingredients to fulfil the **Physical Functions** of the cake.
Write them in the boxes.

Bulking –

Sweetening –   Texturing or Shortening –

Shelf life –   Aerating –

**Filled Tartlets
Named**

Moistening –   Browning –

Coating –   Sandwiching –

Next choose your flavouring ingredients for **Taste**, extra **"Mouthfeel"** or extra **Nutritive Value**.
These might be chocolate chips, chopped nuts, dried fruit, essences, etc.

Flavouring –

Figure 5.5 Be a baker!

than others for specific properties of the cake. The baker will need ingredients that will hold the air or gas, which is beaten in or introduced by chemical means, to make the sponge a light texture. He or she will also need moistening ingredients and those that will brown. Ingredients that will sandwich the pastry to the sponge will coat and decorate the top, add flavour, 'mouthfeel' and nutritive value are investigated. This information is reinforced by the pupils developing a database on the computer identifying the properties of the ingredients they have meet. The database is then available for a *search* of, for example, *aerating ingredients* when the pupils carry out their 'Design and Make Activity'.

Pupils are then taught how to use 'star graphs' to establish an aim and to evaluate the finished product. The new word 'descriptors', or adjectives or phrases which best fit the hoped-for result, is introduced to pupils, and an example of a star graph (Figure 5.6) for a sponge tartlet is used to illustrate the process. Pupils are also introduced to hedonic testing and screening algorithms.

Section 2: Design and make activity

The teachers uses the brief, '*A Food Technologist, specialising in bakery, wishes to develop a cake to add to the company's range of individual, sponge tartlets boxed in packets of six*', to help assess pupils' design and technology capability and level of attainment at the end of key stage 3. An assessment grid (Figure 5.7) is produced, which relates the design activity to level descriptors in D&T Attainment Target 1 (*Designing*) and D&T Attainment Target 2 (*Making*), which enables teachers to assess pupils' progress and achievements.

Pupils are given the criteria for the sponge cakes and asked to follow the processes and practices of supermarket chains while developing their own food product. They are able to work at their own level, following more sophisticated procedures to achieve the higher national Curriculum D&T assessment levels. For instance, to achieve Level 8 they can produce a 'Nutritional Information Label' for their product using the computer program 'Nutrients' with 'Labeller' (Hampshire, 1994).

Summary

This case study has illustrated a number of important features in food product development in the classroom. These are:

- Case studies developed by pupils require a sound base of basic food technology knowledge understanding and skills.
- The knowledge, understanding and skills are acquired within a framework of structured focused activities across Key Stage 3.
- An assessed design and make activity requires a more open-ended approach where pupils are involved in the decision-making process.
- A brief based in a bakery (Figure 5.8) is an ideal, realistic way of pupils beginning to develop an awareness of practices in the food industry.

Star diagrams

A star diagram is used by the food industry to describe the looks and taste of food and other products. It is an easy way to compare products as you can quickly see the differences on the star graphs. You can compare several factors at once such as the sweetness and crunchiness of a biscuit. From the star diagram you can write a **product profile** describing how it looks and tastes.

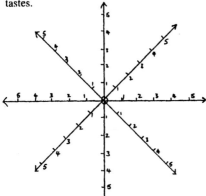

How to draw a star diagram
1. Draw a graph with 8 lines as shown.
2. Label each line with a word (sensory descriptor) which describes the food or product such as "sweetness" or "crispness". Use the **Tasting Word Bank** to give you ideas.
3. Mark each line on the graph with a scale from 0 to 5 where 0 = not at all, 3 = OK and 5 = very ....

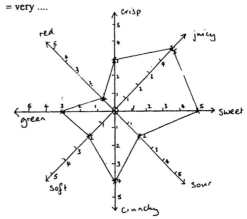

How to fill in the star diagram
1. Taste the food and give each word a score out of 5. If the word is "sweet" a zero score means the food does not taste sweet at all, and a 5 score means that it is very sweet.
2. Mark each score on the graph and draw up the lines to form a star diagram to show the product profile.

Example
8 words to describe an apple:

crisp, juicy, sweet, sour, crunchy, soft, green, red.

This is the star diagram describing an apple. The graph can be used for a written description of the apple:

" The apple is green with a little red, quite crisp and very juicy, very sweet but just a little sour, very crunchy and not soft."

To do
Carry out an apple tasting.
You need:
4 different types of apple cut into small pieces
Method
1. Draw 4 star diagrams each labelled with scales for the tasting words you will use for the apples. Taste each apple and fill in the star diagrams.
2. What is the difference between the taste and looks of each apple? Write a sentence to describe the taste of your favourite apple.

Figure 5.6 Star diagram

ASSESSMENT GRID

Year Group **Nine** Tech Grp _____ Form _____

Course _____

Date _____ Teacher _____

Pupils' Names

LEVEL DESCRIPTIONS

Level 5			Photocopy at A3
	AT1 Designing	1. Draw on external sources & understand the characteristics of familiar products. 2. Clarify ideas by discussion, drawing and modelling 3. Use your knowledge & skills. (Progs. of Study) 4. Understanding of the context, function & constraints.	Eg. Market survey & testing. Use of a computer data base etc.
	AT2 Making	1. Work from own plans & modify if necessary. 2. Use tools & materials safely. Be precise & check. 3. Modify design when necessary. 4. Evaluate artefact compared with original design.	"Plans" include own developed recipe with the method & timeplan or flow chart
Level 6			Aesthetics & taste?
	AT1 Designing	1. Sources used include those unrelated to task. 2. Consider appearance, function, safety and users of the product. 3. Make models to test thinking. 4. Use formal drawings to communicate	"Models" include first trials of basic recipes & first trials of a developed recipe.
	AT2 Making	1. Plans show implications of your design intentions. 2. Show alternative methods if first fail. 3. Skilful with techniques, tools & materials. 4. Evaluate products in use and identify improvements.	"Implications" - green & environmental issues. Reason for your product on the
Level 7			Wide selection of sources but showing discrimination from the start.
	AT1 Designing	1. Identify appropriate information to generate ideas. 2. Investigate form, function, production of familiar products to develop your ideas. 3. Design for a variety of users & evaluate progress. 4. Use "knowledge & skills". Communicate their design's use using a variety of media.	Study existing products.
	AT2 Making	1. Produce plans which predict time needed for stages and processes. 2. Match you choice of material with tools, equipment and processes. 3. Provide sound reasons for changes in production. 4. Evaluate by appropriate methods & say how performance could be improved.	Show awareness of time & deadlines. Use technical testing methods.
Level 8			Aim to show that your product has advantages over existing products.
	AT1 Designing	1. Use range of strategies to generate appropriate ideas 2. Compare existing artefacts in use with their own. 3. Understand physical & working function of materials 4. Analyse conflicting demands on designs & identify these when communicating their design.	Scientific understanding of materials.
	AT2 Making	1. Plans identify where decisions have been made. 2. Plans show alternative methods of manufacture. 3. Organise work for high degree of precision & high quality. 4. Evaluate procedures. Indicate improvements & implement these improvements.	See "Exceptional Performance" notes in the Orders.

Figure 5.7 Assessment grid Part 1

ASSESSMENT GRID

Year Group _____ Tech Grp _____ Form _____

Course _____

Date _____ Teacher _____

Pupil's Names

Photocopy at A3

LEVEL DESCRIPTIONS TRANSLATED FOR THE COURSE

Level 5

AT1 Designing
DS1 Analyse constituents such as bulking & sweetening of existing, similar cakes.
DS2 Draw cross sections of 3 cake designs with notes showing contents.
DS1 Use obvious understanding of this work, do in K&S
DS2 Show understanding of context and constraints.
DS3 Plan your recipe & method plus drawing.

AT2 Making
Teacher's observation - Use tools & ingredients safely - checking with precision.
DS4 Star Test result, comparing it with original

Level 6

AT1 Designing
DS1 Make lists of ingredients under 'bulking', 'sweet' etc.
DS2 Show which ingredients perform which function.
DS2 Star test for each type of cake.
DS2 Good formal drawings.

AT2 Making
DS3 Plan shows that it works in time & equipment when making a small number of cakes.
Teacher's Observation - Adust plan if necessary. Skilful techniques used.
DS4 Identify improvements after Hedonic tests.

Level 7

AT1 Designing
DS1 Investigate shops & find cakes to research.
DS1 Show which of the commercial range comes nearest to the star test.
DS2 Do algorithms on each to prove them fit for the brief.
DS2 Communication of test results shown very clearly.

AT2 Making
DS3 Plan shows plan of production timing.
Teacher's observation - Uses suitable methods for time etc.
Provides sound reason for changes.
DS4 Says what could be improved in technical language.

Level 8

AT1 Designing
DS1 Shows advanced evidence of own research into shop cakes.
DS2 Makes a nutrients label for one cake and compares it to shop ones.
DS2 Using test results compare own designs with shop.
DS2 Shows real understanding of physical function of ingredients.
DS3 If changes are made they are noted on the sheet.

AT2 Making
DS3 Notes the alternative methods if changes are made.
DS4 Idicates full improvements using technical language and if time allows, makes the cakes including the improvements plus new ingredients label.

Enter each pupil's name along the top.
Assess each of the criteria on the left, marking:
0 = Not attempted
1 = Attempted but not achieving the level.
2 = Satisfactory for the level
3 = Very good for the level

The "working towards" level is assumed at the point where the pupil fails to be awarded a bulk of 2 or 3.

At the end of the Key Stage this is moderated with the levels achieved in Textiles and CDT materials, to decide the Technology level achieved.

Figure 5.7 Assessment grid Part 2

FOOD PRODUCT DEVELOPMENT

THE DESIGN BRIEF

A Food Technologist, specialising in bakery, wishes to develop a product to add to the company's range of individual, sponge tartlets, boxed in packets of six.

Criteria

Like the others, already in the range, the new cake should be medium sweet, have a fairly high N.S.P. (dietary fibre) content, be moist, have varied "mouthfeel", look attractive, have a good flavour, have reasonable shelf life without artificial preservatives and use the creamed sponge method and shortcrust pastry.

WEEK 1

Class work.

Introduction to the Design Brief. You will be working in just the same way as Tesco or Sainsbury's develop a new product for sale.

1. Revise the meaning of the technical words you have used in the "Knowledge and Skills" lessons:

a) Ingredients for "bulking, "sweetening", "moistening", "aerating", "binding", "texturing", "browning", "coating", "sandwiching" etc.

b) What is "Shelf-life? Which ingredients would give cakes a long shelf-life?

2. Observe and taste the shop bought cake provided and study the ingredients and nutrition labels on the packet. Study the other, empty, cake packets which are provided. (The process of analysing ready made products is called "disassembling")

HOMEWORK

Observe and research packeted cakes, other than those you have been shown. Collect the packets if you can.

Think and observe the varied ingredients you could add to a Sponge Tartlet design.

Figure 5.8 Food product development – pupil sheets

WEEK 2

Design Sheet 1

NOTE:
All of you must attempt Stage 1. If you are working beyond Stage 1, read all the instructions in a Design Sheet box before you start.

Stage 1 *(Level 5)*
i) Draw or describe the cakes which were in the empty cake packets you are shown.
ii) Write notes to say what properties they have, showing that you understand some of the technical terms used in baking technology.

Stage 2 *(Level 6)*
iii) [You may need a new sheet numbered 1 b] Draw a table headed with the different properties discussed in the introduction (see page 1). List all the appropriate ingredients you can think of which go under each heading and can be included in sponge tartlets.

Stage 3 *(Level 7)*
iv) [You may need a new sheet numbered 1c] Show the cakes you researched for homework, with notes to show the properties you think they have.
v) Draw a Star Test for each, using the criteria of the Brief as the adjectives. Estimate which type of commercial cake comes closest to the criteria and write a conclusion to explain.

Stage 4 *(Level 8)*
As Stage 3, but showing real evidence of advanced independent research during homework time.

| NAME | FORM | TITLE *"Design Opportunities for Sponge Tartlets"* | SHEET No. 1 |

Homework

From your basic formulas for shortcrust pastry, creamed sponge and from appropriate additional ingredients, plan three types of sponge tartlets, in your rough book.

They should have a pastry base, a sandwiching layer, a flavoured sponge top and decoration.

Figure 5.8 continued

WEEK 3 Design Sheet 2

Stage 1 *(Level 5)*

i) For homework, you planned three different sponge tartlets of your own. Divide the sheet into four sections. Draw 3D cross section drawings of each of your cakes, in three of the sections.

ii) Write notes around each picture about the ingredients.

Stage 2 *(Level 6)*

iii) Make sure you do good, formal drawing. In the notes around your pictures, include information about the properties of the ingredients.

iv) Add a Star Test beside each showing how nearly that cake meets the criteria of the brief.

Stage 3 *(Level 7)*

v) [You will probably wish to use another sheet, numbered 2b] Do Screening Algorithms for each cake to see which will be the best product to add to the range.

vi) In the 4th section on Design Sheet two, using the technical language, write a conclusion to the Star Tests and Screening Algorithms to show which cake will be best overall.

Stage 4 *(Level 8)*

vii) Use the computer "Nutrients" program to show the nutrient label for the cake which has come out best so far. Compare your label with one from a packet of shop bought cakes. Glue the two labels to your sheet.

viii) Include this information in the conclusion you write in the 4th section, saying which ingredients make your cake particularly healthy and nutritious.

| NAME | FORM | TITLE *"Developing Design ideas"* | SHEET No. 3 |

Homework

You should now know which type of cakes you will make. You may mix ideas from two or three of the cakes on sheet 2.

Investigate the ingredients you will use and find out which will be tastiest or healthiest etc. Keep notes in your rough book.

Make sure you have worked out how much pastry and sponge you will make for 6 to 8 cakes. Make notes in your rough book.

Figure 5.8 continued

WEEK 4 Design Sheet 3

Stage 1 *(Level 5)*
i) Draw a 3D picture of the cake which has come out best. (Use an isometric grid guide sheet behind the paper if it is helpful.) It can be larger than those on sheet 2 and you may have combined some of the ideas, so it is no longer exactly like any of those on sheet 2.
ii) Write the exact recipe and method for 6 to 8 cakes, so that anyone picking up you sheet could understand and follow it and make your cakes.

Stage 2 *(Level 6)*
iii) In Show the main timings beside the method, to show that you can finish in 70mins.

Stage 3 *(Level 7)*
iv) As Stage 3, but make a more exact time plan and make sure you keep exactly to it when you cook. Remember clearing up time.

Stage 4 *(Level 8)*
vi) Leave an empty space on the sheet headed "Alterations".
Immediately after you cook, write about anything you did differently, with the reason and say whether your time planning was correct.

NAME   FORM   TITLE *"Product Specification for Sponge Tartlets"* SHEET No. 3

Homework

You should make sure that you collect the ingredients for your practical test session.

Some of you will wish to practise at home to be sure of what you are doing and to make sure you can work quickly enough, but you do not have to do this.

IF YOU HAVE FINISHED THE DESIGN SHEETS YOU ARE NOW READY TO COOK

Arrange which week you can cook.

If you have finished the Design Sheets and have to wait to cook, take another sheet and number it 3b.

Design the packaging for your product.

HOMEWORK   **Make a front cover for the project.**

Figure 5.8 continued

WEEK 5/6
COOKERY SESSIONS in as near practical examination conditions as
   possible.

Photograph six cakes on a small plate for each pupil, but preferably line
   up three plates in one photo to save expense. The prints can be cut to
   make a small picture each.

FREEZE ONE CAKE EACH FOR THE EVALUATION. TAKE THE REST HOME.

WEEK 7 Design Sheet 4

Stage 1 *(Level 5)*
i)   Defrost your cake and look at it.
ii)   Glue your photograph on to the sheet.
iii) Draw a Star Test on the Design Sheet, beside the photo, using the same
      criteria as before.
iv)   Cut the cake into quarters and eat one piece.
v)   Test your cake on the Star Graph to see if it matches the criteria required
      by the brief.

Stage 2 *(Level 6)*
vi)   Get together with two other pupils (groups of three). In turn, eat a piece
      of each others cakes and conduct a Hedonic test on them. Each make a
      copy of the Hedonic test and glue it to your Design Sheet.
vii) In a section of your sheet, write the heading "Conclusion to Tests" and
      comment on how your cake came out in the Star and the Hedonic tests.
      Suggest any improvements you could make.

Stage 3 *(Level 7)*
viii) As Stage 2 but make sure you use the technical language when writing
      you comments – e.g.. "it might have have more varied mouthfeel, as well
      as flavour, had I added crunchy chocolate drops instead of just cocoa."

Stage 4 *(Level 8)*
ix)   Leave As Stage 2 and 3 but in detail and in technical language.
      Add a Nutrition Label for the final cake, if it has developed from the last
      one you did. Comment on the nutritional content and the criteria of the
      brief.

| NAME | FORM | TITLE *"Evaluation of Sponge Tartlets"* | SHEET No. 3 |

Put your design sheets together with the cover on top and then sheets 1
   to 4 with any extra a) and b) sheets in the right order.

THE END

Figure 5.8 continued

Section 3

Recent Projects

Section 3 examines a range of teaching materials written and published to support the teaching of food technology in the secondary D&T curriculum.

Chapter 6 explores the philosophy of the Nuffield Design and Technology Project, outlines the materials available and highlights examples that can be used for teaching food technology at Key Stages 3 and 4. Figures and tables reproduced with the permission of the Nuffield Foundation.

Chapter 7 focuses on the Royal College of Art (RCA) Technology Project to explore how it can be used to support the teaching of food technology at Key Stages 3 and 4. Figures and Tables reproduced with the RCS's permission carry appropriate copyright acknowledgements.

Chapter 8 looks at the Science with Technology Project with specific reference to teaching food technology using the units *Understanding the Science of Food and Developing Food Products*. Figures 8.1 and 2 are reproduced with the permission of the Science with Technology Project and the Association for Science Education.

Chapter 6

Food Technology in the Nuffield Design and Technology Project

Judy Hallett and Marion Rutland

Introduction

However we choose to define the subject area of 'food', pupils working in this area have always been been required to prepare, combine and cook food materials. So what is different about food technology? In home economics subjects there has been a long tradition of looking at food as a home-produced commodity. The shift in emphasis in food technology means that pupils are no longer expected to spend their lessons 'cooking meals for the family' but should now be concerned with designing and making food products with market potential.

The Nuffield Design and Technology Project has evolved to meet National Curriculum demands, offering a range of creative resources which provide challenging opportunities for pupils and support for teachers. The Nuffield Key Stage 3 resources were published in 1995 (Barlex, 1995) and those for Key Stage 4 were published 1996 (Barlex, 1996).

The key message from Nuffield is that children 'must be able to design what they make and make what they design', and this designing and making must be securely underpinned by a firm foundation of skills, knowledge and understanding. All the Nuffield resources are closely linked to the most recent curriculum order for Design and Technology, and there has been close collaboration between several GCSE examination boards and the Nuffield Design and Technology Key Stage 4 resources.

The Nuffield Design and Technology Key Stage 3 books provide a range of carefully structured and interrelated materials which can readily be modified by teachers to meet individual requirements.The project recognises the importance of allowing pupils the opportunity to work with a wide range of materials, including food, until the end of Key Stage 3, to develop capability in D&T.

In this chapter we offer solutions to four questions:

- What is a food product?
- What do pupils need to know and be able to do with food?
- What do the Nuffield Design and Technology materials provide for pupils and teachers?
- How does the Nuffield Project support teachers?

What is a food product?

An intuitive answer from our pupils would probably be 'what's on the supermarket shelves'. True! But if we begin to think about:

- scale of production
- types of product
- consumer need
- where and how food is eaten

we begin the process of alerting ourselves to the huge potential when pupils work with food. Food technology could be interpreted as designing and making foods for the supermarket shelf, but there could equally be a focus on fast foods, restaurant food, food for school expeditions, or delivered food for the elderly and many other possibilities.

The Nuffield resources concentrate on what children need to know and be able to do to design and make food products, as opposed to how to produce the packaging they are sold in, or designing the place where they are eaten. While these may all be important considerations, we should not be diverted from the emphasis on developing something that:

- Looks, smells and tastes good: this requires making skills and understanding of food behaviour.
- Is desirable, and affordable by potential customers: this requires understanding of needs of consumers and evaluation of product.
- Has assured quality when produced in bulk; this requires an understanding of safety and hygiene requirements during food production.

What do pupils need to know and be able to do to produce a quality food product?

Pupils need skills and knowledge which enable them to:

1. Identify wants and needs of particular groups of people.
2. Understand and interpret a design brief and then produce a design specification.
3. Make and modify food products.
4. Assess the success and suitability of those products through sensory evaluation techniques.
5. Evaluate the effectiveness of the product by thinking about the environmental, social and economic impact of the production and use of the products.

What do the Nuffield resources provide for pupils and teachers?

The resources provide just enough information so that pupils can get on with designing and making. The Key Stage 3 resources consist of:

- *A file of resource tasks*, or, in National Curriculum terms, 'focused tasks' (DfE, 1995a), which are short practical activities to teach technical knowledge and understanding, making skills and strategic skills, and values. They are designed to help pupils practise and develop particular skills and knowledge.
- *A file of capability tasks*, or, in National Curriculum terms, 'assignments' (DfE, 1995a) which are complete design and make tasks which provide opportunity for pupils to show their D&T capability through a range of materials.
- *A Study Guide* to give advice for pupils on how to do D&T well using resource tasks and capability tasks, and also includes case studies which describe real examples of D&T in the world beyond school.
- *A Student's Book* which supplies technical information, background reading and strategies for designing for all the D&T materials.
- *A Teachers Guide* which gives useful advice on ensuring that each student gains a balanced D&T experience. Various curriculum models are suggested so that teachers can use the Nuffield approach to construct a scheme of work appropriate for their own teaching environment.

The Nuffield project has identified three important types of learning activity:

- Resource Tasks (focused practical tasks).
- Capability Tasks (design and make tasks).
- Case Studies (products and applications, quality and health and safety).

A judicious mix of these learning activities, in which a sequence of Capability tasks is supported by appropriate Resource tasks and Case Studies, permits a D&T curriculum which is broad and balanced, and with sufficient depth to allow pupils to progress.

Focused practical tasks – Nuffield D&T Resource Tasks

As with all the Nuffield D&T materials, when working with food pupils need opportunities to acquire certain designing and making skills, technical knowledge or value appreciation, all of which should encourage progression; these are provided by a series of short focused tasks. These tasks are designed to teach a particular making skill, a specific piece of technical information, or a particular strategy for designing or evaluating. The framework for the resource tasks is identical for each material, in the form of an A4 instruction sheet (Figure 6.1) which gives the following information:

- a statement of what the pupil will learn
- where to find useful information in the student book
- how long the task will take
- a clear list of materials, components, tools and equipment needed
- instructions about what to do
- what to write
- usually includes some extension work to meet needs of more able pupils.

Designing and making with food ➤ Resource Task 4
Preference tests

You will learn

How to use a **preference test** to find out how much people like or dislike a food.

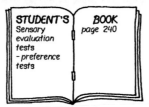

STUDENT'S BOOK *page 240*
Sensory evaluation tests
– preference tests

Find out how much people like different types of scones

You will need

Sample A
* 225 g SR white flour
* 40 g hard margarine
* Approximately 150 ml milk
* 50 g chopped cherries
* 1½ level tablespoons castor sugar
* Pinch of salt

Sample B
* As sample A but; leave out the chopped cherries
replace the SR white flour with SR wholemeal flour
add 25 g of sultanas

Sample C
* As sample A but; leave out chopped cherries and the sugar
add 50 g grated Cheddar cheese

What to do
Work in groups of four or five.

Preparing the samples

1 Put the oven on at 210°C or gas mark 7.

2 Lightly grease a baking tray.

3 Sieve the flour into a mixing bowl.

4 Add the margarine and rub it in lightly with your finger tips.

5 Add the remaining ingredients.

6 Mix to a soft dough with a fork or knife.

7 Roll out the dough and cut it into rounds at least 10 mm thick.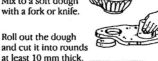

8 Put the scones on to the baking tray.

9 Bake the scones on the top oven shelf for 7–10 minutes.

10 Lift them on to a cooling rack.

Carrying out the test

11 Label the scones ZXY, PLF and VYX and put them on plates.
12 Get together a tasting panel of at least ten people and prepare an answer sheet.
13 Ask the tasters to fill in their sheets describing how much they liked or disliked the scones.

What to write
● Use the results to draw conclusions about how much the panel liked or disliked each type of scone.

Figure 6.1 Key Stage 3 Food Resource Task – Preference tests

To do these tasks pupils need an understanding of the properties and qualities of food; this technical information is found in the Student's Book, together with a series of strategies for designing with food.

Let's take a closer look at some of these resource tasks concerned with designing food products. In the early days of D&T, considerable emphasis was given to designing and making the packaging of food products, with the result that limited time was spent making the product itself! Eye-catching packaging may persuade customers to buy a food product once, but the success of the food industry is about creating products which people will buy repeatedly. What food technology teachers also know, and some of us have learnt this by bitter experience, is that scale drawings and traditional models do nothing to contribute towards high-quality food outcomes! Pupils need particular skills and knowledge when working with food which:

- enable them to understand the needs, wants and likes of consumers, so that
- they can write a design specification for a product and generate ideas for that product before
- finally deciding what to make, so that they are then able to design food products with real market potential.

What are these skills needed to design food products? The Nuffield resources offer a range of strategies and tasks which allow pupils to learn how to design with food in an active and rigorous way. Any discussion with pupils about their eating habits tells us that food choices are based on more than the nutritional value of food and the well publicised connections between food and health ('what's good for me'). Food choice is likely to be related to a variety of *Physical* and *Intellectual Emotional* and *Social* factors. This '*PIES*' approach, as illustrated in Figure 6.2, is a useful strategy that can be employed to help pupils understand and establish the needs and likes and dislikes of people.

Consider for example the needs of an elderly house-bound person. Using the PIES approach, pupils may decide that this person requires regular visits to meet intellectual, emotional and social needs. This may then stimulate discussion about whether it is better to design frozen meals that could be delivered monthly, or to design a range of fresh meals suitable for daily delivery. As with other strategy resource tasks this work is probably best tackled collaboratively (very few designers work in isolation), resulting in a clear chart with key words only. Pages of writing are not necessary or appropriate in D&T and may well reduce the clarity and understanding of the task.

The **image board** (Figure 6.3) is another way of producing a quick visual record of pupils' thinking. This strategy is used in the food industry to help understand what different people might like, and to help understand the style and types of product which might appeal to different people. Following the task instructions, pupils select and assemble pictures from journals and magazines and paste them on a sheet to provide a quick visual image of the consumers, where they live, what they do in their leisure time, what they eat, clothes they wear, where they shop. A teenage image board with its images of an intensely active lifestyle may strongly suggest the need for a food product that can be eaten 'on the move'.

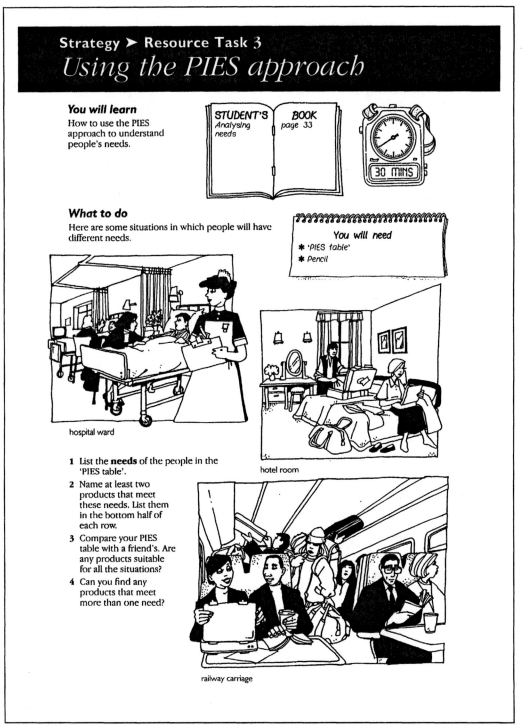

Figure 6.2 Key Stage 3 Strategy Resource Task – Using the PIES approach

Strategy ➤ Resource Task 5
Using image boards 2

You will learn
How to use image boards.

Green or GREEDY?

Do some products, looks, styles or activities make you think of particular ways of life?

What life styles do the words **green** and **greedy** suggest? What images do they conjure up in your head?

Work in groups of about four or five.
You will create image boards that suggest the ideas of green and greedy for some different products. Your teacher will tell you which products to work on.

You will need
* Two large sheets of paper or board
* Glue sticks, PVA or Cow Gum
* Old magazines, catalogues and newspapers
* Scissors

What to do

1 Use images cut out from the magazines and other sources to create *two contrasting image boards* to illustrate the ideas of **green** and **greedy** – for one of the following products:
   - food;
   - furniture;
   - clothing;
   - footwear;
   - transport.

2 When both boards are complete, ask the other groups to work out which is green and which is greedy by answering these questions.

What to write

- What is it about the pictures on the image boards that suggest green?
- What is it about the pictures on the image boards that suggest greedy?
- What are the biggest differences between the green and the greedy image boards?

Homework suggestion

Try to find pictures of products which suggest the words **natural** and **techno** (hi-tech/modern).
Collect several images for each word, and create two image boards. Your boards should not need labels as each image will be 'shouting' either natural or techno.

Figure 6.3 Key Stage 3 Strategy Resource Task – Using image boards 2

Designing and making food products using Nuffield materials

Designing

Pupils need to be able to write and justify a design specification for a product and produce criteria against which one design can be assessed as it develops, and this of course is the case with any D&T material. Whatever the material the specification should describe:

- What the product has to do
- What it should look like
- Any other requirements.

In the case study, Year 7 have been working on the following task, adapted from the *Healthy Heart* task in the Nuffield Capability Task File:

'Design and make promotional items which could be used for a Healthy Heart exhibition stand at the local sports centre.'

This is the specification written by one group of pupils:

- *What the product has to do:*
  - Be low in fat and sugar.
  - Be high in dietary fibre.
- *What the product has to look like:*
  - Inspire people to want healthier lifestyles by being attractive to look at.
  - A small sample – to be given away.
- *Other important points:*
  - Will it keep well without refrigeration?
  - There is not much money available for this promotion.

The next stage in designing is to decide what to make to meet these requirements. A group brainstorming session may produce a long list of possibilities. A quick review of their ideas against the original specification at this stage can help pupils to select an appropriate idea for development.

The Nuffield approach recommends that pupils should be encouraged to pause and consider their work at three critical points in their tasks:

- When the preliminary design proposal is on paper.
- Pupils reviewing the design proposal against the specification to make sure it meets requirements.
- Pupil reviewing the product – does it meet the specification?

These review points give opportunities for reflection, reasoning and cognitive conflict enabling pupils to confront and struggle with problems to develop their thinking skills.

This is a good moment for teachers to remind their pupils of what they are *Able* to do and to dissuade them from selecting a recipe that 'sounds nice' ('Well, I like chocolate!'). It is important for pupils to generate a range of ideas before making a decision, perhaps brainstorming their ideas in groups. Another way of doing this is to look at the characteristics of a familiar product, for example fish fingers or tomato soup, and then generate a range of possible new attributes using an attribute analysis table to develop ideas for a new product.

Pupils may want to sketch their final idea – a frustrating exercise for some of

Strategy ➤ Resource Task 20
Drawing quick 3D views

You will learn

How to produce quick 3D views by starting with flat shapes.

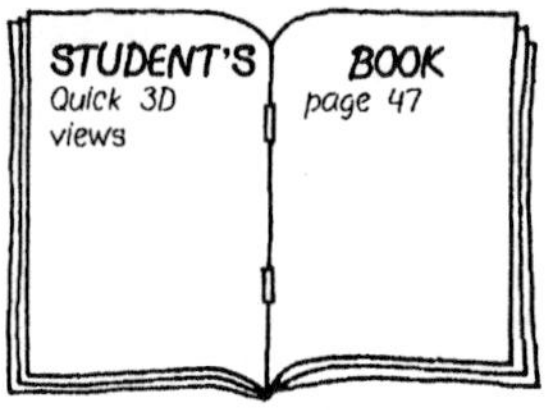

STUDENT'S BOOK
Quick 3D views
page 47

Here are some flat 2D shapes. You are going to add to the shapes to make them into simple 3D views.

What to do

1 Copy each of the shapes shown.
2 Draw parallel lines from each corner or edge (as in the first example), and join up the lines to create a 3D form instead of a flat, 2D shape.

You will need
* Your workbook or drawing paper
* HB (or softer) pencil

Homework suggestion

Draw some flat shapes of your own and then make them into 3D views.

Figure 6.4 Key Stage 3 Strategy Task – Drawing quick 3D views

them, who protest 'I'm no good at drawing!'. Figure 6.4 shows one of the strategy tasks to help pupils produce quick *3D sketches*, a useful skill whatever materials pupils are working with, enabling pupils to design products which not only meet the demands of the brief but are also creative.

Making

How do the Nuffield resources approach the making of food products? On many occasions there is still a need for the teacher to supply clear skill instruction and demonstration coupled with opportunities for practice. This allows pupils to see how things can be done well, and to see the teacher solving problems which the pupils themselves may encounter. There is no need for tried and tested approaches to be cast aside. The teaching of skills through demonstration remains an invaluable teaching strategy, and pupil practice is essential to achieve understanding of process. This approach prevents food being reduced to the testing of existing products, and more importantly permits pupils the enjoyment of 'making'.

The Project recognises how important it is that pupils can read recipes, follow instructions clearly, be able to weigh and measure accurately and work safely, issues that are all addressed in the student's book and resource tasks. Food is a material which teaches particular food-based technical knowledge and understanding through making, cutting, combining and cooking foods to produce high-quality food products. The Nuffield approach emphasises the need for pupils to develop control over their designing and making by making changes to:

- the flavour and texture
- the shape and finish
- the nutritional qualities

and by changing the ingredients and the way the food is prepared and cooked.

The nutritional aspects of food choice in the Student's Book are well related to current nutritional advice and nutritional food labelling.

All the tasks encourage pupils to prepare and cook high quality products that can then be tested for acceptability for a particular market, using a range of sensory evaluation techniques. There are a number of strategy tasks that can be used to evaluate the outcomes. Examples are *User Trips* – finding out what others think of it by eating the food, and answering questions and *Winners and Losers* – a task which alerts pupils to the possibility that some people will gain from a new product while others will 'lose'; it also encourages a consideration of ecology and technology, and energy conservation.

Designing and making assignments – Nuffield D&T Capability Tasks

The Capability Task file contains a series of longer, more open-ended tasks which are designed to teach and reveal pupil capability. The structure of these tasks (see Figure 6.5 for an example) allows pupils to be self-directed, as well as providing a clear plan for teachers in the form of a teaching sequence on a lesson-by-lesson basis. These tasks can, if desired, be interpreted through several, if not all, the D&T materials, encouraging a co-ordinated approach in D&T faculties/departments.

What follows is an outline scheme for a *Food Capability task*, developed for Year

8. The task includes a visit to a burger bun manufacturer so that pupils learn about large-scale production. At the end of the task the pupils submit their written evidence for Bronze CREST awards – an indicator of the rigour and depth achieved by using the Nuffield approach.

Task: **Golden West Foods wants to develop new bread products which will appeal to health conscious consumers. Design and make a range of 'healthy' fast foods suitable for large-scale manufacture**

Week 1　　　*Knowledge:* cereals, staple foods and the nutritional value of flour (worksheets on this for homework). In addition, requiring 2 weeks, devise a short class survey to establish what kinds of bread people eat, and where they are purchased.

Week 2　　　*Technical knowledge and skill:* making bread – demonstration and practical.

Week 3　　　Analyse and communicate survey results, using GRAPHIT. Homework: complete presentation of results.

Week 4　　　*Conclusions and evaluation of survey.* Introduction to capability task and Bronze CREST Award.

Week 5　　　*Attribute analysis:* burger bun (Strategy resource task).

Week 6　　　*Difference test:* burger/baked beans (Food resource task).
Product specification (Strategy resource task).

Week 7　　　*Task plan:* brainstorm ideas and ingredients list – completed for preparation.

Weeks 8–12　*Making and improving the product:* use appropriate sensory evaluation techniques. (Nuffield food resource tasks.)

Week 13　　　*Verbal Presentation to Burger Bun executive* – evaluation of process and product.

Week 14　　　*Completion of all work* in readiness for moderation by CREST officer.

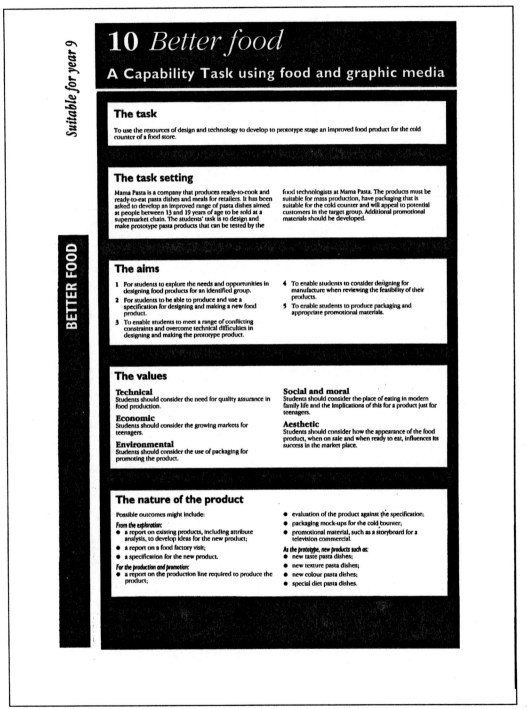

Figure 6.5 Key Stage 4 Capability Task Part 1 – better food outline. Part 2, possible teaching sequence

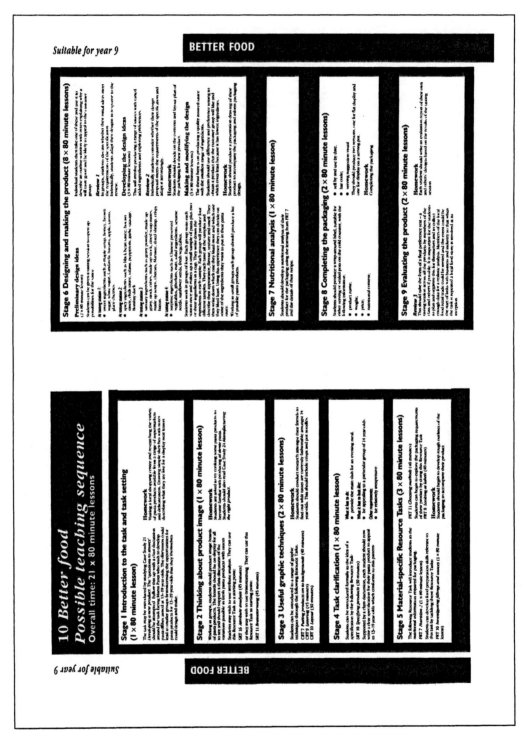

Figure 6.5 Continued

Making links with the real world – Nuffield D&T Case Studies

It is not always possible for pupils to observe D&T in the real world by visits to manufacturers and industry. To compensate for this the Nuffield Case Studies are an important way to allow pupils to reflect on D&T in practice and to appreciate how user needs and preferences may, or may not be met through D&T. They help pupils:

- 'evaluate familiar products and applications' (DfE, 1995a)
- reflect on D&T practice that will affect their own D&T
- appreciate how user preferences may or may not be met through D&T activity.

The following Case Study examples have particular relevance for food:

- *Preserving skills* – Food technology in Sri Lanka (Figure 6.6 shows how women use their knowledge of food preservation techniques to develop products for sale – emphasises thorough research of the needs of their customers).
- *Developing a new product* (from the first idea to the launch – shows the importance of team effort and individual skills to ensure success).
- *Manufacturing the right product* (market research to get the product right, the price right, the packaging right; once more emphasises the importance of team effort).
- *Shopping and choice* (alerts us to the wide choice and persuasion to buy).
- *Food mixers* (Historical development of the food mixer to meet the demands of changes in diet and eating habits).
- *The development of a creative food product:* Pop Tarts.

Throughout the case studies there are questions and ideas for research, making them a valuable way to create understanding of people who have used their D&T skills to meet wants and needs. They provide opportunities for discussing the environmental, ecological and social issues involved in technological change, and to question market needs. Not least these case studies are invaluable as homework exercises, as well as to provide work when teachers are absent.

Teaching Food Technology at Key Stage 4

In general all the Nuffield Design and Technology 14–16 resources aim to provide:

- Dedicated in-depth material for each of the specialist areas of D&T.
- Support for both short courses and full GCSEs.
- Opportunity for pupils to develop the skills, knowledge, strategies and understanding for each of the focus areas.

During Key Stage 3 pupils will have used a wide range of different materials other than food for designing and making, for example textiles, wood, metal, and plastic. A major difference is that at Key Stage 4 pupils are allowed to specialise in a material area. If they choose food technology, as with other specialist materials, they will be expected to work to a higher standard in both designing and making and produce products which are genuinely 'shop' quality. As with other specialist D&T courses, food-based activities must relate to industrial practices and the application of systems and control, with pupils learning about how industry is organised to manufacture goods (DfE,1995a).

Written with the help of INTERMEDIATE TECHNOLOGY

5 Preserving skills – food technology in Sri Lanka

A group of women in Sri Lanka use their knowledge of food preservation techniques to develop products for sale

Many foods go bad if they are not correctly processed, packaged and stored. They can taste unpleasant and are sometimes dangerous to eat. If fruit is left in a warm place for some time it soon begins to smell bad and has to be thrown away.

All over the world, people have developed different ways of preserving fresh foods to prevent waste. Preservation techniques include:

- drying;
- smoking;
- adding salt;
- adding vinegar;
- adding sugar.

These methods work by stopping micro-organisms living and growing. Salt and drying, for example, reduce the amount of water in the food so that micro-organisms cannot live. Vinegar makes the food too acidic for micro-organisms.

Why preserve food?

Food is preserved for two main reasons:

- **To provide food security** – Foods are preserved when there is a lot of them, for example after a harvest. They can then be eaten at other times of the year when there is a shortage.
- **To add variety to the diet** – For example, fruit and vegetables are often made into pickles, chutneys and sauces. These add interest and flavour to food and provide a range of important vitamins and minerals.

The basic methods of food preservation are the same all over the world. However, there are differences in the type of ingredients used, the equipment and resources available and the people's preferences.

▲ *All these preserved foods are found in the supermarket.*

Research

Go to your local supermarket and find foods which have been preserved by each of the methods listed here. Produce a table like this

Method	Food
Drying	Apricots, currants
Smoking	

Figure 6.6 Key Stage 4 Case Study – Preserving skills

The format for the Key Stage 4 Nuffield Design and Technology Project is similar but slightly different to Key Stage 3. There are three resources:

- A Food Technology book for the student
- A Teacher's Guide and
- A set of Resource Tasks for the teacher.

The three types of learning activity identified at Key Stage 3 remain: Resources Tasks, Case Studies and Capability Tasks.

Resources Tasks

These are focused tasks which are short practical activities designed to help pupils develop and practise particular knowledge, skills and understanding. The Resource Tasks are presented as instruction sheets, and the 'Looking at Emulsions' task (Figure 6.7) brings alive the significance of food emulsions, helping pupils to reinforce the information provided in the Student's Book. In this task pupils discover what ingredients are necessary to produce temporary and permanent emulsions, and then think about their choice of ingredients to make their own dressings for salads. Further work encourages pupils to look at the emulsifiers used in many commercially produced products.

At Key Stage 4 there are three types of Resource Tasks. There are:

1. *Recapitulation Tasks* that go over work probably already covered at Key Stage 3.

2. *Extension Resource Tasks* (see Figure 6.8) that take an idea that pupils were probably taught at Key Stage 3 and develop it further.

3. *New Ideas Resource Tasks* that deal with new knowledge, understanding and skills to help the pupils progress.

The Resource Tasks can be used by a whole class, a team or a small group. On the other hand, individual pupils can choose to use a task that is appropriate for developing knowledge, understanding and skills in their own D&T activity.

Case Studies

These are structured longer activities which describe real examples of D&T outside the context of school and provide pupils with knowledge they would not easily access on their own. At Key Stage 4 the Case Studies relate to business practices, the manufacture of food products and their impact on consumers and the environment. There are two types of Case Studies:

- Those that deal with 'large' technologies which tend to significantly affect the way people live. They are frequently associated with a particular period in history and help pupils understand the effect of technology on their lives.
- Those that deal with products that are similar to ones they will develop in school. They describe:
  - how the designs were developed, manufactured, marketed and sold.
  - how the products works.
  - how the products affect the people who make them, those who use them and others.

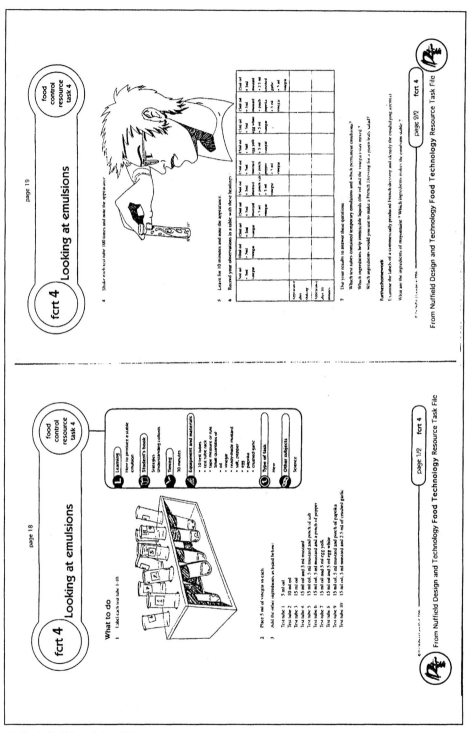

Figure 6.7 Key Stage 4 Resource Task – Looking at emulsions

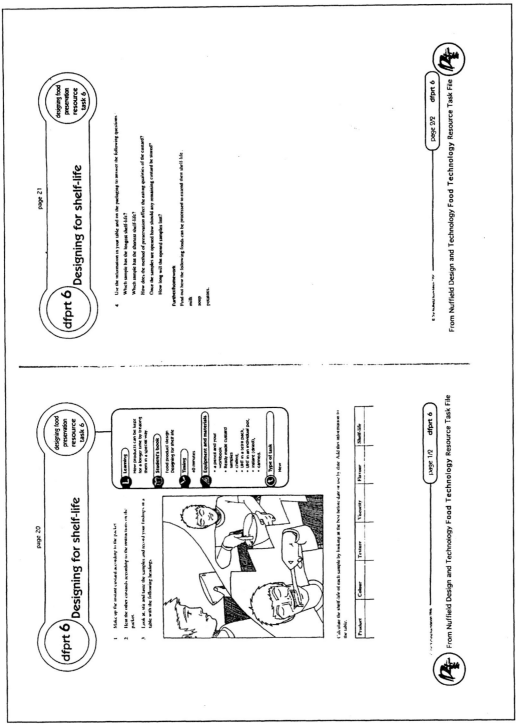

Figure 6.8 Key Stage 4 Resource Task – Designing for shelf-life

A corny story

Popcorn and sweetcorn are two familiar processed cereal products. They look quite similar but are produced from two different types of maize. Popcorn is made from a type of maize that has been selected for its ability to 'pop' when heated. Sweetcorn is a maize that is harvested while still immature for canning, freezing or eating as corn on the cob when it has been boiled. Maize is the second most-grown cereal crop in the world, grown in every continent except Antarctica! The reason it is grown so extensively is because it is extremely useful.

Pause for thought

How many different products can you think of that come from maize? Check out your answer with the illustration below.

Research activity

You can use this activity to find out more about how maize is processed. Collect samples of corn, flaked maize, maize flour, corn oil and two or three brands of cereal. Write a description of each one listing the processes involved in its production. Put your samples in order of the amount of processing, starting with the least.

The birth of a cornflake

How does the seed of a maize plant become a cornflake? Over 100 years ago Dr John Kellogg, a vegetarian and health food specialist, developed grain food products to replace meat- and fish-based meals. He mixed grits (pieces of corn endosperm) with flavoured syrup, rolled and toasted them, boxed them, and the rest is history! But there is a huge difference between making small batches of products and the multi-million industry that breakfast cereals have become – most supermarkets stock over 100 different types!

Focused case studies

③

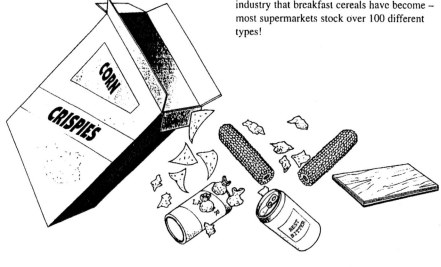

Figure 6.9 Key Stage 4 Case Study – A corny story

The Case Studies are important as they broaden the pupils experience of the food industry (Figure 6.9), provide discussion points and further research activities.

Capability Tasks

These are 'assignments' where pupils design and make products that meet a specification involving the full design process of designing and making. As at Key Stage 3, pupils are expected to use the knowledge, understanding and skills they have learnt through doing the Resource Tasks and Case studies to generate their own design brief and product specification (see Figure 6.10). It is intended that the relevant Resource Tasks and Case Studies are used as part of a full Capability Task.

Lines of interest and design guides

The Project has developed the idea of a **line of interest** and **design guides** as a means of limiting the sort of product that students in a class might design and make. This makes the teaching of a Capability Task much more manageable:

- **A line of interest** describes a particular type of product, and seven lines of interest have been written as suitable for food technology: for the elderly, for the very young, for those at risk, for special diets, from primary foods and from the baker and from the confectioner.
- Each **design guide** deals with the issues that should be considered when designing within a line of interest, for example the knowledge, skills and understanding that are useful for designing food products from the bakery (Figure 6.11). These include an understanding of nutrition, the properties and qualities of food materials, preservation and packaging techniques to design and make an appropriate product. They set an agenda rather than provide the answers, but they always give examples of solutions that successfully address the issues. The design guides provide a straightforward way for students to become familiar with areas of food technology. They can act as a stimulus for pupils who are finding it difficult to decide on their main course work. The products made by pupils could range from a long-life, easy-to-cook, inexpensive meal for a student on a low income to a high-nutrition easy-to-prepare dish for an earthquake victim.

Systems and control in food technology

The Nuffield Design and Technology project developed a clear conceptual framework about systems in Key Stage 3. This is revised and extended at Key Stage 4 through writing about the systems and control in the Strategies - applying science section and by describing systems and control in action in focused case studies (see Figure 6.12).

Examples of this approach can be found in Chapter 12 of this book.

Strategies

As at Key Stage 3, pupils following the Key Stage 4 course are given guidance on a range of strategies they can use and develop in their designing and making with food. These include:

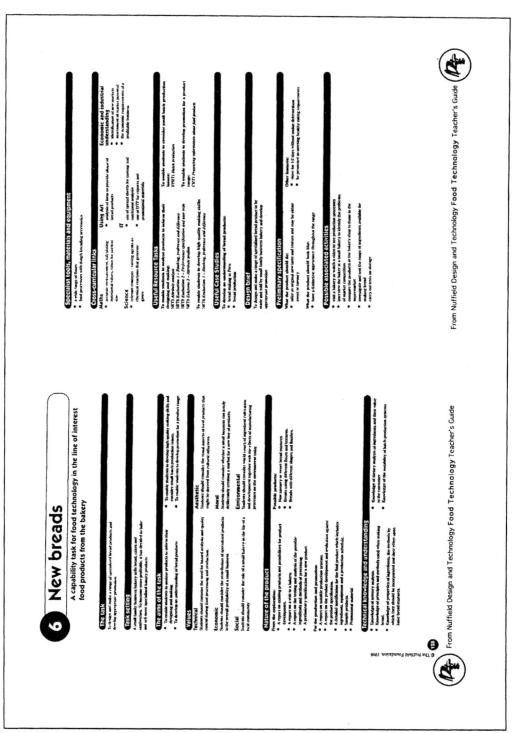

Figure 6.10 Key Stage 4 – Capability Task – New breads

⑥

For breakfast in a coffee shop

Where will it be sold and who is it for?

Resourses checklist

Knowledge and understanding of the problem:
- preferences of coffee shop users;
- nutritional issues associated with fried foods.

Knowledge and understanding for the solution:
- storage/contamination risks;
- cafeteria procedures for serving hot dishes

Useful strategies
- PIES;
- attribute analysis;
- interviews;
- questionnaires;
- evaluation by user trips;
- evaluation by attribute profile.

What are the important background facts?

- The requirements of the customers.
- Opening times of coffee shop, advertising, position and layout.
- Price range of food products, special price deal.

What types of products does the coffee shop sell already?

- fried breakfast (eggs/bacon/tomatoes);
- scrambled/poached eggs on toast;
- cereals, toast and preserves;
- coffee and tea.

What types of products might they develop?

- range of savoury/sweet-filled pancakes;
- muffins, waffles, scotch pancakes, potato cakes;
- hot brioches with butter;
- filled omelettes, kedgeree;
- range of fruit/vegetable juices;
- special muesli and fresh fruit.

What are the nutritional issues?

- What nutrients are best eaten at the beginning of the day?
- The importance of breakfast as a main meal of the day.
- The metabolic rate of the body.
- Problems related to high-fat diets and fried foods.

Figure 6.11 Key Stage 4 Design Guide – from the bakery

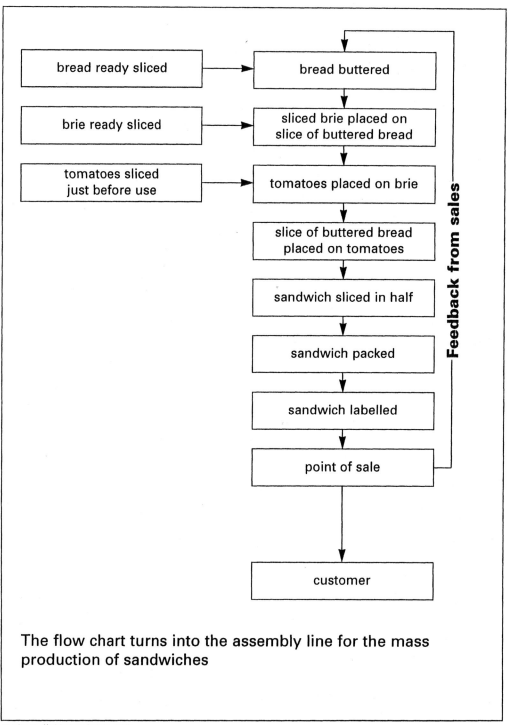

The flow chart turns into the assembly line for the mass production of sandwiches

Figure 6.12 Key Stage 4 Systems thinking

- identifying needs and likes
- writing and collating results from questionnaires
- using image boards
- writing a design brief and a performance specification
- generating ideas
- brainstorming
- observational drawings
- attribute analysis
- refining ideas
- using computers
- applying science
- systems thinking
- planning and evaluating.

Communicating design proposals

Three important areas of communicating design proposals are considered including communicating with:

- the client about the nature of the proposed food product
- the manufacturer about the means of producing the product
- the customer through packaging and advertising the product.

Food chemistry

An understanding of food chemistry is very important at Key Stage 4 to support pupils in their designing and making of quality food products. This helps them make sensible design decisions, and be able to explain why things are sometimes not successful. It is worth noting that food chemistry is not currently part of the National Curriculum Science document, so it is now only in Food Technology that pupils can learn about how food behaves when it is cut, mixed or heated. The materials look at the composition of foods, nutrients, caramelisation, coagulation, gelatinisation, foams, emulsions and food tests.

Nutrition

Understanding and knowledge of nutrition is another essential requirement for pupils following a food technology course at Key Stage 4. Aspects covered include: digestion, role of dietary fibre, dietary needs, nutrients in food, energy and obesity, coronary heart disease (CHD), diabetes, bulimia nervosa, anorexia nervosa and dental carriers.

Food product design

A number design issues are explored including nutrition, cooking methods, flavour, odour, colour, texture, finish and surface colour. Designing for the shelf-life of a product is very important as it is directly related to food hygiene and safety. It is important that pupils understand the methods of extending shelf-life, for example canning freezing and drying. Economic factors such as designing for cost all need to be taken into account.

Planning is a crucial aspect in prototype production and pupils need to be able to draw up a production schedule. For this pupils need to know about the method of preparation, the equipment to use, its application and effect on the product and quality control procedures. This knowledge and understanding will help pupils choose the most suitable food material, cooking and finishing method.

Food production

In addition to pupils knowing how to produce a single prototype, they need to know about the design and manufacture of food products. This includes understanding the methods used in catering organisations such as sandwich bars, cafés, hotels and restaurants.

Catering organisations and hotels

A London-based chain of high-quality food outlets is used to illustrate that, though the processes in producing a single prototype product and catering are similar, differences in the scale of production result in significant variations. As food is produced in batches throughout the day the company must have a systematic approach to preparing the food, otherwise it will be wasted and short-life products such as sliced tomatoes or soft cheeses either will not be ready at busy times or they will stand too long and 'go off'. A flow chart or assemble line for mass producing sandwiches shows how feedback from sales helps the firm plan when each stage should be done for effective production (Figure 6.13).

An example of catering in a hotel is used in similar way to illustrate how systematic planning and organisation are vital when preparing food in large quantities.

Industrial food production

See section 4, Industrial Practice (page 118)

Food poisoning, food hygiene and the law

Causes and sources of food poisoning and its effect on the body are outlined and ways of preventing bacterial contamination considered. Guidelines for proper food preparation procedures are suggested as the key to preventing cross-contamination between raw foods that might have some bacterial contamination and cooked foods where the bacteria have been killed by cooking.

All food technology pupils developing food products need to know about the various Acts of Parliament and regulations related to the protection of the public from food that is unfit to eat. They also need to know about food labelling and regulations about the information that must be shown on a food product. These include the ingredients, nutritional content, date mark, storage instructions, name and address of the manufacturer, place of origin, instructions for preparation, quantity or weight and any special claims, e.g. 'no nut content'. Pupils also should have knowledge and understanding of food additives that affect taste, texture, colour or the shelf-life of the food products.

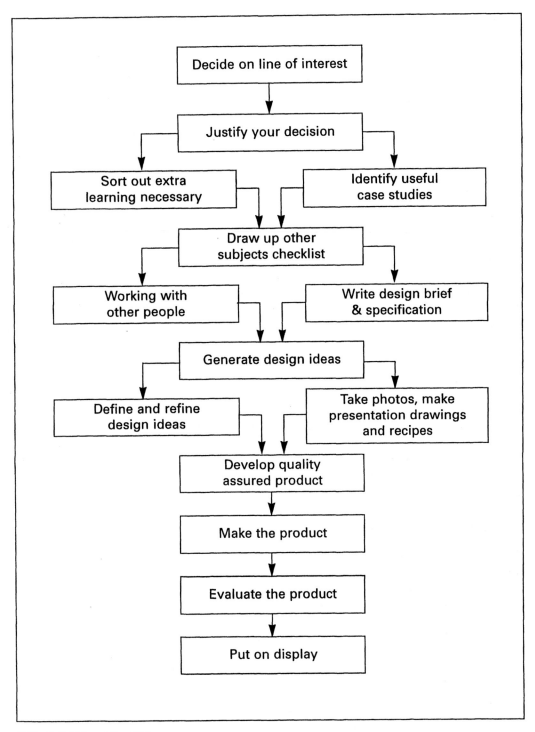

Figure 6.13 Key Stage 4 Flow chart for a Capability Task (sandwiches)

GCSE Food Technology Examinations

It is intended that during the Nuffield course pupils have the opportunity to work in at least three different lines of interest to ensure they have sufficient depth and range of knowledge, understanding and skills of D&T and specifically food technology. It is suggested that in a full GCSE course, three Capability Tasks are tackled from different lines of interest in Year 10. In Year 11 one can be revisited or a new one chosen, and this one is likely to be presented for GCSE coursework. It is acknowledged that it will be difficult to complete three capability tasks in Year 10, and it is therefore suggested that a Capability Task can be stopped at different stages. There could be a different emphasis for each task, for example at least one where all the stages in the process are completing, one where only the first prototype is developed and one where a series of design proposals are devised and presented as recipe suggestions.

In Year 10 a more structured approach may be used where the teacher gives the class a design brief plus a specification and asks pupils to make a product that meets those specifications. On the other hand pupils may be given the brief, the specification and the recipe and asked to make the product so they can learn about the manufacturing process. It is emphasised that pupils carry out the Resource Tasks and Case Studies to acquire the relevant knowledge, understanding and skills.

It is suggested that two shortened and one full Capability Task is completed for the short GCSE course. Advice is given to pupils on how to check that their design brief is progressing satisfactorily, with suggestions for reviewing the design process and evaluating the final product to ensure it meets the specification. Links with other curriculum areas – for example science, mathematics, art and information technology – are highlighted. Resource tasks describe how these links can be made and pupils can choose to develop these links in Capability Tasks. Guidelines provide help for pupils on how to write their own Capability Task and Case Study for GCSE coursework in Year 11.

How does Nuffield support teachers?

Many teachers have been introduced to the Nuffield project through a national network of regional centres within maintained and independent schools. These have been established to create a regional focus for user groups where teachers can meet informally, to provide venues for regional meetings and to create opportunities for making links with industry. A team of 12 Area Field Officers to support the Regional Network and manage the User Support Programme at a local level. This User Network is invaluable with the introduction of the Key Stage 4 materials. The main difference between the Key Stage 3 and 4 materials is the requirement to specialise in a focus area of D&T. Individual Student's Books are available, which match the GCSE examination titles:

- Product Design (resistant materials).
- Food Technology.
- Graphic.
- Textiles.

While class sets of Student's Books will be required, only one copy of the Teacher's Guide (which includes the Capability Task file) and the Resource Task file is necessary, as these are photocopiable.

The Project is well supported by educational suppliers who develop equipment for courses, offer training to teachers attending in service sessions at these centres. It is helpful for these suppliers to see how their products can be used in schools, and to see what improvements can be made to make their products more valuable in the classroom.

Conclusion

At a recent Nuffield training session one of us was introduced as a Nuffield missionary to spread the gospel according to Nuffield! Missionaries traditionally are bringers of good news, and I believe that the Nuffield D&T project *is* good news. These materials, and I repeat this, can enable our pupils to design what they make and make what they design. Some of us are old enough to remember the 'O' level Domestic Science book by Abbey and Mac Donald, which provided pupils with what to learn; the Nuffield Project more importantly and of greater relevance shows our pupils *how* to learn. As teachers this is a main aim: to teach children how to learn. If we can achieve this, we shall be very happy to retire when the next official D&T document appears!

For more information about the Nuffield Design and Technology Project please contact:

Administrator: Nina Towndrow
Nuffield Curriculum Projects Centre
17 Rathbone Street
London W1P 1AF
Telephone: 0171 637 5506/0171 436 3312
Fax: 0171 436 1869

Publishers: Addison Wesley Longman Limited
Edinburgh Gate
Harlow
Essex CM20 2JE

Chapter 7

Food Technology in the Royal College of Art Schools Technology Project (RCA)

Louise Davies and David Perry

Introduction

The Royal College of Art Schools Technology Project is a 3-year programme which started in September 1993 designed to raise the sights and cater for the curricular needs of technology teachers in secondary schools. The Project is funded by the Department for Education, the Esmèe Fairbairn Charitable Trust and Cable and Wireless plc.

The underlying purpose is to improve the quality of technology education throughout secondary schools in England (Figure 7.1). The Project will provide a high-quality course, whereby teachers can better deliver the requirements of and enhance the National Curriculum, and post-14 work, particularly for GNVQ.

'This project will be immensely helpful in developing and promoting high quality education in technology ... to make a significant and lasting contribution. The project will develop practical approaches to help teachers meet the demands of vocational options in the technology curriculum.'

The Baroness Blatch, CBE FRSA,
Minister of State for Education 1993

The Project's small central team is based at the Royal College of Art supporting developments in selected secondary schools with Teacher Fellows on part-time secondment. They are developing a comprehensive technology course for students aged 11 to 19 published by Hodder and Stoughton Educational. The team is working closely with business organisations and major industrial companies to ensure a curriculum which is relevant to the worlds of business and commerce.

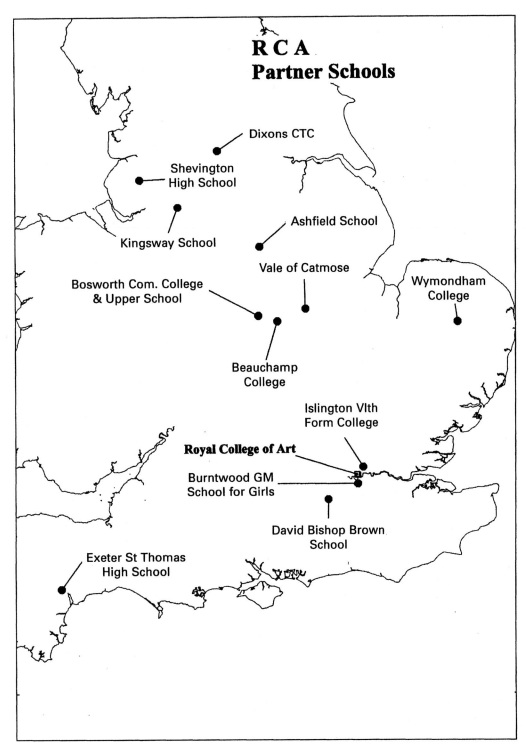

Figure 7.1 RCA Partner Schools

Approaches to Food Technology Key Stage 3 and 4 as part of a D&T Course

The Royal College of Art Schools Technology Project publishes material to support a cohesive and progressive course in D&T throughout the secondary age range, 11–18 (Perry, 1995, 1996). The course has been founded on a set of thoroughly thought-through principles which are reflected in the structure of the course as a whole and every constituent part.

The Project aims to meet and go beyond the demands of the 1995 National Curriculum D&T through a course which:

- is relevant to adult worlds of D&T
- acknowledges, and develops from, a prior learning base
- is meaningful to children in today's and tomorrow's world
- supports attention to individual's needs and potential
- stretches to the limit those with most ability, and serves as well all others
- progressively builds in students:
  - capability
  - responsibility
  - autonomy
  - awareness and understanding of and pride in their own learning
  - knowledge and understanding
  - awareness of others' needs
  - understanding of how D&T activities affect others
  - creativity
  - sensitivity
  - self-confidence
- makes a technologically complex mode of living approachable
- draws in and makes useful and meaningful matter studied in other subjects especially science, mathematics, and art
- draws out the relationship between the nature of designing and learning
- encourages teachers to work together.

Some of the key features of the Royal College of Art Course will be familiar from the National Curriculum Orders (DfE, 1995a):

- designing and making assignments (DMAs)
- focused practical tasks (FPTs)
- investigating and evaluating products and their applications (P&A).

The Royal College of Art Schools Technology Project learning approach is constructed around these three elements. The Units pay careful attention to the new demands of the National Curriculum and address food as a material for designing and making. These Units build a Food Technology Course which provides:

- an understanding of where food comes from
- development of basic practical skills
- an awareness of cross cultural issues related to food
- understanding of how food can be manipulated as a material (food science)
- case studies which raise awareness of industrial contexts and the manufacturing environment

- use of IT
- rigorous evaluation of products (including sensory analysis and consumer testing)
- opportunities for team delivery with other specialists (e.g. systems and control in food production).

Designing and making assignments

Units of learning activities each revolve around a central designing and making assignment. These are presented as Challenges, each of which is a rounded or holistic activity which starts from an awareness of needs and clarification of purposes, and concludes with a product and evaluation of both this and the learning achieved.

The challenges

- establish the context of the assignment
- give snapshots of similar activities in the adult world
- clarify purposes, giving students ownership
- set out initial criteria for success
- explore related values issues
- help teachers and students set out a planning framework.

An example of a challenge is given in Figure 7.2.

Eat Italian – Your challenge!

Italian food is very popular and ready-to-eat meals can be seen in every supermarket. There is a wide range of dishes using typical Italian ingredients – meat, mozzarella cheese, tomatoes, herbs. Pasta is especially associated with Italian food and there are many different shapes to choose and use.

A manufacturer wants a new fresh pasta dish for its cook-chill line. Your challenge is to design and make a prototype of a typical Italian dish.

You might be able to simulate a production line to see how your dish would be made in larger quantities. You may also design or use some special equipment to help in the production of your dish.

Layer by layer – Your challenge!

Supermarkets sell lot of chilled desserts such as yoghurts, trifles, cheesecakes and mousses. Some are the same texture all the way through, others have a variety of textures – crunchy, smooth, chunky, soft, chewy. New types are tried on consumers frequently but some do not last long.

Food manufacturers carry out a great deal of research to find out what consumers like. Recent research shows that some people like small, individual layered desserts with fresh fruit in them. They are trying to develop a new product to meet this demand.

Your challenge is to design a layered, chilled dessert containing fruit, for one person. You may present it in a vacuum-formed package which shows off the layered effect.

© Royal College of Art Schools Technology Project. Reproduced with permission

Figure 7.2 Your challenge! Part 1, Eat Italian; Part 2, Chilled desserts

Focused Practical Tasks

These accompany the DMAs, some being set out in the students' books and further ones in the photocopiable section of the teachers' books. They cover the underlying knowledge, skills and understanding needed for the DMAs, including some drawn from investigating and evaluating products.

They are generally teacher-directed, to be used as necessary, preceding or at points during or after the main DMA. In all cases these relate to a specific DMA, though they may be relevant in others.

One use of product evaluation is to investigate products which respond to needs similar to those the students are to address in a DMA. In this case, a product evaluation session is presented as an FPT. There are also other times when to investigate products is of general value, encouraging pupils to look at how materials have been used, manufacturing techniques, or design priorities. This type of approach is also supported in RCA materials, an example of which is given in Table 7.1.

Designing and Making Assignments (DMA)	Focused Practical Tasks (FPTS)
Creative salads	• Finding out about fruits and vegetables • Preparing fruits and vegetables • Marks and Spencer Ribon Vegetables Case Study • Researching what people like or want • What is a salad and what is a salad dressing? • Understanding about healthy eating • Food tests – changes in fruit and vegetables
Pastry Product development	• Generating ideas – bright ideas • Market researching – what already exists? what do customers want? • Investigating pastry fillings • Sorting out the good ideas – concept screening • Writing a specification • Prototyping • Consumer testing and sensory analysis • Costing and spreadsheets • Quality control • Ginsters Case Study – Cheese and Onion Pasty

Table 7.1 Focused tasks chart

Structuring a sequence of units

The Course Guide and Teachers' Books give advice on structuring a sequence of units so that students progress smoothly in a number of aspects of D&T as they move through the course. Programme of study (PoS) mapping charts, such as the one shown in Table 7.2, are included to help teachers ensure that National Curriculum requirements are met.

The sequence and content of the KS3 Food Technology units are based on the progression map (Figure 7.3). There is a choice of Units for schools to choose the most appropriate to their situation. This will depend on:

Activity	Skills		Knowledge and Understanding					
	Designing	Making	Materials	Systems & Control	Structures	Products & Applications	Quality	Health & Safety
	a b c d e f g h i j k l	a b c d e f g h i j k	a b c d e	a b c d e f g	a b c d e	a b c d e f	a b c d	a b c
Novelty Chocolates	* * * * ? ? ? ? * ? * *	* * * * * * * ? ? * *	* * ? * *	? ? ? ? ? ?		* * ? * * *	* * * *	* * *
Puppets	* * * * ? ? ? * * ? * *	* * * * * * * ? ? * *	* ? ? * *	* ? ? *		* * ? * * *	* * * ?	* * *
Wall Hanging	* * * * ? ? * * * ? * *	* * * * * * * ? * * *	* * * * *			* * * * *	* * *	* * *
Door Buzzer	* * * * ? ? * * * ? * *	* * * * * * * ? * * *	* * * * *			* * * * *	* *	* * *
Disk Case	* * * * ? ? ? * * ? * *	* * * * * * * ? * * *	* * * *		*	* * * * *	? ?	* * *
Creative Salads	* * * * * ? * * * ? * *	* * * * * * * ? * * *	* * * *			* * * * *	? ?	* * *
CAD/CAM Puzzle	* * * * ? ? ? * * ? * *	* * * * * * * ? * * *	* * * *			* * ? ? * *	? ?	* * *
Pasty Product Dev	* * * * ? * * * * ? * *	* * * * * * * * ? * *	* * * * ?			* * * * *	? ? ?	* * * *
Can Crusher	* * * * ? ? * * * ? * *	* * * * * * * ? ? * *	* * * * *	* *	*	* * * ? *	* *	* * *
Electric Buggy	* * * ? ? ? * * * ? * *	* * * * * * * ? ? * *	* * * * *	* *	*	? ? ? ? ? ?		* * *
Art Deco Jewellery	* * * * ? ? ? * * ? * *	* * * * * * * ? ? * *	* * * * *			* * * * *	*	* * *
Events Kit	* * * * ? ? * * * ? * *	* * * * * * * ? ? * *	* * * * ?			* * ? * * ?	*	* * *

*   all aspects addressed
?   some aspects addressed
☐   not addressed

1995 Order
Key Stage 3 Programme of Study

© Royal College of Art Schools Technology Project. Reproduced with permission from *Course Guide for KS3*, published by Hodder & Stoughton Educational

Table 7.2 Year 7 PoS map

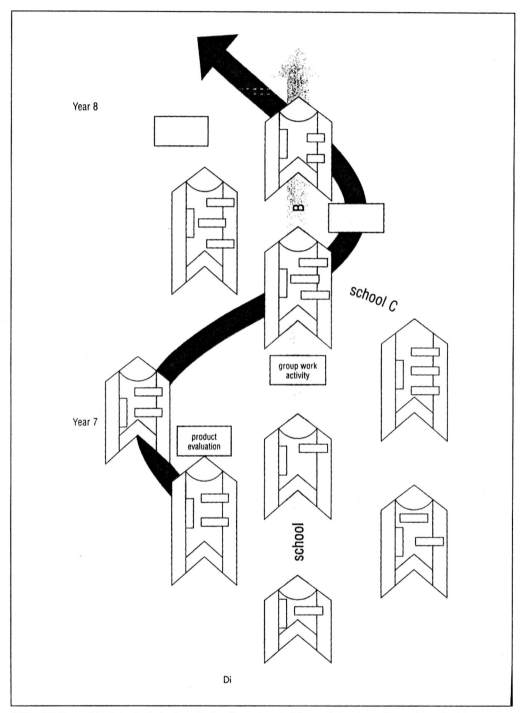

Year 8

Year 7

product
evaluation

group work
activity

school C

school

B

Di

Figure 7.3 Different schools' route through RCA STP course

Skills, Knowledge and Understanding		
Technical Issues	**Human Interactive Issues**	**Making Issues**
Year 7 • Recognise, group and compare a wide range of foods. • Know about the links between diet and health and understand the main healthy eating recommendations. • Use hygienic practices. • Recognise the working characteristics of basic foods and use them to design products which have a variety of colours, tastes and textures. • Recognise that changes in quantities affect the form and texture of he product, and that changes are caused by combining ingredients in different ways under a variety of temperatures.	• Explore colours, smells and tastes of familiar foods and serve food attractively. • Evaluate the product, consider people's opinions and use appropriate sensory descriptors. • Know about and understand symbolic meanings and uses of food. • Work out the cost of the ingredients for a product.	• Measure foods accurately. • Mix and prepare foods. • Use equipment which allows a degree of precision (e.g. hand whisk/grater). • Select and combine raw, pre-cooked and processed foods to create products. • Make a product to meet a set specification.
Year 8 • Be able to make recommendations and practical adjustments to food and food choice to achieve a healthy diet. • Experiment with ways of combining foods to create and modify products to improve sensory characteristics. • Know that micro-organisms are affected by critical temperatures.	• Know that food choice is affected by nutrition, culture, customs, religion, availability and cost. • Evaluate consumer acceptability of products by using tests with verbal and/or pictorial scale. Be aware of moral and social issues concerned with product development. • Carry out simple market research as part of product development.	• Know about a range of popular foods from production to consumption and identify the effects of technology at each stage. • Know how to ensure consistency in batch production. • Know about a range or preservation methods and additives and their affect on food. • Match equipment and processes to components being used and outcomes required.
Year 9 • Understand the nature of nutrients and take into account nutritional content of a product in meeting the needs of the users (e.g. DRVs). • Use functional properties of food constituents (protein starch, fat) to achieve desired effects: shape and textural characteristics of a product (e.g. setting and thickening). • Be able to use food tables and specialist computer programmes to analyse diet and nutritional values of products. • Be aware of product development for larger scale production (manufacturing).	• Understand how social and economic factors influence food choice and diet. • Evaluate food products using difference and attitudinal sensory tests e.g. triangle and hedonic ranking. • Be aware of environmental issues affecting food production, storage and choice of packaging. • Work out the cost of the product and variations to ingredients.	• Select and use processing and cooking methods/equipment to match design intentions. • Generate own design specification. • Sequence steps of food production and processing including safety and hygiene checks (for a small scale production run). • Understand that heat treatment freezing and additives prolong the shelf life of foods, and apply knowledge of temperature control when storing and working with food.

© Royal College of Art Schools Technology Project. Reproduced with permission from *Course Guide for KS3*, published by Hodder & Stoughton Educational

Table 7.3 Progression

			Event Kits / Other Materials
Y7 Manageable Closely relate to themselves Simple ingredients	**Healthy Eating** Creative Salads Promoting healthy eating – Fruits and vegetables Aesthetics: Understanding origin of foods. Product Development Food Science: emulsions Food tests, enzyme activity Changes in Food Nutritional analysis M & S Case study	**Pasty Product development** Product development, limited to filling Researching, prototyping Understanding industrial approaches Sensory analysis – star diagram taste panels Simple Quality Assurance., Costing – spreadsheets Ginsters Case Study	**Event Kits** Festive food Food contamination Hygiene Celebration Portion control *Other Materials* ***Novelty Chocolates*** *Production in quantity. Moulds and casting. Product evaluation. Food science-tempering case study* Graphics Pneumatics
Y8 Larger Scale production work in/across other material areas (not compulsory) Closer to prototyping in test kitchen	**Pasta Production** Research Product evaluation Understanding scales of production Cook-chill Prototyping Production line simulation Consumer research evaluation Pennine Foods/Heinz case study Optional input - Resistant materials & systems and control	**Fruit Dessert** Generating ideas – Blue sky design Food Science – Understanding fruit, foams, gels Healthy eating – sugar Experimenting (combine flavours, textures and colours. Specifications Twin pot ice cream Case study Optional input – Resistant materials – Vacuum formed complimentary packaging (volumes)	***Moving Display*** Food and culture Research Food photography control graphics ***Product Range*** *Simple design across a range of materials CAD/CAM*
Y9 Closer to manufacturing Introducing industrial practises	**Specialist Products** Re-designing a menu item for mass production (for restaurant chain) Hygiene HACCP Individual groups nutritional needs Case study of airline meals etc Additional links across resistant materials and systems and control	**Bread Manufacturing** Nutritional needs Food Science: Raising agents, flours, gluten Preservatives and shelf life Manufacturing Case study Greenhalgh's bakery	**Creative Food** New product from existing ideas Consumer evaluation Scaling up production Case Study – Dohler ingredients *Manufacturing to Sell (cross material entrepreneurial DMA)*

© Royal College of Art Schools Technology Project. Reproduced with permission.

Table 7.4 Food units at Key Stage 3

1. Previous experience of the majority of students.
2. Resourcing – rooms and equipment available.
3. Staff expertise and interest.
4. Time allocated for the year.
5. Delivery model – Some units provide opportunities for team delivery with other specialists (e.g. systems and control in food production, graphics in food packaging, vacuum forming for production).

Figure 7.3 illustrates different schools choosing different routes through STP material to meet their needs. It recognises that schools will have different starting points and finish points – some will have the time and resources to go well beyond basic National Curriculum demands. Others will only just meet them.

The first need for any English school will be to meet National Curriculum demands. The most likely problem for many schools will be having enough time available to do only this. Other schools, such as technology colleges, may be using non-National Curriculum time, extended school days or school years to go much further.

As Tables 7.3 and 7.4 illustrate, much effort has been devoted to showing how individual students and the set of units available to them should progress in a coherent way, such that higher levels of activity build on basic achievements. The principle is made real – every child's potential is fulfilled.

Empowering students

A particular concern of this project is to enable students to build a sense of ownership, of their learning, of their progress through the course, of the purposes behind their designing and making and of their future directions. This is seen as fundamental to design and technology. If students are not gaining ownership of their designing and making purposes, they are not designing but merely going through the motions. This is the key to success over the years of a D&T course. If a teacher instils in students a sense of engagement and purpose in what they are doing, it becomes more than likely that high-quality learning will result, whatever the other constraints, facilities, time or resources.

Summary

The project's approach:

- Set up the Challenge in a way which motivates students and allows them to make a personal response, to take ownership of the task (Figure 7.4).
- Be adequately flexible allowing a spontaneous response, for students to identify and follow their own purposes, to follow what they think is interesting and creative, and to value it (Figure 7.5).
- Allow maximum autonomy, either individually or to teams as the task demands.
- Intervene only when it is judged likely to be in the students' best interests – perhaps in the long rather than short term. Allow constructive failure, ensure eventual success.

Why this activity is useful

- You will find out about the types of ingredients which go into Italian dishes, and how pasta is made.

- You will experiment with different ingredients, combining them to make a new product or improve an existing one. This is important for future new product development.

- You will think about how production systems are designed to produce a dish on a larger scale.

- You may work with other materials as well as food.

Why this activity is useful

- It is all about developing new products.

- You will learn some food science such as how different ingredients can cause different effects like thickening and setting.

- You will understand about different types of fruit, how they can be prepared for eating in interesting ways and why they are important in everyone's diet.

- You will experiment with different textures, flavours and colours and how they can be combined to make a new dessert.

© Royal College of Art Schools Technology Project. Reproduced with permission from *D&T CHALLENGES Green Book*, published by Hodder & Stoughton Educational

Figure 7.4 Why this activity is useful

- Emphasise the process skills in designing as well as a concern for underlying knowledge and understanding.
- Structure the learning such that required skills and knowledge (e.g. from the NC programmes of study) are achieved through active designing and making.

For more information about the Royal College of Art Schools Technology Project please contact us at the Royal College of Art, Kensington Gore, London SW7 2EU 0171 584 2391 (Fax 0171 584 2062). To place an order for the publications please telephone Bookpoint on 01235 400405.

To be successful

You will need to:

- use your research into traditional Italian foods and existing products to design and make a new pasta dish,

- design and produce your own pasta shapes,

- explore plenty of ideas so you will finish with one that is excellent,

- think carefully how you can combine ingredients to make a dish which will appeal to consumers,

- understand how your prototype dish could be made on a larger scale.

To be successful

- Your research into existing products, your ideas and experiments with ingredients will result in a dessert which:

  contains fruit,

  combines different layers, colours and textures,

  looks attractive,

  tastes wonderful!

- You will apply your understanding of how different ingredients may be used to set and thicken food products to create a popular dessert.

- You will record your product development process thoroughly.

- You will evaluate your product and consult other people appropriately.

- Any packaging you make will be attractive and complement the appearance of the dessert, keeping it free from contamination.

Figure 7.5 To be successful

Chapter 8

Food Technology in the Science with Technology Project

Jim Sage

Introduction

The Science with Technology Project was a joint initiative of the Association for Science Education (ASE) and the Design and Technology Association (DATA). The Project was also supported by the National Association of Teachers of Home Economics and Technology (NATHE) in the food and textiles areas. The project was established to produce curriculum materials and to develop strategies to support schools making links between science and technology. These materials are aimed at students in the 14–19 age range and can be used with GCSE, GNVQ and A/AS level courses. Developing these curriculum materials often involved working with industry to develop accurate, relevant and interesting contexts for work in science and technology, illustrating the 'seamless web' that links these subjects together with mathematics in 'real life' contexts.

The Project's strategies

Through working with a wide range of schools and colleges, including both teachers and students, a number of key issues about collaborative working were identified covering:

- Logistical issues – timing and sequencing of topics, timetable problems, student groupings and so on.
- Philosophical issues, subject cultures and teachers' attitudes leading to barriers and blocks that make collaborative work difficult.
- Students' conceptual development in different subjects.

The Project team felt that the last of these was the most important issue to be addressed, but in doing so we agreed that we would also give attention to the other two particularly in identifying and developing a range of strategies that could be used to make collaborative work successful.

As a consequence of this, one of the problems tackled by the project was the complex process of transferring knowledge, understanding and skills effectively from one subject to another. In the case of science and design and technology this involves a construction of a scientific understanding which has to be firstly de-constructed and then re-constructed before it can be applied to a new situation. This explains the difficulties encountered by students when they try to apply their understanding of science to their work in design and technology (D&T). Often the way a concept is developed in science does not lend itself to an understanding that can be applied in another subject; mathematical skills are developed to serve the purposes of mathematics, not D&T. The contexts used in science and mathematics are often constrained and simplified to make the development of students' understanding more straightforward. D&T by its nature has to address 'real world' problems and deal with the constraints and all of the other complex issues that surround designing products for use by people.

Students' work on designing and making is considerably enhanced by an understanding and application of appropriate key scientific and mathematical principles. A number of the units produced by the Project are designed to develop students' understanding of key scientific concepts that can be utilised in designing and making and turn this understanding into 'knowledge for practical action'. This often includes developing key mathematical and IT skills at the same time. This is demonstrated clearly in the project's *Understanding the Science of Food* unit which contains a range of activities that can be used in food technology to help the students both develop and apply their scientific understanding.

If the transfer from one subject to another is to be effective, appropriate teaching and learning strategies have to be employed to support the students. The Project team developed a range of strategies for collaborative work between science and D&T. The easiest and often the most effective of these to implement involves increasing awareness of what is being taught and learnt in the other subject, discussing the different approaches used and taking account of this in planning activities and assignments for students. This will help to ensure that the students have a coherent learning experience. Different approaches to teaching-related topics may still be used, but if these are part of a planned and co-ordinated approach, it will lead to enhanced understanding rather than confusion and conflict in students' minds. This approach has been applied in the *Developing Food Products* unit.

The Project's approach to food technology

The Project's starting point was always to identify areas where science and D&T naturally relate to one another and not to force a relationship that was likely to be unsuccessful. For this reason, it was always intended to produce curriculum materials in the food area. However, as the Project developed, it became clear that there were other very sound reasons for developing resources in food technology. The industrial sponsors of the project included a number of prominent food companies, and we wanted to reflect the important role of the food industry in the manufacturing sector. It also became very clear that producing a unit about developing food products provided opportunities to introduce students to key issues about product development, and hence develop their overall D&T capability. Linking this with science took us naturally into the areas of food science and food technology.

The food technology units

The Project produced two units related to food technology:

- Developing Food Products.
- Understanding the Science of Food.

Developing Food Products

This unit covers all aspects of developing a new food product and scaling up production. It is based on the soya product tofu, but all of the activities can be easily transferred to the development of other food products. The unit is summarised in Figure 8.1.

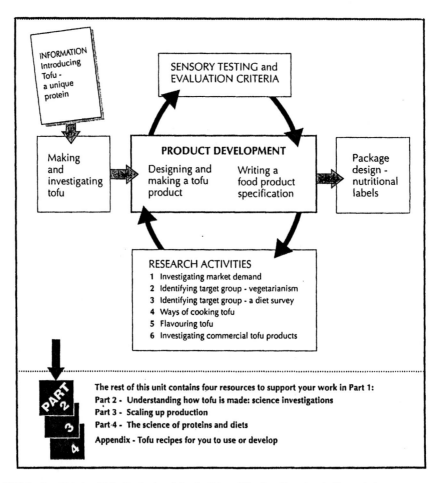

Figure 8.1 Product development

This approach shows how a designing and making assignment can be integrated with a range of focused practical tasks and activities involving evaluating existing products.

There are several advantages of basing this unit on tofu:

- A large proportion of students in the 14–19 age range are vegetarian; there is a section in the unit presenting research on vegetarianism and a focused task designed to help students identify the target group for their food product.
- Tofu is the only non-meat food product with a 100% protein quality – it contains all of the indispensable amino acids. This allows issues related to the quantity of protein required in a diet and the quality of the protein to be discussed; this is an issue ignored in most, if not all, information about 'healthy eating'.
- Tofu in its raw state is very bland and allows for the development of a wide range of interesting new food products; its working properties need careful investigation, leading to a range of focused practical tasks.

The science investigations help students understand the processes used to make tofu and the scientific principles behind these processes. This understanding is vital to appreciate the issues that have to be considered in scaling up production. The information used was provided by Cauldron Foods, the company that manufactures most of the tofu and tofu products available in supermarkets and health food shops. These investigations can, and have, been used in science to provide an interesting context for this work.

This unit has been used with GCSE and 'A' level courses as well as GNVQ Manufacturing and GNVQ Health and Social Care programmes at Intermediate and Advanced level; it could also be used at Foundation level.

Understanding the Science of Food

This unit covers:

- the nutritional function of food and how this is related to digestion;
- the science behind the physical function and the working properties of food;
- the effects of cooking food on the nutritional function of food;
- using microbiological tests to asses food hygiene and safety.

Figure 8.2, taken from the introduction to the unit, shows how these are related to food product design. This is reinforced through each part of the unit with references to how this relates to industrial practice.

The nutrition part of the unit contains an activity using a spreadsheet as a tool for designing food products to meet specified nutritional requirements. This demonstrates how IT is integrated into other activities and how relevant contexts can be used to develop IT skills. Students, of course, need to identify clearly these nutritional requirements for their target group and the unit contains full explanations of both DRV and RDA. They are also provided with a number of possible areas to research including meals for a range of hospital patients with very different nutritional requirements.

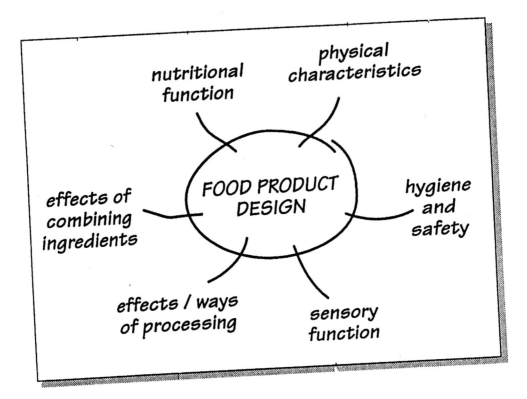

Figure 8.2 Food product design

Summary

A successful co-ordinated approach:

- *Understanding the Science of Food* has been used by both science and food technology teachers and, together with *Developing Food Products*, provides a good model for a co-ordinated approach to these subjects.
- A common context is agreed through discussions involving teachers from both subjects; in this case it is also useful to include a mathematician as work on DRV and RDA requires a mathematical understanding.
- A major activity is developed to which all subjects will contribute; here this would be based on the development of a new food product.
- A series of 'structured inputs' are then developed to support the 'core' activity to provide data and information and act as resource activities and focused tasks to develop skills and understanding. The 'structured inputs' provide a range of different learning experiences for students, which can be matched to the syllabus requirements of the subjects involved.
- These inputs can then be covered in the different subjects in a planned and coherent way or be used as part of a more integrated activity.
- This model provides great flexibility in the range of strategies that can be used to suit the needs of different schools and colleges.

● Both of these units have been used as the basis of INSET courses for practising teachers and for those in training. The feedback from these sessions has shown clearly that these materials are extremely useful in developing, enhancing and supporting food technology courses as well as contributing to the professional development of teachers.

Science with Technology units are available from ASE Booksales, College Lane, Hatfield, Herts AL10 9AA. Telephone 01707 267411, fax 01707 266532.

Other units that may be of interest:
● Developing Textiles Products
● Investigating and Designing Control Systems
● Control in Action: Designing a fermenter
● Teamwork: solving problems and improving quality
● Product Development – innovation, design, production and quality
● Project Management
● Human Factors in Design

Section 4

Industrial Practice

This section focuses on the National Curriculum D&T requirement for an increased emphasis on knowledge and understanding of industrial practices.

Chapter 9 considers practices in food product development through the eyes of industry.

Chapter 10 provides an example of a school-based vocational GNVQ course in Manufacturing with a focus of food technology.

Chapter 11 examines the RCA Technology materials to see how they support and provide guidance for teachers and pupils following the new D&T food technology courses.

Chapter 12 considers how the Nuffield Design and Technology project enables pupils to develop an understanding of the processes and procedures of the food industry.

Chapter 9

Food Technology: An Industrial Perspective

Brenda Jamieson

Introduction

There are many aspects of food technology in the National Curriculum related to food retailing. The introduction and acceptance of a new product, from the first stage of conception to the point of consumption (Figure 9.1), is a good illustration whereby classroom investigations and evaluation can reflect industrial practice, from quality control and sensory evaluation to marketing and advertising.

Food retailing is a rapidly moving business. Changes in lifestyle affect the way people shop and consequently the type of stores, facilities and products that retailers offer. New products come on to the market every week; often these are modifications of an existing food product but technological developments sometimes help to create new products.

New products are developed to reflect the changes in home and society. The nineteenth century saw the commercial introduction of canning and as a result, fruit, vegetables, meat, fish and dairy products readily became available in canned varieties. In the 1950s as more homes acquired freezers, frozen foods became popular. In the 1980s changing demographics, in particular such factors such as more one-person households and fewer family meals, together with changing tastes, made ready meals popular. The pace of change has accelerated sharply in recent years, and over the last decade the UK has seen several changes in society which have opened up a whole new consumer market.

More wives and mothers working means less time for meal preparation and a greater demand for convenience, quick cook and microwave foods. Convenience meals were developed by modifying the cook–chill techniques of mass catering pioneered for hospitals. The 1990s have seen an increasing sophistication of consumer tastes, bringing a demand for higher quality and greater variety, with customers prepared to pay extra for convenience and higher quality. Cultural diversity is now a significant feature of British society. The increasingly cosmopolitan

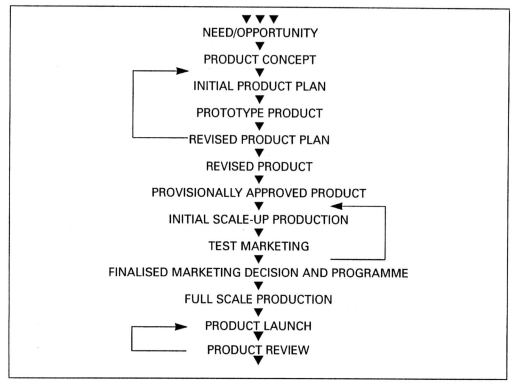

Figure 9.1 Product development

nature of our society influences the range of products supermarkets offer, and increased travel has led to interest in foreign eating habits and a widened interest in foreign foods and wines.

The importance of eating a balanced diet has become better understood by doctors, the food industry and by customers. The dietary changes recommended by the Committee on Nutritional Aspects of Food Policy (COMA) report of May 1994 reinforced the message of the 1991 and previous COMA reports:

- reduce total fat
- reduce sugar
- reduce salt/sodium
- increase fibre intake.

This has resulted in the development of modified foods such as reduced sugar, salt and fat, or increased fibre alternatives to standard lines. Consumer lifestyles continue to change and are reflected in changes in eating habits, such as 'grazing' and tele-meals.

Manufacturers who have to develop products to appeal to clearly defined market sectors must increasingly think of the circumstances and lifestyles they are catering for. New product development is the systematic process for developing and marketing a new product, from identifying the market opportunity and the development of an original concept, through to test kitchen trials, evaluation and re-formulation, to production, packaging and the launch of that product on the market and in-store presentation to the customer.

Research

The key to producing any successful product is to identify a gap in the market and to fill it with a high-quality product at a reasonable price. The commercial buyer is responsible for negotiating with the supplier and overseeing the strategy, and the technical division oversees the technical aspects of production ensuring that highest standards of hygiene and safety are enforced.

New products may be developed by brand leaders, by manufacturers who supply proprietary brands, or by supermarket retailers. In the case of manufacturers, new ideas are likely to come about as the result of research and development work undertaken on the manufacturer's own account or on behalf of a client. Retailers are always studying the market, monitoring competitors' new ideas and trying to identify gaps in the market. Being in touch with customers and having a day-to-day knowledge of the market is dependent upon the expertise and technical ability of the retailer and manufacturer. A continuous supply of market research data from established sources such as AGB and Nielson helps identify new product ideas. In addition, sales data from supermarket scanning checkouts can be analysed to show which types of products are selling well, or how a new proprietary brand product is selling.

Understanding the reasons for food choice is a complex field influenced by many factors. A knowledge of the factors and how they relate is essential to manufacturers and retailers. A producer must be aware of his potential customers and attitudes to his products as well as the various economic or social factors which influence them when purchasing. Without such information it is impossible to optimise product ranges, successfully create new products or direct advertising to where it will be effective.

Innovation

New product development is an intriguing and creative process which incorporates sound scientific techniques plus a 'feel' for a product's potential based on intuition or on experience. Innovation covers:

- New concept development – a completely new concept often incorporating new technology.
- Range extensions – this covers all new flavour extension work over innumerable ranges of products. Successful range extensions are a vital follow-up to every new concept.
- Improved products – even successful products need their 'images' lifted from time to time.
- New positioning concepts or new market segments.

Once the type of product to be developed has been identified, the next stage is to make up the recipe. The development of the product is a two-way process between the retailer and the supplier. This may start by briefing a supplier to produce samples; the supplier will submit samples to be tested and then modify the recipe in the light of reactions. This process may be repeated several times. Products which require a lot of processing, for example canning, may change considerably during processing. Sometimes changing an ingredient can affect the product in unexpected ways.

Additives are the ingredients that are not usually regarded or used as foods themselves, but which are used in or on foods to affect its keeping qualities, appearance, taste, texture or other properties, or to assist in processing. This is an area where there has been considerable effort within the European Union to promote 'harmonisation' to ensure that the same rules apply in each member state. The introduction of the 'E' numbers was an attempt to simplify additive listing on ingredient labels across Europe. They are normally used at very low levels, but their importance is far greater than the amount used would suggest. In general, food additives are used for three main purposes:

- To preserve and prevent the growth of harmful organisms such as bacteria, thereby improving the keeping qualities and hence the safety of the food. Natural preservatives such as salt have been used for hundreds of years: bacon and ham are preserved by a curing process which requires the use of nitrates which give bacon its characteristic flavour and colour.
- To modify the consistency and texture of processed products such as soups, cakes and cooked meats. Emulsifiers must be used where a fat and a liquid need to be blended together: salad cream, mayonnaise and low-fat spread all need emulsifiers. Stabilisers act in a similar way and prevent separation.
- To add colour or flavour to many foods. This affects the sensory perception and appreciation. There are hundreds of flavouring substances, and it sometimes takes several of these blended together to obtain the finished flavouring required.

Evaluation

The sensory quality of food products can have a significant bearing on their commercial success. The consumer's decision to purchase or re-purchase a new product is determined by many factors, and of prime importance are the appearance, flavour and textural quality of the product. Appearance either succeeds or fails to stimulate appetite. Once the food has been tasted, appearance becomes secondary to taste and texture. Taste will remain the overall consideration when food is purchased, and so whatever trends may occur over the years, the product must taste good if it is to survive. Evaluation of the organoleptic qualities of a product during development stages results in greater chances of success in the market place. Laboratory taste panels provide standardised conditions for vigorous tasting techniques. This is known as *sensory appraisal,* correctly defined by the Institute of Food Technology as 'a scientific discipline used to evoke, measure, analyse and interpret reactions to those characteristics of food and materials as they are perceived by the senses of sight, smell, taste, touch and hearing'. Modern sensory evaluation techniques require careful experimental design to ensure efficient use of the powerful statistical methods for analysis now available in computer packages. The ready availability of computer hardware and software for data collection, storage and analysis has led to an interlinked computing system. The sensory evaluation techniques include:

- *Difference testing* which determines whether a product modification such as a substitute ingredient, produces a perceptible change in the product (to what level, for example, can fat levels be reduced before the change is detected?).
- *Product profiling* which uses panels extensively trained to score sensory attributes of products, resulting in a visual representation of the data in the form of a star diagram or spider's web plot.

Evaluation of the organoleptic qualities of a product during development stages results in greater chances of success in the market place. Consumer tests are also essential to assess the potential acceptability of a product. The actual consumer test chosen will depend upon the type of product, and it is important to select the appropriate consumer test to answer the objective. *Consumer preference* measures the appeal of one product when compared against the other. If the requirement is to know which product is preferred, a *paired comparison* or a *ranking test* may be chosen. These involve the consumer selecting the preferred product, or ranking the products in ascending order of preference. Consumer *acceptance* measures the degree of liking of individual products. To evaluate acceptability, *hedonic* scales are often used. The hedonic test directly measures the degree of liking or acceptability of a product. A typical 9-point hedonic scale would consist of descriptive words such as 'like extremely' (9) to 'dislike extremely' (1). For children, picture scales are more appropriate.

In addition, market research may also be carried out. *Quantitative* research involves surveying a representative sample population, usually through the use of a numerically coded questionnaire with a limited range of answers. Consumer surveys using a carefully worded questionnaire can provide information such as frequency of purchase and likely repeat purchase, and also investigate market variables such as name, packaging and price.

Qualitative research includes more in-depth and 'open' questioning, particularly useful for exploring feelings and attitudes. In-depth focus discussion groups provide information on how consumers think about a product in their home and among their friends. They look at the product from a totally impersonal view; their evaluations are dispassionate and their comments are honest.

Trial run

Once the sample has been agreed, the supplier will draw up a specification and submit samples from a trial production for analysis. The specification contains details of the recipe, how it is to be processed, and what the final appearance of the product should be. Cost indications enable agreement of a retail price for the product within an acceptable profit margin.

A trial run is a small-scale production run designed to test how the product will perform under normal conditions. Numerous tests are carried out to check for everything from unwanted ingredients to foreign bodies, the processing effectiveness, acidity levels and drained weights. Problems may arise at this stage which mean going back almost to square one! A product, for example, may have been developed with a characteristically rich sauce, but the trial run stage may show that it is too thick to pass easily through machinery. An attempt would therefore have to be made to decrease the viscosity of the sauce while maintaining the rich flavour.

Packaging

In today's highly competitive food market, packaging has a wide-ranging role. New methods of packaging and packaging materials are continually being developed, and there are many new technologies becoming available. Ready meals are a good example of this, with many products now packaged in microwaveable containers. During the last 5 years, sensitivity to the environment has been one of the major factors responsible for the significant increase in both the development and the profile of packaging. There is no doubt that all of us are becoming more environmentally sensitive, with many people prepared to change their purchasing habits to reflect environmental principles.

Materials commonly used for packaging include paper, metal, glass, and many types of plastic, often in various combinations. The choice of packaging material depends upon a number of factors – the nature of the product to be packaged, the cost of packaging materials, environmental impact and presentation required. The choice of the right type of packaging for a new product is an important part of its development because:

- The most important function of packaging is to protect the product from the environment, by acting as a barrier to reduce deterioration from the point of production to consumption. The protective role of packaging reduces waste and prolongs the shelf life of goods.
- Packaging is also a means of giving customers information. It identifies and describes the contents and assists the customer in their choice of product.
- Packaging is necessary to present the product to the consumer in a convenient form. As packaging has become more complex and the materials evolved, problems have arisen, such as 'openability'. However, a number of considerations have to be taken into account when researching alternative packaging materials for the purpose of easy opening. The easier it becomes to open products, the greater the risk of spoilage – weakness in the material being unable to withstand transportation, increases in the number of tampering incidents requiring greater product protection and tamper-evident seals.
- Marketing and selling the product is an area where packaging and design have an important role to play. Products must look attractive on the shelf and stand out from the competition. No matter how good a product is, it will not sell if it does not look good on the shelf. Packaging has been called the 'silent salesman' as eye catching designs help to advertise and sell products. The artwork for packaging may involve photography or drawing illustrations.

Food labelling

All packaged food sold in the UK must carry labelling which conforms to the Food Labelling Regulations (1984). In addition, a European Commission directive on nutrition labelling came into effect in the UK on 1 March 1995. Points required by law include:
- *The name of the food* – The easy part is finding something short, memorable, easy to pronounce and different; the hard part is avoiding unfortunate

connotations in other languages and cultures, and making sure it can be protected as a trademark. If this name does not explain the nature of the food a subtitle must be added, for example Jump, a chewy cereal bar.

- *Weight* – Most foods may be packed in any weight the manufacturer chooses; there are some foods, however – such as tea, biscuits, butter, milk and bread – which have to be sold in specified weights.
- *List of ingredients* – Which must be listed in weight order. Additives must be declared and should be preceded by the name of the additive group to which they belong.
- *Minimum durability* – Regulations under the Food Safety Act 1990 require most foods to carry a durability mark, for example 'use by' on highly micro-biologically perishable foods (such foods are normally stored in chill cabinets), and 'best before' used on all other products. The 'best before' date given is the date by which the food can be enjoyed at its best, taking into account the storage conditions printed on the pack.
- *Instructions for use* – Many products need explanations for their use, for example cooking instructions, mixing instructions etc. If other ingredients are required to make up the product, these must be stated on the outside of the package, e.g. 'cake mix – add an egg and butter'.
- *The name and address of the manufacturer or supplier* of the product.
- *Particulars of the place of origin* of the food if the name might be misleading, for example Italian pizza – made in the UK.
- *Nutritional labelling* – at present, there is a legal obligation to provide nutritional information only if a nutrition claim is being made. Criteria for nutritional claims are taken from Ministry of Agriculture, Fisheries and Food (MAFF) Regulations. Where nutritional information is given, it must be set out in a prescribed format, for example EC Directive 90/496/EEC prescribes the format to be used when nutrition information is given on pack. All information is given per 100 g or 100 ml for easy comparison, but where there is space, the information is also given per serving or per unit (for example, per biscuit, per sausage). This detailed information is useful for those who are on special diets – calorie counted, diabetic, salt free, low fat.
- *Bar codes* are incorporated on the packaging of most products sold today. When the bar code is passed over the window at the check-out the scanner reads the code and charges the correct price. Scanning can also be used to help with stock control and to generate orders.

Production

Once the artwork is completed and the packaging is ready, a first production run will be organised. Once a product is given the go ahead, the supplier is asked to describe the *flow process* in detail showing precisely what happens to the ingredients from the time the raw material arrives at the factory until the finished product leaves. The flow process can be broken down into a number of distinct stages: hazard analysis; quality control checks on raw ingredients; storage of raw ingredients; raw ingredients washing, cutting and weighing procedures; cooking procedures; transfer to high-risk area; cooling process; assembly process; labelling and coding; storage in chill chain.

A hazard analysis is carried out on this process to be sure that the safety checks and procedures are adhered to and monitored. Food technologists at the factory ensure everything runs smoothly; they will check that procedures are carefully followed, monitored and recorded, and that the product tastes just as it should.

'Traceability' is very important, as each ingredient has its own history recorded and the finished product is coded so that it can be traced accurately. Many products can be produced in bulk and stored until required, for example canned and frozen foods. Others need to be produced on a daily basis because of their relatively short shelf life, typically cook–chill products. This means that a particular product may only be in production for half an hour; at the end of this short production run, the lines will have to be cleaned and prepared for a new product.

Advertising

Understanding the reason for food choice is a complex field, influenced by many factors including marketing and advertising, even the brand name, price and availability. It is difficult to imagine life without advertising. The average Briton now watches two and a half to three hours of TV commercials a week (the equivalent of two feature films!). To this must be added the considerable exposure of newspaper, radio and poster advertising, which when combined means the consumer is exposed to some 200 'messages' every day.

The Advertising Standards Authority controls the content of print and cinema advertisements and stipulates that advertisements must be legal, decent, honest and truthful. Advertising may be classified as:

- *Informative* – to generate awareness of a new product in the market place.
- *Competitive* – to protect against competition.
- *Persuasive* – 'lifestyle' advertising;
- *Corporate* – to give an image of quality and innovation aimed at long-term customer loyalty.
- *Generic.*

There is an important difference between *brand* advertising to encourage shoppers to buy a particular product and *retail* advertising which uses products to attract potential customers to purchase a variety of 'shopping basket' items. The choice of media advertising is determined by a number of factors:

- *Target audience* – to reach housewives, women's magazines or TV AM might be appropriate; whereas, to reach business people a broad-sheet newspaper or TV advertising during '*News at Ten*' might be better.
- *Advertising budget* – television is the most powerful and fastest growing advertising medium claiming 31% of advertising expenditure; radio advertising has also increased, but only claims about 2%. Although advertising in the press has declined, it still retains the largest market share at 62%.
- *Marketing mix* – promotion includes all those activities which are designed to improve customer awareness and understanding of the product. Advertising is the most obvious and direct method of promotion, but special offers, free gifts, competitions, merchandising, personal selling and publicity also play an important role.

Merchandising will decide how much shelf space the new product needs and there may be a possible introductory offer, and from then on it is all left to the customer. Research recently estimated that more than 50% of food purchase decisions are made while individuals are in the supermarket; consumers therefore need useful in-store information to help guide their food purchase decisions.

Summary

- Consumer needs are constantly changing and the pace has accelerated in recent years.
- Food manufacturers must constantly review their product ranges to keep pace with sophisticated taste requirements and meet customers heightened expectations.
- Customers will continue to insist on *quality, convenience* and *innovation.*
- The demands made for more variety and higher quality will be met by an array of powerful technologies, related to rising educational standards, to meet the demands of shopping and eating in the twenty-first century.

Chapter 10

Food Technology – GNVQ Manufacturing

Pat Moore

Introduction

Bodmin Community College is not, as might be expected, a typical rural school. Many families from Rodmin a small, former market town in North Cornwall and an over-spill town, have inner London origins and pupils have some of the problems that might be more associated with an urban school. For example, we have over 90 pupils with statements of special needs. Bodmin has a population of about 14000 and we are the only secondary school, with over 1200 on roll; currently over 200 are in the sixth form and more than 250 mature full- and part-time access students. Sixth form students follow a variety of courses, including a mix of 'A' levels, General National Vocational Qualifications (GNVQ), GCSE retakes, RSA Certificates, Certificate in Child Education or a combination of these alternatives.

Bodmin no longer has a market or a garrison or even a railway station, and the biggest employer, St Lawrence's, the largest mental hospital in the South West, has now almost disappeared. Bodmin does have, in the old military lines and the new industrial estates close to the A30, a variety of small businesses and industries at the most employing between a few and a hundred people. The largest employs just over 500. The manufacturers represent just about every Council of British Industry (CBI) sector, including a bookbinder, a wet-suit manufacturer now diversifying into other leisure markets, a label manufacturer, a high-specification warp knitter, a high-precision electronic controls and components manufacturer, several traditional bakers and ice cream makers and a Cornish pasties and pie manufacturer.

Suffice it to say that we treasure the relationships and partnerships with our employers, which have grown over a very long time. We regard them almost as part of the family silver. A week of work experience has been a feature of the Year 11 curriculum at Bodmin Community College for some years, but not for the sixth form. Work experience is not a mandatory part of any GNVQ subject, but the college believes that students would not achieve a really good understanding of what their courses are about unless some form of work-based learning was built into the course structure.

Introducing GNVQ

In 1993 the college was looking for something to replace the Certificate of Pre-Vocational Education (CPVE) and was considering BTECs, City & Guilds Diploma and the new General National Vocational Qualification (GNVQ) introduced by the National Council for Vocational Qualifications. Our brief was to investigate, set up and train the deliverers, find the students and be approved by the awarding body.

In the same year we offered GNVQs in Health and Social care (H&SC), Leisure and Tourism (L&T), Science, Business, Art and Design, and Manufacturing, recognising the latter one as a broad base which encompassed everything from a T-shirt to a tank! That year we registered 45 students, mostly at Intermediate level in Health and Social Care, Leisure and Tourism, Science. However, Business and Art and Design did not run because of lack of take-up by the students.

In 1994 we increased the registration to 67 for GNVQ, and had, by this time, discontinued Science, recruited for Business at all three levels and recruited more advanced students for the other subjects.

By 1995 seventy seven new students had been recruited in Manufacturing, Leisure and Tourism, Health and Social Care and Business and Art at intermediate and advanced levels. There were three students on foundation Health and Social Care and eleven students on the Certificate of Child Education course (CACHE). We are now seeing progression for our own students, with a handful moving from foundation to intermediate, and larger numbers from intermediate to advanced.

The introduction of GNVQ has helped to broaden the opportunities for the sixth form and offered alternative ways of achieving success and qualifications for the students, good reasons for coming back to study at any age. We have a mother and daughter on one of the Advanced courses!

Why GNVQ Manufacturing?

The statistics are interesting and provide an answer to this question. It is estimated that 4,551,600 of the total UK work force are employed in manufacturing, and that each worker employed in manufacturing provides a job for at least another worker in the service sector (CBI, 1994). Manufacturing earns about 65% of the UK's foreign currency with the food industry as the largest sector.

At Bodmin, we had twelve of the total 2,140 student numbers for Manufacturing GNVQ in 1994–5 (Table 10.1), a factor that has interested the National Council for Vocational Qualifications (NCVQ) and the Confederation of British Industry (CBI, 1994). We decided not to concentrate on one industry and have encouraged a gender balance of students since the beginning of the scheme.

We achieved this success through a team approach There is a specialist vocational input from textiles, food, electronics and construction teachers and all the students have a timetabled support period for information technology, application of number, or contextualised mathematics! Communication is accommodated within the vocational time.

ART & DESIGN	17,359
BUSINESS	55,257
HEALTH & SOCIAL CARE	36,028
LEISURE & TOURISM	30,086
MANUFACTURING	2,140
SCIENCE	5,044
CONSTRUCTION & THE BUILT ENVIRONMENT	3,047
HOSPITALITY & CATERING	4,098
PILOT SUBJECTS	7,839
TOTAL	**162,825**

Table 10.1 GNVQ student numbers

Students must show knowledge and understanding of at least two manufacturing sectors and scales of production. Two weeks of work placement has been built into the course in addition to industrial visits, though a reasonably resourced technology faculty without highly specialised equipment can be used very effectively on the course. The work placement and industrial visits are ideal for pupils to learn about continuous or batch production, 'just-in-time' or quality circles by observation; or, best of all, by hands-on working on an assembly line or in a manager's office. All these activities do not necessarily require major industry on the doorstep.

Links with industry

One of the links we have established with industry has been with Proper Cornish, a company with 65 employees and an annual turnover of £2,000,000 (Figure 10.1).

Figure 10.1 Proper Cornish logo

During two successive years two of our students have organised themselves a work placement of one week with the company, making all the arrangements themselves and completing a work experience log book. The work experience is carefully planned and students have to identify the core skills elements and vocational elements they intend working towards on the placement. They were able to see and participated in the manufacture of high-quality pies and pasties, which in Cornwall have to be traditionally made if they are to be taken seriously. In practice this means starting with the skins on the vegetables, pieces of meat, and basic ingredients for pastry, and the pasties have to be crimped by hand, baked, blast-chilled and packaged for delivery. The students experienced quality assurance procedures at first hand with, for example, supervisors slowing the production line to achieve high quality. All these factors are important as manufacturers cannot afford to make mistakes in a fickle market. Our students are able to take in these processes and gain a real insight into the manufacturing costs of materials, labour, equipment, distribution. For example, while our students were on the placement, they observed at first hand Proper Cornish improving their buildings to meet European Community (EC) standards to ensure the business would not close. An added bonus was that this work experience also contributed to their achievement of the Institute of Environmental Health Officers (IEHO) Basic Food Hygiene Certificate, all of which is taken into account for the student's assessment for the award of GNVQ Manufacturing.

GNVQ Course Structure

All GNVQs have three mandatory core skills units of communication, application of number and information technology, with six units at foundation and intermediate level for GNVQs and twelve at advanced level. Most of the mandatory units (Figure 10.2) have attached end-of-unit tests.

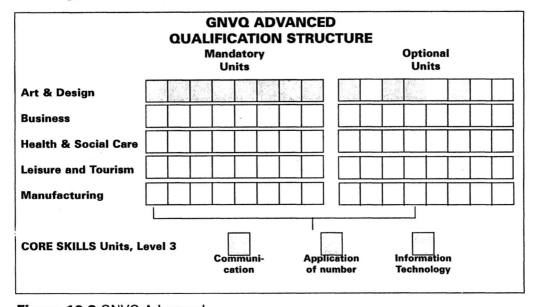

Figure 10.2 GNVQ Advanced

Integration is the current buzz-word, firstly for the core skills and secondly for the approach to substantial parts of the whole award. It could be argued that the GNVQ structure could militate against integration as certification can be at unit level or for the unit tests themselves, though theoretically students should not be able to pass the test unless they have covered the unit. Also, in our experience there are some GNVQs which lend themselves better to a linear unit-by-unit approach, for example H & SC and L & T. We have adopted a more integrated approach in Business and Art and Design and a hybrid in Manufacturing. An overview of the intermediate course (Figure 10.3) and details of the units need to be made clear to the students, or unpacked, and certainly experience has shown us this can be done. Details of each unit, which can be seen in Figure 10.4, are composed of elements providing further details of what needs to be covered.

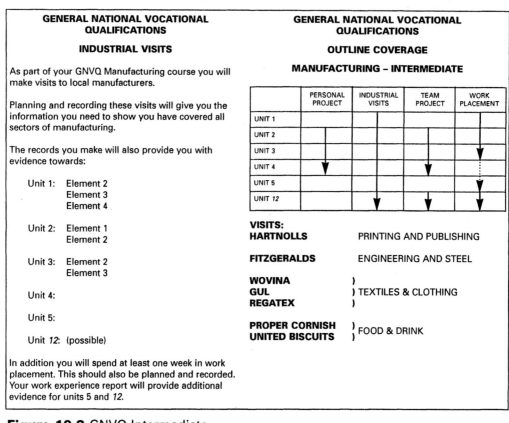

Figure 10.3 GNVQ Intermediate

Teaching styles

We start the the course by following a unit and a style of teaching that is familiar to students. We have 'class lessons', which is reassuring to staff and students, as we all at first have difficulties with the approach, the language and the assessment.

As the course progresses it is intended that the students will develop a pace and independent style that results in them becoming autonomous in their learning. This can present difficulties for some staff, as at times it is only the student who knows their precise stage of development within the course. We aim to be involved in individualised learning, tutorial style sessions with guidance geared to the precise needs of the students by the end of the Autumn term.

Intermediate Manufacturing GNVQ – unit summary

UNIT I:THE WORLD OF MANUFACTURING (INTERMEDIATE)
Element 1.1: Investigate the importance of manufacturing to the UK economy
Element 1.2: Investigate production systems
Element 1.3: Describe manufacturing organisations
Element 1.4: Identify the environmental effects of production processes

UNIT 2: WORKING WITH A DESIGN BRIEF (INTERMEDIATE)
Element 2.1: Originate product proposals from a given design brief
Element 2.2: Finalise proposals using feedback from presentations

UNIT 3: PRODUCTION PLANNING, COSTING AND QUALITY ASSURANCE (INTERMEDIATE)
Element 3.1: Produce production plans
Element 3.2: Calculate the cost of a product
Element 3.3: Investigate quality assurance

UNIT 4: MANUFACTURING PRODUCTS (INTERMEDIATE)
Element 4.1: Prepare materials, components, equipment and machinery
Element 4.2: Process materials and components
Element 4.3: Assemble and finish materials and components to specification
Element 4.4: Apply quality assurance to manufactured products

---

Figure 10.4 Unit details

Assessment

An example of an *element* is shown in Figure 10.5. We start with the evidence indicators, look at the performance criteria which must be covered, and use the evidence indicators to provide the evidence for student's portfolios. The range statements are attached to the performance indicators, though from September 1995 we have not had to track all of the range of statements, except for the core skills. An essential aspect is that the assessment should not be 'atomistic'.

We use a variety of assessment methods and collect evidence though a variety of means (Figure 10.6). Reports, for example, do not have to be written, they can be oral or by presentation and we are beginning to apply accreditation of prior achievement (APA), particularly for mature students. We do not expect them to cover these achievements again, as long as they can provide evidence that they have covered the aspects specified for an element or unit.

Planning

Action planning is essential if all the above factors are to be taken into account. The one we use (Figure 10.7) contains performance criteria (PC), because in our view these have to be covered implicitly even if they are not explicit in the evidence indicators. Students use the back of the action plans for noting any adjustments, or monitoring. We have abandoned 'logs', except for work experience, as there was too much of 'then I did, then I did' as a plan or record!

We want our students to achieve grades of merit or distinction and we think planning is one way of ensuring good grades. If students have planned and adjusted where necessary they will find they have relevant information to include

Element 1.2: Investigate production systems

PERFORMANCE CRITERIA

A student must:

1 describe each **key stage of production** for a given product
2 describe **scales of production** for a given product
3 produce a block diagram of the **production system** for a given product
4 identify the **quality control** points within a given **production system**
5 explain how changing scales of production **affects** the organisation of manufacturing systems

RANGE

Key stage of production: material preparation, processing and assembly, finishing, packaging

Scales of production: continuous, line, batch (small, repetitive), jobbing (one-off)

Production system: sourcing and procurement, processing, handling and storage

Quality control: quality indicators, inspection and testing methods, data recording formats

Affects in terms of plant layout, work practices, cost, numbers of products produced

EVIDENCE INDICATORS

A report which includes general descriptions of key stages and scales of production with general notes explaining how changing scales of production affect the organisation of manufacturing systems.

A block diagram illustrating the production system for a given product, which must include comment on quality control points that are required to produce the product to specification.

AMPLIFICATION

Key stage of production (PCI) the common production cycles involved in the manufacture of most products.

Scales of production (PC2 and PC5) differentiating between these will highlight the difference between manufacturing in volume and craft (e.g. continuous biscuit making and local shop production).

Production system (PC3 and PC4) covers in basic terms the different systems needed to produce products that satisfy the customer, are produced safely to the correct quality, and are profitable.

Affects (PC5) students should be specific rather than discursive here about how changing scales of production affects the organisation of systems.

GUIDANCE

This element asks students to follow a product from the sourcing of materials to finishing and packaging. PC3 places production in the context of production systems. Students should understand these systems that underpin all scales of manufacturing. For example, access to resources may have a direct impact on the scale of production or production processes themselves. Students should then explore in PC5 how altering the scale of production might affect these systems. Throughout this element, reference should be made to quality assurance.

A single product (or local opportunities) may not provide appropriate cover of all range items. This may be overcome if, within a teaching group, students investigate and present their findings on different products. Evidence of the coverage of range could then take the form of students' general notes.

Figure 10.5 An element

in their evaluation. Teachers are able to identify relatively easily the quality of outcome and synthesis, but good evaluation can be more problematic as they should have the two strands of outcome and process.

When we organise the students' work we adopt a fairly simple approach: Assignment = Evidence Indicator + Action Plan (A = EI + AP)!

However, we certainly do not send students away to 'sink or swim' with their units. At the beginning of a unit the students and teachers brainstorm what we think the

Matching forms of evidence to assessment methods

Evidence may be tangible or ephemeral. It is not necessary for all evidence to be recorded for GNVQ assessment. Whatever form it takes it is important to match the assessment method to the form. In group work it will he important to be able to differentiate the performance and contributions of individual students.

Forms of evidence

Written such as:

> diary/log
> essay
> letter/fax
> hand written notes
> questionnaire
> printed report

Images such as:

> diagram
> film/video
> graphs/charts
> photograph picture/sketch
> storyboard

Three-dimensional work such as:

> model/prototype
> product/artefact
> produce
> sample/mock-up

Visual such as:

> demonstration
> display/exhibit
> [ephemeral work may be supported as appropriate by simple plan, evaluation notes notes on key points, record of feedback]

Oral such as:

> debate
> discussion/conversation
> interview
> commentary
> performance
> presentation
> role play
> [ephemeral work may be supported as appropriate by simple plan, evaluation notes notes on key points, record of feedback]

Methods of assessment

Observation of student performing activity
Oral questions put to the student
Scrutiny of images and three-dimensional work
Scrutiny of written work
Written questions put to the student

© Chesterfield House 1994 Assessment Checklist February 15, 1995

Figure 10.6 Evidence for assessment

words mean and work out how best students can access information, present work and find resources. This becomes the assignment and provides the students with the basis of their individual action plan; they are encouraged to take a progressively proactive role in the process.

Prioritise the Actions by Number	Action	Evidence	Performance Criteria	Resources	Time

	Adjustments to Plan

Figure 10.7 Action plan

We find that students are able to plan their own visits, set up workshops and arrange for visiting speakers. For example, a talk about pollution from the local environmental department links directly into intermediate Manufacturing unit 1 and advanced unit 8. The vocational sessions help identify opportunities for providing evidence of the core skills. A copy of the current assignment, unit or element is given to the core assessors, so everyone knows when students might be working on surveys, spreadsheets etc.

Tracking and recording of Core Skills

We have designed our own set of student owned tracking or record sheets (Figure 10.8). It is a student's responsibility to claim that an assessment is complete. He or she records where the evidence can be found in column A and the core tutor signs column B. We have found that planning together for integration in the early stages is better, as teachers can identify and develop opportunities that arise naturally from students' work. We try to avoid bolt-on activities and have, for the most part, been successful. These records are then put into the students' cumulative assessment record which contains details of all the students activities for when they will be needed for verification.

The future?

- This review has provided a snapshot of the present position of GNVQ Manufacturing at Bodmin Community College and an overview of the rationale that prompts us to work in our chosen manner.
- At present we are very much in control of assessment, although we value and do make use of witness statements and observations, and for the future we look towards working more closely with our employers.
- We envisage a situation where a student might cover one or more units in 'the field' or outside school and that the assessment of that unit is managed by the employers.
- We know what we want to achieve but, sometimes like our students, we have not as yet quite worked out the process we need to follow to achieve our goal.

Since this chapter was written GNVQ is changing in response to recommendations made by Sir Ron Dearing on the whole of post-16 education and Dr John Capey on the role of assessment in GNVQ. These changes include:

- Core skills are known as Key Skills as from September 1996.
- External assessment of the Key Skills will probably be introduced.
- In three subjects, two or three units have been rewritten with assessment taking place at the level of a unit.
- A pilot is currently taking place with both internal assessment and the new style external assessment, in the form of externally set assignments and new style external tests.

Changes in GNVQ should be in place by September 1998.

INFORMATION TECHNOLOGY LEVEL 2

2.1 Prepare information

PERFORMANCE CRITERIA – All must be covered

	A	B

1. Select information appropriate to the task
   - information taken from existing sources
   - information developed during input
   - text
   - graphics
   - numbers

2. Enter information into software in ways that will make it easy to edit
   - inputting source information accurately
   - making immediate corrections to errors noticed on entry
   - putting right simple equipment faults
   - using manuals and on-line help facilities
   - asking for help as appropriate
   - for text
   - for graphics
   - for numbers

3. **Keep source information** required for the task

4. **Store input systematically** & make backup copies
   - naming files sensibly to indicate the contents
   - locating files conveniently for subsequent use
   - creating & using directories to group related files
   - saving work before and after important changes
   - saving work when all the information has been input

Types of evidence P = Paper evidence Q = Question and answer
D = Demonstrated

Column A – Identity a piece of work which you think covers that part of the range.
Column B – Your assessor should write a P, Q, or D, the date and their initials
when they are satisfied that you have achieved that part of the element

Element completed Signed   Date

COMMUNICATION LEVEL 2

2.3 Use images

PERFORMANCE CRITERIA - All must be covered

A student must:

1. select **images** which clearly illustrate the **points** being made
2. use **images** which are suited to the **audience, situation** and purpose
3. use **images** at appropriate times and places

RANGE

1. **Images:** taken from others' material, produced by the student
2. **Points:** on straightforward subjects
3. **Audience:** people familiar with the subject who know the student; people familiar with the subject who do not know the student
4. **Situation:** in written material; in one to one discussions, in group discussions

EVIDENCE INDICATORS

	A	B

- in text: people familiar with the subject who know the student
- in text: people familiar with the subject who do not know the student

- in one to one discussion

- in one to one discussion with a person who does not know the student

- in group discussion

- in group discussion with people who do not know the student

Column A – Identify a piece of work which you think covers that part of the range
Column B – Your assessor should write the date and their initials when they are satisfied you have achieved that part of the element.

Element completed. Signed   Date

Figure 10.8 Record sheet

Chapter 11

In Partnership with Industry for Curriculum Development – The RCA Project

Louise Davies, Barbara Mottershead, Anne Constable and Mary Moran

Introduction

The Royal College of Art Schools Technology Project has developed close links with industry and community to develop a D&T course for 11–19 year olds which meets the demands of the revised National Curriculum Orders for D&T and the new GCSE examination courses. 'A' level requirements are also being reviewed as this is written, and a growing number of schools embarking on GNVQ manufacturing. Taken together these demand a new approach in the delivery of food technology, and new skills and understanding for many teachers who have a background in Home Economics education rather than in industry.

Extracts of Key Stage 4 statements from the National Curriculum D&T Orders (DfE,1995a: 10–11):

> Pupils should be given the opportunity to develop their design and technology capability through ... assignments in which they design and make products. Taken together these assignments should require activity related to industrial practices and the application of systems and control.

> 'Pupils should be taught:
> Designing skills ...
> c) to design for manufacturing in quantity
> Making skills ...
> d) a range of industrial applications for a variety of familiar materials and processes'
> e) how products are manufactured in quantity, including the application of quality control and quality assurance procedures
> f) how computer aided manufacture is used both in manufacturing in quantity and

in the production of single items and small batches
g) to simulate product and assembly lines

Knowledge and understanding
b) materials can be combined and processed in order to create more useful
properties and how these properties are utilised in industrial contexts
c) how materials are prepared for manufacture allowing for waste and fine finishing
Quality
Pupils should be taught to distinguish between quality of design and quality of
manufacture ...
e) how far it meets manufacturability and maintenance requirements'.

When we are teaching food technology, pupils are developing food products that
are suitable for selling. Teachers and pupils have considerable experience of the
concept development phase, but the development of the 'chef' product or test
kitchen prototype for volume production presents a new challenges.

This new focus means that pupils must have a clear understanding of the industrial
process to be successful in their own designing and making. This understanding
needs to be built up over Key Stages 3 and 4, and taught in a way that is interesting
and relevant to pupils. The ideal would be for every child to be able to get out into
the industry, but this is not realistically achievable on a large scale for all pupils. The
Royal College of Art project has provided resources to 'bring industry to the pupils'.
The project has worked in partnership with industry to provide appropriate
examples and information. It is hoped that this will help teachers update their own
professional practice and provide a richer experience for all their pupils.

Developing partnerships with industry

In the development of the course, the project team and teacher fellows promoted a
number of links with industry. These included visiting companies and factories,
experiencing teacher placements, meeting product designers and product managers,
discussing processes, following a product being developed, collecting information
and writing together. The reciprocal arrangements of partners in industry visiting
schools and becoming involved in the education of the next generation meant that
both parties had a much clearer understanding of the other's work.

This experience for our teacher fellows meant they:

- improved their own teaching and were able to write focused practical tasks and
  designing and making assignments which were more accurate and realistic
- gained access to resources for their lessons and for the Project's publications
  which were not otherwise readily available
- updated their professional expertise and changed their viewpoint, including
  stereotypical images of the industry and common misconceptions
- were able to use the company's final product and standards to provide a
  framework for student folio work
- gained confidence in the classroom to address these new areas as they were able
  to talk to pupils about what they had seen and experienced
- developed a shared understanding of manufacturing, e.g. resistant materials and

systems and control, when they visited teachers of other specialisms, leading to many common starting points and joint projects.

Introducing industry to Key Stage 3 and 4 pupils:

The following mechanisms can be used to introduce pupils to industry in any scheme of work and are a feature of the course:

1. Designing and Making Assignments in an industrial context.
2. Case studies from industry of product development and manufacturing.
3. Products and application activities – examples from industry.
4. Introducing industrial standard equipment.
5. Visits and outside speakers.

DMAs in an industrial context

'Your Challenge' from Pasta Project Year 8 book

A partnership with Pennine Foods has resulted in a rich DMA where Year 8 pupils are asked to design and make a new cook chill pasta dish (Year 8) as a prototype for manufacture. The unit of work features focused practical tasks and a case study written in collaboration with Pennine Foods. Our work with them highlighted the importance of pupils becoming more exact about the type of materials, the quantities and the processes used and the controls that come into operation during the production, as well as cost implications. They provided us with much needed information about production planning, Hazard Analysis of Critical Control Points (HACCP), flow diagrams, process control, scaling up, and so on.

We developed simple focused practical tasks which included simple materials specifications and quality assurance. An example, given in Figure 11.1, introduces the idea that just asking for 'tomatoes' would not be sufficient since there are a wide range of tomatoes available!

A plan of a factory layout is useful, so that pupils are able to understand a complete food production system in operation from the intake of raw materials to the output of the finished product. Within this system there will be sub-systems, for example where part of the product are manufactured and then combined on an assembly line (e.g. paste plus sauce plus flavouring foods, chicken and mushroom). Within each sub-system there will be various controls that must operate and these will be part of the quality plan or safety plan for the product.

With a food specialist in our team, we developed a task where pupils set up production line simulation. A systems and control specialist developed a task which mirrored the weight control mechanism to check the weight of all the made-up pasta dishes on the production line, and which could be quite easily be simulated by Year 8 pupils. A resistant materials specialist devised a way for pupils to make a ravioli board, as seen in the test kitchen, to test ravioli shapes and fill them more accurately.

Controlling the raw ingredients

When a pasta dish is made in large quantities, each finished dish has to look and taste the same. This is harder than you think because the raw ingredients vary enormously. Manufacturers choose their ingredients carefully and buy particular varieties and types of ingredients. On the production line strict procedures make sure each dish is prepared in the same way.

When you make one dish, you can use measures such as one onion or one can of tomatoes, but if you are going to make large quantities you will need to think about controlling your raw ingredients. Here are some investigations that you might like to try.

Activity 1 How many tomatoes are there in a can?

> You will need:
>
> 6 different brands of canned tomatoes
> sieve
> measuring jug
> weighing scale

1   Carefully open one can of tomatoes
2   Pour the contents through the sieve
3   Measure the tomato juice in the jug and the tomato solid on the scales
4   Record your results on the chart.
5   Repeat with each can.

Activity 2 Which is the tastiest tomato?

> You will need:
>
> 6 different cans of tomatoes or 6 different varieties of fresh tomatoes
> plates
> spoons

1   Set up a taste panel for the 6 tomato samples
2   Taste each sample and then rank them on a scale ranging from sharpness/acidity to sweetness.

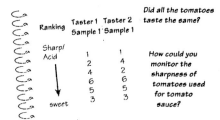

Activity 3 How big is an onion?

> You will need:
>
> one bag of onions (containing approximately 10–12 random selection)

Weigh each onion and record your results on a chart. You could also peel and chop each one to see how much is left after preparation.

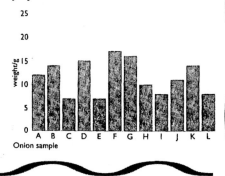

Name .... **Class** .... **Date** ....

Figure 11.1 Controlling the raw ingredients

Case studies from industry of product development and manufacturing

Our case studies consisted essentially of photographs, slides or video footage, with accompanying text about a specific company or product. They are extremely valuable because they open up the adult world for pupils and can be used in a number of ways by teachers, for example:

- As a basis for discussion to show how their designing and making mirrors the adult world.
- To build an awareness of differences between domestic, catering and volume production.
- To highlight the difference between designing and making for yourself and prototyping.
- As a visual resource, a photostory or life story of a product to gain understanding of the scale of production.
- To pose further questions (e.g. research for homework) or activities (e.g. students go to supermarket to find out about existing products).
- To explain difficult and otherwise abstract concepts (e.g. critical control points, sensory analysis, selection of materials according to properties, effect of temperature).
- To give examples of real specifications, mood boards, costings, market research. marketing, quality assurance schemes, flowcharts.
- To simulate production/assembly lines.
- To set targets for able pupils (e.g. linking more closely to an industry specification).
- To examine materials (e.g. compare fresh/processed flavourings).
- To use prior to a visit or a talk by a company.
- To help with evaluating existing food products (e.g. disassembly).
- To introduce industry standard equipment (e.g. multi-moulds, weigh machines, conveyor ovens, mixing machines, pasteuriser), and industrial terminology and procedures (e.g. sensory analysis, HACCP).

Case study: Gourmet Chocolates (Year 7 Student Book)

At Year 7 pupils are introduced to the idea of volume production in a very simple way by producing chocolate novelties which are cast in vacuum formed moulds. The case study which accompanies this DMA helps the pupils to understand that their designing and making is a mirror of what happens in industry and volume production, such as accuracy in control when 'tempering' the chocolate, which they can relate to their own experience of using the microwave or bain marie.

Products and application activities – industrial examples

The National Curriculum Orders for D&T (DfE,1995a: 10) state that:

Pupils should be taught to investigate, disassemble and evaluate a wide range of products and applications, in order to learn how they function, and relate products to:

a) their intended purpose,
b) the choice of materials and components, and the ways in which they have been used
c) the processes used to produce them
d) the scientific principles applied
e) the views of users and manufacturers
f) a range of alternative products.

Looking at existing products is a valuable way to explore how pupils think things might be made. They can use their experience of products to add to their skills and knowledge and draw on this in their own designing and making. Many product designers use a taste panel of all the competitor's products as a starting point for their designing.

Information about industrial examples can be used with pupils to:

- Identify functional parts – why is this product like this?
- Understand the demands which were placed upon the product developer.
- Look at the criteria used to judge the products and how improvements were made.
- Understand how products change over time and reasons for the changes.
- Give them ideas to draw upon in their own designing and making.

Case study – Ginsters Pasty (Year 7 Student Book)

The case study of Ginsters developing a new Cheese and onion fillings (see Figure 11.2) shows how difficult it was for the manufacturer to get the cheese in the filling just right. They did not want their product to be too oily and so they had to mix different cheeses with different characteristics to get the right result. This meant that they ended up with a blend of three cheeses, after a lot of testing.

Case study: Salads (Year 7 Student Book)

The ribbon vegetables case study opens up opportunity to look at machinery for cutting fruits and vegetable for a salad, e.g. how the scaling up of a piece of catering ribboning equipment allows 1 tonne to be produced in a day. There are opportunities to work in resistant materials to look at cutters and volume production.

Industrial examples of where products have come from are also interesting for pupils. Greenhalghs bakery looked at their waste puff pastry from the manufacture of their pies and developed a new product to use it up as the left-overs were costing a lot of money. Pennine foods developed a Gaucamole line to use the avocados that were too ripe for prawn and avocado sandwiches.

Introducing industrial standard equipment

In addition to securing information to support the project materials, we felt it was important for teachers to have the right equipment in the classes and to have worked with a number of suppliers partly to help develop their products in an appropriate way for the classroom and partly to support them with projects in our

PASTY PRODUCT DEVELOPMENT

Consumer testing

Do your potential customers like the product? How will you find out?

Taste panel

List them in order of preference

List them in order of preference

RESULTS 1 2 3

Favourite

What price for a pasty?

Even if your pasty is very good, consumers will not buy it if it costs too much. Use a **spreadsheet** to work out the cost of your product.

Designing skills: Modelling spreadsheets 104

Using a spreadsheet on a computer to work out the unit cost

Ginsters Ltd

Ginsters are **brand leaders** in the pasty market. Graham Cornish (Product Development Manager) tells us how they developed their new pasty.

The Cheese and onion pasty

Our vegetarian pasties were selling well, but our sales team told us that people had asked for one that was bigger than our 'Ploughman's Pasty', and which really tasted of cheese and onion.

We carried out a lot of research and tested different recipes to get the right filling.

The cheese was important – it had to taste good and to melt when it was cooked, but without being too oily. We use a mixture of three different cheeses and a hint of Dijon mustard.

Once the recipe was right we worked out how we could produce it in large numbers to the same standard. This involved some new production techniques for preparing the cheese and decorating the pastry.

A Ginsters cheese and onion pasty

Figure 11.2 Ginster

books which make effective use of the equipment. We have also encouraged suppliers to provide training and support (e.g. a help desk) for teachers to feel competent and confident to use equipment. This has included specialist companies who supply monitoring equipment, e.g. pH, HACCP software and training resources, systems and control, specialist bakeware, and measuring equipment.

For example, Dohler supply specialist ingredients, such as flavourings, for the food industry. Armfield already supply training equipment for Higher Education and the industry and have developed a number of scaled-down processing units which will be invaluable for schools (such as a miniature pasteuriser). With this equipment schools really can model manufacturing processes.

Visits and outside speakers

Students would clearly benefit from visits to factories manufacturing food products, but time constraints make this difficult at Key Stage 3. Also, companies are sometimes reluctant to accept students under 15 years old because of insurance considerations as well as health and safety factors. In any case a friendly factory may not stay friendly and welcoming for long if inundated with hundreds of pupils from local schools. For those students specialising in food technology at Key Stage 4 and post 16 this is less of a problem and visits are to be encouraged if at all possible. An alternative solution is for teachers to make the visit themselves and then to transmit the information to the pupils. Another possibility is for a company to come to talk to students.

Teacher visits

Teachers visiting a factory should take sequenced photographs of the industrial processes to display, enlarge and use with students to help explain how a product is made. Particular photos can be enlarged and highlighted to make a particular point, e.g. 'this photo shows people assembling a pasta dish', 'this shows the thermometers used to check the temperature of the soup', 'look at how many people are used to put this product together'. Some companies have training or promotional videos and it is worth asking what is available.

Company speakers

This works best where the speaker has been properly briefed. If possible, let him or her come to a lesson beforehand; if not, show examples of the pupils' work so that they are able to judge the level and discuss with them how to pitch their talk. Encourage them to bring slides or a video and samples and other visual aids. Many speakers have children of their own and are able to relate well to pupils when well prepared.

Student and teacher visits

Visits must be well planned and a visit beforehand by the teacher is recommended. In this way a teacher can look at the product in detail and understand the different stages: machinery used, the control systems, temperature sensors and control. Discussion beforehand with the pupils is essential – what they will see, what to look out for. A worksheet asking students questions relevant to the visit, picking out particular aspects, is also useful, e.g. how a machine is used to make the containers, how foods are stored in the warehouse, how the product is date-stamped.

It is also sound practice to take another D&T teacher with a different specialism with you. Two areas can then be covered in one visit and the food specialist can extend his or her knowledge of control, mechanisms and pneumatic systems. It is also important to relate the visit to work in other areas of the D&T curriculum, e.g. if students have made something using a control system, link and use it to explaining about the control systems they will see on the visit.

Conclusion

How schools can build and make the most of their industrial links

Every secondary school has a local community including parents, primary schools, local further education colleges, people involved in the business, large or small, charitable institutions or bodies working on their behalf, and some type of access to industry; and every student and teacher in the school has some knowledge or contact, with some, or all of the above. It therefore makes sense to utilise these contacts to form a network of both short- and long-term potential for industrial and community links. For example:

- Keep a list of contacts:
  - parents
  - work experience
  - feeder primaries
  - further education
  - local business
  - charities, local hospitals, nursing homes
  - industry
  - support for agencies or projects
  - media.

- Match existing projects to potential links:
  - local bakery with bread project
  - local biscuit or scone manufacturer
  - local jam producer
  - frozen food manufacturer

- Examine the opportunity for development:
  - Is their product of interest to the pupils?
  - Can they provide materials to enhance the project in schools?
  - Are their production methods of interest?
  - Can their staff offer useful expertise?
  - Would the nature of the school project interest the manufacturer?

- Speculate on what you would like to happen:

- Focus on one high profile event:
  - lunch for visitors
  - a community evening

- an industrial launch
- a competition.

- Invite key figures:
  - Utilise known and existing contacts
  - Establish the idea of partnership
  - Form a nucleus of your network.

- Involve your contact in as many school events as possible:
  - Gradually your contact will identify with the school, and act as an ambassadors on your behalf.

- Share your resources:
  - Links are a two-way process with benefits for both sides
  - What can you and the school offer to the community and or industry?

Chapter 12

Understanding Industrial Practice in Food Technology through the Nuffield Design and Technology Project*

Marion Rutland

Introduction

All GCSE or GNVQ examination courses in food technology must ensure that pupils understand the relationship between their food product development, designing and making activities in the classroom and industrial practices and systems and control. It is at this stage that the food technology lessons at Key Stages 1, 2 and 3 culminate in examination courses that have moved away from home economics and the domestic arena of 'cooking family meals' to a new emphasis of commercial and industrial practice, first suggested in the document *The Proposals for the Secretary for Education for Technology for Ages 5 to 16* (DfE, 1992).

This requirement at Key Stage 4 for activities which relate to industrial practice is the same for all examination courses, whether pupils specialise, for example, in resistant materials, textiles or food (DfE,1995a). It is not intended that pupils will copy industrial practice in the classroom, rather that they should develop knowledge and understanding of large-scale production processes, learn about ways in which firms and businesses design and manufacture goods and how these goods are marketed and sold.

Systems and control

So how do the Nuffield Design and Technology Project materials help pupils develop an understanding of industrial practices? During Key Stage 3 pupils are introduced to 'systems thinking' as a way of helping them understand the way food

---

*Figures 12.1–12.5 are reproduced by permission of the Nuffield Design and Technology Project, who are the copyright owners.

products are produced. This is further developed in Key Stage 4 and related to designing a food production system in the context of a fast food outlet, using familiar generic control terms, for example *inputs* and *outputs* to illustrate the process. It is explained how a designer will break down the system into subsystems to see how these inputs and outputs need to be arranged.

The fast food outlet example in Figure 12.1 is used to illustrate how the output of one subsystem becomes the input of another, creating feedback of information. For instance, if there is an increase in the number of people buying food, there is *feedback* from the service area to the cooking area telling the cooking area to produce more food, or conversely less food if there is a decrease in the number of people buying food. It is explained that this type of feedback is called a *closed-loop system*, again a familiar control term. Additional terms used in industry are introduced, including *operator* and *user interface, human and machine interface.*

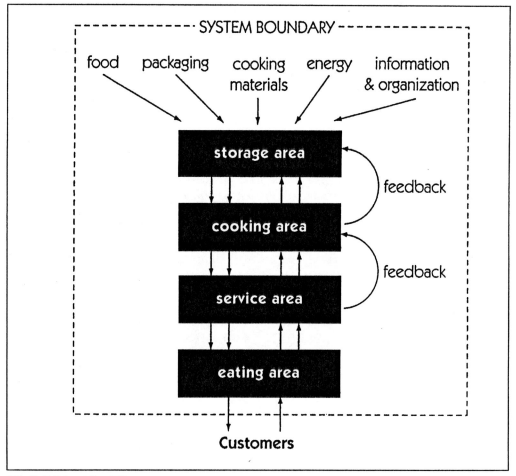

© The Nuffield Foundation, 1996

Figure 12.1 Systems diagram of a fast food service

The chip-fryer in the cooking area of the fast-food outlet is used to illustrate feedback and control in greater depth (Figure 12.2). As a common cause of fires, it is very important that the fryer does not overheat and that the fat or oil remains at a temperature that will safely cook the food for consumption by the customers. A similar example is used with a freezer, also in Figure 12.2, which shows how temperature sensors are used effectively to control the cooling unit of the freezer.

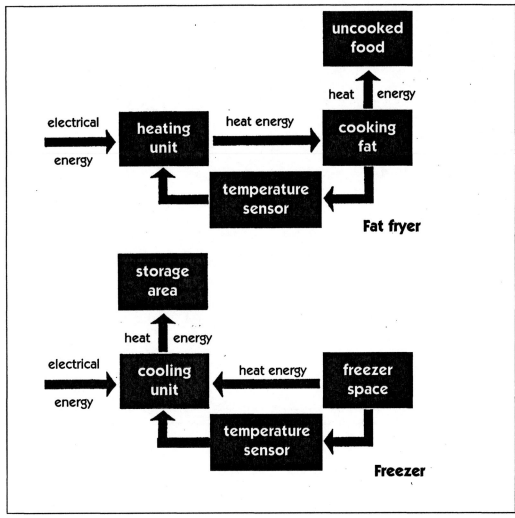

© The Nuffield Foundation, 1996

Figure 12.2 Temperature control system for fat-fryer and a freezer

Industrial production

In industrial food production, pupils need to know how quality can be achieved through the use of control systems. They need to understand that when an individual food product is made, it is a *person* who is the control system. He or she weigh out ingredients, attend to the oven and use their personal skills to make judgements. In large-scale food production in industry, all these processes are controlled by computer systems. Sensors detect any changes that take place when the food is processed and passes the information back to the central processing unit (CPU). This information is then used to initiate another process, for example open a valve at a given temperature to allow the mix to move to the next stage of production or allow a new raw material to be added. Large-scale versions of domestic equipment such as a mixer are an essential part of the production line. Heating and cooling of food during production is all controlled by the CPU, with Hazard Analysis of Critical Control Points (HACCP) used by the food industry as a means of quality assurance. This involves the manufacture analysing and identifying any possible hazards, in terms of food hygiene and safety that may occur during production. A critical point is a point where a control procedure is applied to prevent or reduce a hazard. This process can be used to reassess a process by helping identifying areas requiring improvements, leading to the modification of the design of the existing control system.

Manufacturing jam

The Key Stage 4 materials of the Nuffield D&T Project help pupils to make the link between preparing jam in the home, with the importance of achieving the right proportion of sugar and fruit, and carrying out this process in industry. They are told that manufactures tend to use a vacuum boiling process where the bulk of the excess water is removed at 60°–79°C under reduced pressure. It is explained that less heat energy is required to boil the jam by this method; also at this lower temperature there is less caramelisation, so reducing the unwanted flavours and undesirable colour changes. Pupils are taken through the stages of jam manufacture including boiling the mixture, filling the jars and finishing off.

Frozen vegetables

Industrial practices related to the freezing of vegetables are outlined, including the role of enzymes and how industry ensures that they do not to produce loss of colour and unacceptable flavours during freezing. The importance of quick freezing, careful storage and the use of quality food are emphasised to help reduce nutrient loss and produce high-quality food products for the consumer.

Modified atmosphere packaging

It is often difficult for teachers to access the most recent developments in food production and packaging. The Nuffield Key Stage 4 Students Book includes sections on some of the most recent major advances in industrial processes, for example, extending the shelf life of products by modified atmosphere packaging. The materials cover the effects of using different gases on a range of foods (Figure 12.3).

One food technology teacher in the project noted that her pupils found this to be a complex process, demanding considerable scientific conceptual under-standing. Designing a task, in the Nuffield style, has helped these pupils towards a clear understanding of the gases used in this process. It was found that with the help of a sympathetic science faculty and an available laboratory, pupils can extract the gas from the range of products and, using a standard test, identify what gases are present in significant amounts. As the teacher commented 'this is a real case of seeing is believing'.

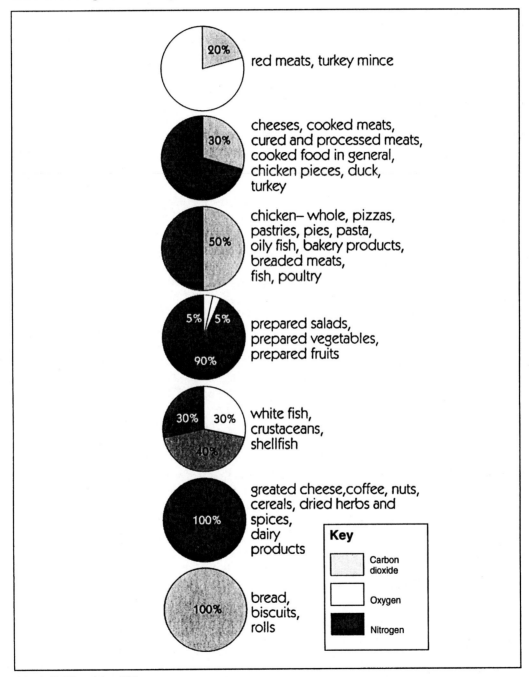

red meats, turkey mince

cheeses, cooked meats, cured and processed meats, cooked food in general, chicken pieces, duck, turkey

chicken– whole, pizzas, pastries, pies, pasta, oily fish, bakery products, breaded meats, fish, poultry

prepared salads, prepared vegetables, prepared fruits

white fish, crustaceans, shellfish

greated cheese, coffee, nuts, cereals, dried herbs and spices, dairy products

bread, biscuits, rolls

Key

Carbon dioxide

Oxygen

Nitrogen

Figure 12.3 Gas mixtures for modified atmosphere packaging

Industrial based Case Studies

The Case Studies in the Nuffield materials provide pupils with the knowledge and understanding of industrial practices that it is not possible to emulate in the classroom. The Case Studies describe systems and control in action and real examples of D&T and food technology in the world outside school. Pupils are encouraged to read the Case Studies, discuss the ideas with friends, answer the set questions and carry out the additional Research Activities at home.

General Case Studies

These Case Studies deal with 'large' technologies which affect the way people live and work. They look at environmental issues to do with our surroundings, materials we use, places of entertainment, communication including the radio and television, the use of computers. medical issues, manufacturing aircraft, city public transport including changes from the horse to buses and the underground, space travel and its benefits including Teflon and microwave cookers.

Focused Case Studies

There are a number of focused Case Studies that enable pupils to learn about industrial practice in greater depth. The Focused Case Study called '*Wrap it up*' explores changes in the packaging of food over recent years in greater detail. The advantages of see-through packaging is discussed, including its safety when in direct contact with food and the consumer.

The Case Study '*Soup beautiful soup*' (Figure 12.4) looks at a firm called New Covent Garden Soup Company that manufactures soups intended to be as good as home-made varieties and made with only natural ingredients with no preservatives, colourings or additives. Pupils are asked to research the most popular flavour of fresh soup and are provided with information on how a firm would manufacture soup on a large scale. They are asked to compare the industrial process, with the help of a systems diagram for automated bulk soup production, with making the soup at home. Pupils are then given the range of ingredients the company would use and asked to research each ingredient and suggest quality assurance procedures that could be carried out to ensure that they are suitable for bulk soup production. Packaging and storage of the soup is examined with thought given to a suitable temperature, packaging materials and style of carton.

The focused case study called '*A corny story*', (Figure 6.9, page 90) examines the history and stages in the production of corn flakes. It is suggested that pupils investigate breakfast cereals and present their findings in a formal style. Another focused Case Study looks at '*Bread production*'. It explores the range of ingredients used and their effect on the final bread product. Again, a link is made between making bread in the kitchen, a familiar activity for many pupils, and making bread in industry. The importance and advantages of the Chorleywood process is explained and the need to produce loaves of bread of a standard weight using objective measurements, as well as subjective measurements such as taste, smell and appearance.

The focused Case Study '*Making minced meat*' (Figure 12.5) takes the pupils

Focused case studies

③

Soup, beautiful soup

New Covent Garden Soup Company

The New Covent Garden Soup Company was set up to manufacture soup that is as good as home-made, prepared with only natural ingredients with no preservatives, colourings or additives. The patented production process is unique and took two years to develop! The ideas for the first 30 types of soup initially came from employees, and were primarily vegetable. They were cooked as samples and modified until the recipe pleased most people. Now the company has extended its range to include meat and fish. The 'home-made', all-year-round range is complemented by summer and winter specials that are based on seasonal vegetables. The company also makes a soup-of-the-month, a clever idea to introduce new and unusual flavours to the market.

D *The label is stuck on so the basic carton can be used for any type of soup*

P **Pause for thought**

Do you like soup? What is your favourite flavour? How often do you eat it? Would you say it is a snack or a meal?

R **Research activity**

Tomato is the most popular flavour of tinned soup. Why do you think that is? Is it the most popular flavour in your class? You can find out like this. Copy out the table below. Working in a group of six complete the table.

Person	Do you like soup?	Which is your favourite flavour?	When do you eat it?	Which of the following sorts do you eat?			
				homemade	tinned	dried	chilled carton
A: You							
B							
C							
D							
E							
F							

Figure 12.4 Soup, beautiful soup

through the manufacturing process of producing dried minced meat. The process involved in the design and development of a new meat pump is outlined with explanations of the criteria that had to be taken into account in the design. Pupils are asked to investigate the manufacturing process of extrusion, the action of the crank, and explore, giving reasons, other food products that could be produced in this way.

③

Making minced meat

Good to eat, but hard on machines

Bachelor's Foods (now part of Vandenberg Foods) produces dried minced meat for large catering outlets such as company canteens. The mince is used to make up dishes such as shepherd's pie, lasagne and spaghetti bolognaise.

In bulk, minced meat has a consistency like bread dough and it is often called 'meat dough' by the processing companies that handle it. A machine called a meat pump is used to process the meat dough and produce minced meat. Large quantities of meat dough can be handled – the machine in this Case Study processes 800 kg per hour. The overall process is summarized in the diagram (below). As the mince is pushed out of the meat pump it is chopped into small pieces which fall onto a stainless steel conveyor belt. This takes them through a dryer before reaching the packaging stage. The dried minced meat is sent out to customers' catering outlets all over the country.

Designing a new machine

Bachelor's existing machine had become worn and corroded, as minced meat is quite abrasive and the fat in it has a corrosive effect on some metals. The machine would have taken a long time to clean and it was also very noisy. Irwin Desman Limited was therefore commissioned to design and make a meat pump to replace the one that had worn out.

Pause for thought

How often do you eat minced meat in a week? Do you know how it's made and processed?

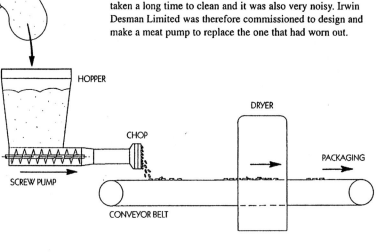

Figure 12.5 Making minced meat

The focused Case Study 'Cool control – *manufacturing the Vienetta*' enables pupils to learn about the particular issues related to the manufacture of ice cream. They are helped to understand the physical properties of ice cream, how it can be extruded on to a moving conveyor belt to get a wave pattern into the frozen ice cream and then layered with chocolate and other fillings.

Summary

- In an ideal world schools should be able to make their own contact with industry and arrange partnerships, visits, projects and speakers for their pupils to learning about industrial processes and practices.
- Many schools find this very difficult to achieve for several reasons.
- Issues such as timetabling constraints, large pupil groupings, expense of school trips and companies who would like to accommodate pupils but have production targets and safety regulations make such activities difficult to set up.
- The Nuffield Design and Technology Food Technology resources provide a sound basis for pupils to make the link between their knowledge of familiar small-scale food production and issues related to large-scale industrial manufacture.
- Pupils are presented with case studies and a range of information in realistic contexts and these can be developed further during their GCSE examination courses.
- It is this balance, between interesting and realistic case studies and developing the knowledge and understanding needed by pupil when developing their own GCSE course work, which makes the industrially based Nuffield materials a resource that can be used very successfully in the secondary classroom.

Section 5

Food Technology and IT

Chapter 13 looks at the present and also looks into the future. The use of IT in teaching food technology has considerable potential which, it acknowledges, is not yet fully developed. Realistic opportunities for the use of IT in food technology are suggested and advice given for the developing of its use in our teaching today, with glimpses of what we could do in the future.

Chapter 13

Using IT in the Teaching of Food Technology

Roy Ballam

Introduction

It can be argued that to be 'high-tech' when working in design and technology (D&T) in schools, you have to be using 'all singing and all dancing' machines linked to computers doing computer-aided design (CAD) and computer-assisted manufacture (CAM) activities that emulate industry. The reality is that in schools it is more common to find most computers being used for such activities with plastic, wood and metal, although it must be said that textiles are slowly being tackled, albeit through embroidery, with computer-aided sewing machines such as POEM and BROTHER. However, if the same kind of financial and political emphasis placed on resistant materials was directed towards resources and equipment for food and textiles technology, then surely the same types of activities would occur in the classroom, resulting in high-quality products being produced by pupils, emulating food and textile industrial practices.

Why not IT in food technology?

An explanation for IT being absent from food technology in schools this could be that in the past the teaching of food has been driven by the context of the home. It is important to realise that food technology is not home economics, and neither can you describe home economics as food technology, though some would say that the same teachers are teaching this new subject area and that this is the problem! Home economics covers more than just food. Its breadth and depth is wider, and the subject probably merits it own curriculum time, now made possible in the 20% 'freed up' time outlined in the Dearing Report (1993b). Home economics prepares pupils to become good home makers and be able to cook for themselves, all desirable life skills I would agree. However, the use of computers or IT was rarely mentioned in this context.

Food technology, unlike school-based home economics, is industrial in content and context, focusing on one element or material within the broader dimension of D&T. It is specific, design driven and scientifically based. Food technology should not be thought of as just 'food', but rather in the broader context into which it fits as it relates to the holistic approach to design. No one owns it, it is a material that is there to be used and exploited to its full potential by the user. Our own imagination is the only limiting factor when we consider what we can achieve in food technology.

Computers have been used in other areas of D&T because industry has dictated their use. Examples from the resistant materials area of D&T include the original BBC computers in schools used for controlling lathes and the programming language LOGO taught to enable pupils to control output devices, for example turtles and robot arms. Food has never really been associated with computers in schools, even though attempts have been made in this direction. Nutritional analysis was the first major use of IT in D&T and this is still true in many schools. The use of computers in this area offers the chance for pupils to enhance their work; it relieves them of the tedious and mundane and gives a 'high-tech' alternative, enabling pupils of all abilities to perform this complex type of analysis.

Another reason for the lack of use of computers in food may be the traditional gender split found in technology. The National Council of Educational Technology (NCET) produced a paper (NCET, 1992) on gender differences based on evidence from research studies and statistical publications. It concluded that access to technology at home, suitable role models, for example girls taking a passive role, subject participation, educational materials and subject focus and classroom management all played a part in generating a gender difference in the use of IT. This led to the NCET and Women into Information Technology (WIT) starting a developmental project to attract girls into IT (NCET, 1994).

I could give other examples, but my point is that we are still at the starting point, whereas other areas of the curriculum have had time to develop and 'show off' their use of IT. DfEE figures for 1995 show that there were on average 85 computers for each secondary school compared with only 13 in 1984. This represents 10 pupils for each computer, and an average expenditure of £21,000–£30,000 annual expenditure in each school on IT. This increased popularity and proliferation in IT ownership is illustrated by the attendance figures for the 1995 British Educational Technology (BETT) Exhibition, which showed that 30.4% of the visitors were involved with the subject of D&T, with a further 5.5% defining their interest as home economics (BETT, 1996). This clearly indicates that D&T teachers are interested and motivated to look for the potential uses of IT in their classrooms.

Food technology today

The statutory requirement in the new Orders (DfE, 1995a) to teach D&T, with the option to include food as a material at Key Stage 3, has meant that practising teachers and student–teachers are expected to teach a subject which is totally new to them, often with little extra training or funding. In addition, reference is made to areas, such as 'systems and control', again an area where many food teachers have received little or no training.

Within this element of the programmes of study for D&T, there seem to be two strands of argument emerging, each with a particular focus and backed by a voice of authority. One argument is that the programmes of study prescribe concentration on the hardware and software requirements of a control system. The other, which I tend to favour, is that it should be the product and process that dictate the criteria for a control system. For example, when an engineering background is considered, the criteria for the control system needed will focus on the need to produce a consistent product. It is when 'systems and control' is seen as conveyor belts, bright lights, gears and pulleys that the product being produced loses its meaning and has little relevance, as it could be a coat hanger or meat pie. I agree that aspects of D&T should provide the opportunity for pupils to study this area of unit operations, yet clearly the machinery exists to produce a specified product. It is the working characteristics and properties of the materials that you are manufacturing that matter, and it is these that dictate the requirements of the production line, from the uniformity of lasagne sheets and the enrobing of biscuits to the sterilisation and septic heating sealing of packaging.

I would argue that this is what makes food an excellent example of *process control* and the systems that need to be developed, maintained and monitored to produce products efficiently and consistently to a specification. These controls may be in the form of pH and temperature sensing, micro-bacterial counts, size and thickness of product (e.g. pastry, pasta) and foreign body detection (e.g. metal detector).

National Curriculum Information Technology

It is intended that the Information Technology Programmes of Study (DfE,1995c) should be cross-curricular and integrated into most areas of the curriculum, with certain strands presenting themselves naturally for inclusion in food technology. For example:

1. Given opportunity to:
   use IT equipment/software autonomously.
2. Communicating and handling information:
   (a) Create good quality presentations – integrating several forms of information.
   (b) Select appropriate IT equipment/software.
   (c) Obtain accurate and relevant information from a range of sources.
   (d) Collect and amend quantitative and qualitative information for a particular purpose, and enter it into a data-handling package for processing and analysis.
   (e) Interpret, analyse and display information, checking its accuracy and questioning its plausibility.
3. Controlling, measuring and modelling.
   (c) Use IT equipment that responds from data from sensors – (temperature probe connected to a computer).

Undoubtedly, computers are going to be increasingly important in children's education. Factors indicating this are:

- CD Rom and internet access, along with tailored educational software, will expand.
- Class sizes could increase.
- Teachers may need to take a more advisory role.
- Increased use of computers for homework.

A research study (Watson, 1993) commissioned and funded by the DfE, set out to evaluate the impact of IT on pupils' achievement at both primary and secondary level. It found that IT did make a contribution to learning but that this was not consistent across subjects and age groups. It was argued that the outcomes of pupils' learning were substantially influenced by teaching. Aspects of organisation, management, teaching styles, philosophy and pedagogical practice and their links with the effective use of IT were found to be important contributors.

A key point to emerge was that teacher understanding, a willingness to experiment and understand the underlying philosophy of the software to be used by pupils made a significant contribution. In-service provision, or lack of it, was identified as a major concern. It has also been shown (Daniels *et al.*, 1993) that pupils find it highly motivating to use a computer and spend time discussing results, and are able to process information more quickly than using other techniques. Clearly this evidence shows that the incorporation of IT in schools, and specifically in D&T, is here to stay, with teachers, students and the DFEE showing the dedication and direction to move forward.

IT enhancement in D&T

Steenstra (1995) argues that IT is used successfully in any subject (including D&T) when it is firmly rooted in the aims and objectives of the teaching taking place, with the computer being used as a tool where and when it is appropriate. Starting from this point, it is a good idea to map out the use of IT in D&T to see exactly what can be achieved. Then, an analysis of the work produced should be carried out to see if it has been enhanced, or whether the work simply has been subjected to an electronic cosmetic change.

Enhancement of student work, and hopefully achievement, through the use of IT must be the major goal. IT should not be used to make work look pretty or simply to perform a task in the fraction of the time otherwise needed. Nor should the use of the computer or other elements of IT be used to keep pupils quiet or 'baby sit' them. A danger here is that students can appear to be at work using a computer because they are quiet, but really they are not making any progress in meeting the learning targets.

Industrial applications of IT in food technology

As the focus in food technology is on industrial rather than domestic production, it is wise to examine the industrial applications of IT in food manufacturing (see Chapters 9 to 12). The evolution of computing technologies in the past two decades has meant quantum leaps in hardware and software developments. This in turn has affected food manufacturing industries internationally, including the whole management and implementation of the food production chain. Areas such as farming, harvesting, processing, storage, product development, marketing and final consumption have all been modified so that they can be monitored, controlled and made more efficient through the use of modern technology.

Other effects of this computerisation have been related to environmental issues such as:

* reduced overall energy consumption
* manufacturing processes are more efficient (less wastage)
* optimised packaging materials for food products.

The use of modern technologies has also re-introduced working from home, using the computer for its range of telecommunications capabilities, with no need for people to travel in to an office. The availability of Small Office, Home Office (SOHO) software, or small-scale versions of major software intended for home use, have provided additional opportunities in the use of computers (Seaman, 1995).

It is important that teachers have an appreciation of the use of IT in the food industry, so that relevant aspects can be emulated successfully in the classroom, though not all aspects of the industrial process may be modelled due to lack of financial, physical and human resources, for example setting up a robotics process control system. The teacher's role is to tease out of those components that will enhance learning, so enabling students to use IT as a tool in developing knowledge and understanding for the design and manufacturer of food products.

Food industry applications of IT

The following is by no means a definitive list, but should be used as a guide to highlight industrial applications and possible emulations that could be carried out within the school context.

Storing and retrieving data

By using database programs, details of product specifications, production quotas, sales patterns/predictions or quality control parameters can be stored. This information can then be accessed and amended as needed. The data may be in the form of market research trends, written briefs or from data logging devices for example temperature, pH and oxygen sensors in the manufacturing process. The data may be utilised by the user in the form of written reports, statistical displays (for example, bar charts) or by controlling machinery on the production line. Nutritional analysis databases are of immense use to the industry as they allow technologists and food scientists to calculate the nutrient content of products (see Modelling and simulation below). Searches for published work also takes place using CD ROM or on-line service technologies, for example the Internet, World Wide Web or Compuserve.

Control

Manual control has often in the past resulted in errors and increased labour costs. Automation in controlling all aspects of the manufacturing process, from checking glass jars by laser to regulating the flow of chocolate in a pipe, has meant that a consistent product can be achieved to a specified quality threshold. The control of biotechnology (for example pH, temperature and oxygen levels), heat processing (for example extrusion), sterilisation and product formulation, have benefited from automation. It has resulted in:

- a reduction in material wastage
- labour savings
- energy efficiency in manufacturing
- avoidance of 'down time', for example stopping a production line because of irregularities
- constant monitoring and control of quality assurance.

Robotics

The use of robotics rather than humans for repetitive actions, has increased efficiency and raised output. Robots have the advantage of being able to work 24 hours a day, they have greater strength, can be very precise and have great speed. However, in certain situations robotics can decrease efficiency on a production line, and there are some operations which do call for the human intervention. For example, a manufacturing line producing 20 varieties of biscuit needs flexibility to cope with the range; robots would need extensive programming and increase 'down time' of the production line.

Artificial intelligence

Expert systems are an amalgamation of rules, previous production problems and hazard analysis techniques, which a company or single operator may need to call upon if experiencing difficulty in production, or if they wish to optimise production capability. The control system can analyse the current situation from data fed in by trained staff and use information from its database to offer possible solutions. This is then a 'troubleshooting' package.

Accounting

The use of a spreadsheet has enabled a range of people from accountants to food technologists to calculate the costs of products and production both before and during manufacture.

Modelling and simulations

The spreadsheet has also enabled buyers, home economists and food technologists to model the 'what if?' factors in relation to costing and scale of production of products. The nutrient profiles of a product can also be modelled using nutritional databases, for example what happens to fat content if peanuts are replaced by raisins? Some expert industrial systems enable people to model 'shelf life' of specified products, for example MicroModel.

Least cost formulations

Food technologists can determine the amounts of ingredients needed to produce a product at the lowest possible cost retaining desirable eating characteristics using as a base line the specified organoleptic qualities of a food product. Variations can also be modelled with changes in ingredients availability or cost fluctuations, uses that can extend to improving consistency and uniformity of production of food products.

Hazard Analysis Critical Control Points (HACCP)

Throughout the production of food products, risk and hazard analysis of critical points in process are necessary to produce consistent and safe food. Using appropriate software, these points can be identified and appropriate action taken to prevent physical, chemical and micro-organism contamination (and recontamination) as well as nutritional loss.

Sensory analysis

IT is used for data input and statistical analysis of results collected from sensory sessions, for example when tasters are in the sensory booths their results are feed directly into computer terminals. This may be through a variety of mediums, such as:

- *Keyboard* – to type a descriptive response to a question or give a score rating to a particular food attribute.
- *Mouse* – to point to a rating panel, line or set of descriptors on screen, though checks need to be made that all tasters are competent in using a mouse.
- *Light pen/touch screen* – to point directly to a particular spot on the screen and record the tasters rating of the sample.

Once all sensory sessions have been completed, all data can be processed by computer and results displayed in charts and graphs or printed out.

The 'electronic nose' is another developing area, which can be programmed to distinguish any smell. The food industry expects to make good use of this technology, especially where aroma is important in consumer acceptability, for example in tea, coffee and other beverage development. Campden & Chorleywood Food Research Association (CCFRA,1995) reported a new development in baking industry software, where the programme will diagnose faults, for example textural problems, in bakery items. Images are scanned on to the computer, and the computer lists possible solutions to the problems using a database of faults compiled from other bakery items.

Image analysis

Imaging devices, such as microscopes or video cameras and digitised images can be used by the computer for a variety of applications. These involve particle size and shape analysis, air bubble size, for example in aerated chocolate or ice cream, or (used in conjunction with robotic devices) checking that ready meal components are the same.

Computer aided design (CAD)

This can be used for designing food manufacturing plants to packaging shapes as it allows the designer to create, model and modify a design. Expert systems also allow the modelling of food production processes, for example the FLAIR 'shelf life' system produced at the Leatherhead Food Research Association. This can analyse a food product, including the raw materials and production process used, and suggest possible shelf life.

Desk top publishing (DTP)

A range of software can be used to produce text, graphs and pictures in reports and presentations. Spell checks, a thesaurus, translators, hand writing and voice recognition are all useful tools in making sure that reports and presentations are professionally produced. The ability to produce multi-media presentations for prospective clients and company directors is now also a reality.

The food industry is one of the largest influences in the UK manufacturing and business sector. IT has enabled it to profit from increased productivity, product consistency and ease of consumer response, yet it would be foolhardy to assume that schools could quickly follow suit. What now follows, however, are some notes and suggestions which help pupils towards an understanding of the issues.

The use of IT in food technology within the school context

Hardware

The computer: Three main types of computer are in general use in schools. There are the IBM PC and compatibles, for example RM Nimbus; Apple Macintosh; and Archimedes. Each brand has its own operating system and specific features, and recent developments enable new Apple (PowerMac) and Archimedes (RiscPC) machines to have the added bonus of being able to emulate IBM PC compatible software, allowing the users to have access to a greater range of software titles.

Hardware which your school/college or local authority may possess:

- printers
- CD-ROM Drives (check type and speed – single, double, quad)
- modem (check speed at which it can transmit and receive data)
- scanners – flatbed/hand held
- digital camera
- microphone/speakers
- keyboards/mouse
- data logging devices
- robotics.

The recent miniaturisation of computers to lap-tops, personal digital assistants (PDA) and notebooks has increased the range of computers available to students within a school. The 'portable' computer has added flexibility in that it can be used around the classroom, for example measuring during experiments, or it can be taken taking home to complete design work. It could be argued that lap-tops are more expensive, and may have a shorter life span at this point in time. However, it is surely the increased number of computers per student and their flexibility which may lead in the future to more use of portables in education (Frost and Wardle, 1995).

Software

There is generally a problem or concern with the compatibility of software with the different platforms or brands available. You may see a title which would be suitable, only to find out that it will not run on your machines!

Below are a selection of *generic* software packages which can be found on most platforms:

- word processors (WP)
- spreadsheets
- data bases
- painting
- drawing
- desk top publishing (DTP)
- communications (if a modem is attached):
  - fax
  - e-mail
  - on-line services
- 'office' package (WP, spreadsheet, drawing, painting and communications package combined)
- presentation package – slides, OHPs
- multi-media authoring program
- nutritional analysis
- kitchen planning
- simulations.

In food technology these packages may be used for:

- *Data bases* – e.g. Nutritional databases.
- *Graphics* – To produce data collection sheets/visual specifications AND dimensions.
- *Plotters* – To produce plans and sheets for viscosity tests.
- *Cutters* – To produce plastic projects, i.e. moulds.
- *Milling* – To produce a former so that it can be vacuum formed i.e. a chocolate/jelly mould.
- *Survey work* – To record data, charts, writing.
- *Scanner* – To record structures of products i.e. bread structures or egg foams.
- *Costing* – For recipe modification.
- *Research* – Using a CD-ROM.
- *Presentation and marketing* – Using hyperstudio.
- *Interactive* – For example the Meat & Lifestock Commission (MLC) software 'Fast Food Diner'.

The increasing sophistication of software and hardware has meant that they are constantly being up-dated and superseded by 'improved' products. However, it is the use and application of what you have in a school that is of importance. The quest may be to reach an ideological 'dream' scenario, but 'getting on' with what you have is far more practical, and can instantly benefit pupils.

The following ideas for the use of IT in food technology, as with the industrial applications of IT, is not a definitive list as variations in types and sophistication of hardware and software available to schools will differ around the country. They are suggestions so that you, as the practitioner, can make selective choices and decide what is best for your situation in school.

The original concept was to produce a guide to using IT throughout the 'design process'. However, as many steps are revisited during D&T work, a loose and more workable format was chosen. Each heading looks at a software area broadly and discusses the types of activities that can be undertaken at particular stages of food product development, with particular reference to hardware and software.

School applications of IT in food technology

Nutritional analysis

Nutritional analysis is frequently discussed when the use of IT in food lessons is mentioned, but more detail is needed. Nutritional analysis can provide a wealth of teaching opportunities in the classroom. Past students and teachers will remember sitting down with a copy of McCance and Widdowson food tables, trying to find a particular food, filling in hand-drawn tables, working out 100 g sizes, then converting it into a more easily understood average portion size. All this was performed using a trusty pen and ruler, and hopefully a calculator!

Life is now far simpler. Tap in a few details about the foods and the number of portions (or weight) and within seconds a detailed analysis is produced. Nutritional analysis is now a possibility for teachers working with mixed ability groups, pupils with special educational needs or just those with lower ability. IT has removed the boredom of working with vast arrays of figures and calculations, and allows pupils to concentrate and utilise the data collected more effectively.

Even more astounding is the application of nutritional analysis in product design and development. One specification may require 'high calcium', to match the criteria. Details can be entered into the software and the results produced on screen and/or on a printer. Changes can then be made to the varieties or weights of the ingredients, with the nutritional differences being displayed almost instantly, clearly an excellent example of modelling. However, students should always be reminded that changing ingredients in this way may indeed produce the specified nutritional characteristics, but the appearance, smell, taste, texture and function of the product may change dramatically.

Using IT within this areas of food technology may enhance work by:

- speed of processing and providing data to work with
- accuracy of figures
- modelling capability
- gender access
- data handling skills.

It may also aid progression in respect to an understanding of nutritional analysis and the application of the results to product design, and, some may say of even more importance, the application to general diet and health issues.

An example of a food technology school curriculum

Year 7: –Look at pupils' own diet in relation to health and nutrient needs.
     – Analyse of a simple recipe for a limited range of nutrients.

Year 8: –Look at another person's diet.
     – Analyse a product designed and made at school and suggest ways of making nutritional changes

Year 9: –Analyse a product a pupil has made, model the effects of different ingredients for nutritional content

GCSE:– Organise, record and interpret a food diary of a specified person, look at nutrient intake, lifestyle and links to Daily Recommended Value DRV's

– Analyse a designed food product, model the nutrients, modify, look at *Health of the Nation* targets

Post-16: As for GCSE, depending on course, for example 'manufacturing' – detailed specifications, consumer demands, market opportunities or 'health/catering/nursing' – dietary analysis of individuals, needs, Dietary Reference Values (DRVs).

Data from nutritional analysis can be recorded by:

- *Past intake* – assessed by a interview or questionnaire.
- *Dietary recall* – students can interview friends or family and ask them to recall all food and drink consumed over the past 24 hours, including average portion sizes. It is useful to keep a log or diary with quantities.
- *Diet history* – students could interview friends or family and build up a picture about the typical foods that the person or group of people eats. This usually builds up a picture of a 7 days eating pattern. The information could then be exploited in research work, identifying design opportunities based of patterns of food consumption.
- *Food frequency questionnaires* – here students give their participants a list of foods, and are asked how often each is eaten, for example daily/weekly/monthly. This could provide data on specific products to see whether there is a market for extending a product range.
- *Present intake* – records are kept at the time of eating.
- *Menu record* – this method is usually used to analyse the frequency in consumption of particular foods/nutrients.
- *Estimated record* – here a record is kept with portions described in household measurements, for example bowl, tablespoon. In scientific tests this method may also combine diagrams or photographs to help – this is a good way of introducing the idea of dietary analysis, especially for GCSE classes.
- *Weighed record* – all the weights of the portions of food are recorded, along with the waste. (While at home, average portions have to be used on the food eaten outside the home.)
- *Precise weighed record* – here all the ingredients used in the preparation of meals are weighed, including inedible waste, total cooked weight and individual portions, including plate waste
- *Cardiff photographic record* – participants take photographs of the foods that they are eating, and these are later analysed using comparison photographs of known portion sizes and weights. This could be emulated at school using electronic cameras, such as the Canon Ion.

All recipes are weighed in grams during food product development and most software programs only accept metric measures, even for liquids. It is important that recipes are worked out before the student starts entering data. When using a *control* recipe, it must be detailed so that any modifications can be measured accurately. Students may need to be reminded that it is advisable to change only one variable at a time, for example examining the total fat content in modified samosas, rather than trying to look at both fat and fibre simultaneously. Each nutritional analysis of each modification should be printed out and clearly labelled for use in design work.

Portion size

Calculating portion size of newly designed or modified products is another area in which nutritional analysis, and its methodology, can be exploited. For many students, this is a difficult concept to grasp as portion size varies from person to person. However, some standards can be found and one useful method is to start students thinking about situations when portions sizes are always identical, using, for example, areas such as ready meals, airline or fast food.

One other possibility is to explore the range of views of different people on portion size, and why they change from one person to the next. When designing a food product, especially if it is a whole meal or snack, manufacturers need to work out the portion size of the final product for economic considerations, consumer acceptance of size and suitable processing techniques to employ.

Students can easily set up focused practical tasks (FPT) to investigate portion sizes for the products they design in Technology. An example of a portion size FPT is as follows:

- Materials: 1 can baked beans.
- Equipment:
    - Weighing scales (electronic)
    - 2 identical plated serving spoons
    - Tablespoons
- Method:

1. Place beans in serving bowl.

2. Allow only one person to supervise and another to participate at any one time.

3. Place plate on weighing scale – correct it so that it reads zero.

4. Ask the participant to serve him/herself a small portion of baked beans.

5. Record the weight.

6. Place another plate on the scales and zero the dial.

7. Ask the participant to serve themselves a large portion of baked beans.

8. Record the weight.

9. Work out the average of these weights – this is then the average portion for this individual.

It is a good idea to allow more than one person to take part in the investigation. When they have calculated the average for each person, then they can work out the average for the whole group and this information could be entered on to a spreadsheet program. A database of portion sizes can be created for future product development work.

The use of IT in nutritional analysis clearly has benefits, allowing students of all abilities the chance to find out and learn about the nutritional qualities of the foods around them. For health education and promotion it encourages students to look at diets in detail, link this to recommendations and make informed food choices. In food technology it allows the manipulation of ingredients to design and make products with desirable nutritional properties and satisfying portion weights. The pocket computer Psion 3a (Page, 1995) can be fitted with a Comcard nutritional analysis system which allows students access to analysis wherever they are, for example on a work bench, at home or even researching on the street.

Spreadsheets

These programs have been available for a number of years in schools and in recent time have become extremely powerful and sophisticated. At its simplest form, a spreadsheet is a glorified calculator, with any number of rows of numbers which can be manipulated. However, one magical aspect in a spreadsheet is in the ability of the user to change the range of variables in a calculation, for example multiply by 4 instead of 2, and to be able to to see the effect of this change instantly. 'What if?' and 'I wonder?' questions can be devised and asked with possible solutions to sometimes difficult problems simulated in the spreadsheet and solved quickly.

Examples of use
Performing a simple function – i.e. calculating the cost of a food product (Figure 13.1).
Calculating the cost of a product, including staffing (Figure 13.2)
In the above examples, the computer performs the calculations in the last column according to the formula entered.

COST OF RECIPE				
FISH CAKE RECIPE MAKE 10 SMALL PORTIONS				
INGREDIENT	AMOUNT NEEDED (G)	COST OF FOOD	LESS COST OF FISH CAKES	
TUNA FISH	2.50	2,50	£0.89	£0.89
POTATO	250	500	£0.40	£0.20
MARGARINE	50	250	£0.30	£0.06
BREADCRUMBS	100	250	£1.10	£0.44
EGG	50	300	£0.60	£1.69
			£3.29	£1.69
			COST OF 1	
			FISH CAKE	£0.17

Figure 13.1 Spreadsheet – simple function

Raw market research data used to produce professional graphs (see Figure 13.3 for a really complex example!)
   On an introductory level, a spreadsheet can be used to record raw data from a survey or questionnaire. Two columns are entered, then highlighted and the graphics option chosen. This produces a bar graph, depending on the platform used. With additional work, both of the axes can be labelled and a title given. The joy is that the chart can be modified into another type of charts or graph immediately simply by choosing one from the graph menu. Figure 13.4 shows a set of raw data which has been transformed into various types of graphs and charts.
Star diagrams – Another exciting aspect of working with a spreadsheet is that all

COST OF RECIPE				
FISH CAKE RECIPE MAKE 10 SMALL PORTIONS				
INGREDIENT	**AMOUNT NEEDED (g)**	**AMOUNT BOUGHT (g)**	**COST OF FOOD**	**COST OF FISH CAKES**
TUNA FISH	250	250	£0.89	£0.89
POTATO	250	500	£0.40	£0.20
MARGARINE	50	250	£0.30	£0.06
BREADCRUMBS	100	250	£1.10	£0.44
EGG	50	300	£0.60	£1.69
		TOTAL COSTS	**£3.29**	**£1.69**
LABOUR COST TO MAKE FISH CAKES				
STAFF TIME (HR)	0.5			
COST OF STAFF(£/HR)	£3.00			
TOTAL COST	£1.50		**SUB TOTAL**	**£3.19**
ENERGY COSTS				
ELECTRICITY	£0.12		**TOTAL**	**£3.31**
			PER F.CAKE	**£0.33**

Figure 13.2 Spreadsheet plus staff

students can produced professional looking charts and graphs based on the raw data entered. This is also true of product star diagrams used in sensory analysis, where all too often in the past these have been drawn without a ruler by pupils, so losing their precise edge and the ability to use them effectively.

The procedure for using a computer is exactly the same as for producing star diagrams in sensory analysis sessions, with the score, or rating for each identified attribute entered into the spreadsheet. Microsoft Excel (4/5) can be used by pupils to enter the data on to the spreadsheet, then Chart Wizard is able to produce a perfect star diagram. Using the computer in this fashion allows pupils to see the relationship between computers and food and it also allows pupils, no matter what their ability, to enhance their work through the use of IT. Wizards are a new concept from Microsoft packages. There are a step-by-step sets of instructions, with options, which appear on the computer to make it easier to use the software. A few clicks of the mouse and a brilliant star diagram is produced for use in further development work. Figure 13.5 shows a computer-generated star diagram.

Star diagrams may be produced at the beginning of a design brief when devising a specification of a food product and a set of criteria for the development stage. Additionally, modifications can be plotted and overlaid on the original, and areas visually identified for further developmental work, as in Figure 13.6.

The use of spreadsheets have an additional bonus in that the student is not limited to eight descriptors, as is often used on hand-drawn worksheets. Some students may only be capable of deciding on three descriptors, whereas others may be capable of ten or more. The data can be entered and the chart produced according to the pupils' ability, so encouraging them to use their own vocabulary and not feel under pressure. Examples using many and few descriptors are shown in Figure 13.7.

The added flexibility of a spreadsheet means that time plans can be produced

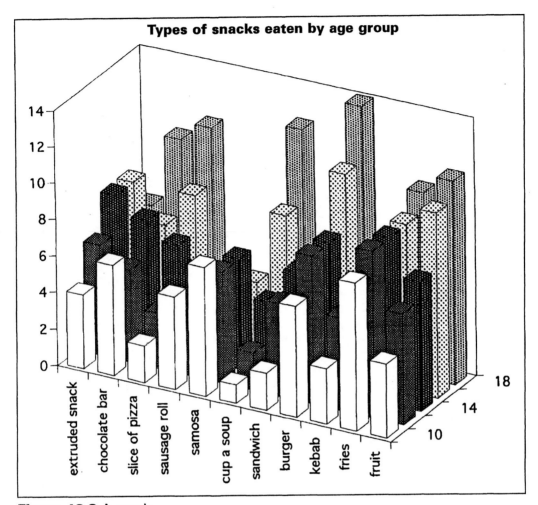

Figure 13.3 A graph

and then monitored during development work. These may be detailed, minute by minute, or an overall plan of the stages of development for a number of weeks can be made (Figure 13.8).

The latter is important, as it gives a clear idea of development and provides a useful check for students to know whether they are running to time. It can also be used by the teacher to guide students and help keep them to an organised plan. An enlarged version could be produced as a wall plan.

Modelling/simulations

Modelling involves the manipulation of tens, hundreds and even thousands of numbers to simulate a process or to pose a 'what if?' question, and it allows several trials and experimentation of a set scenario to be replayed, with changing variables until the ideal solution has been found.

This application of numbers may seem rather confusing, yet it is of paramount

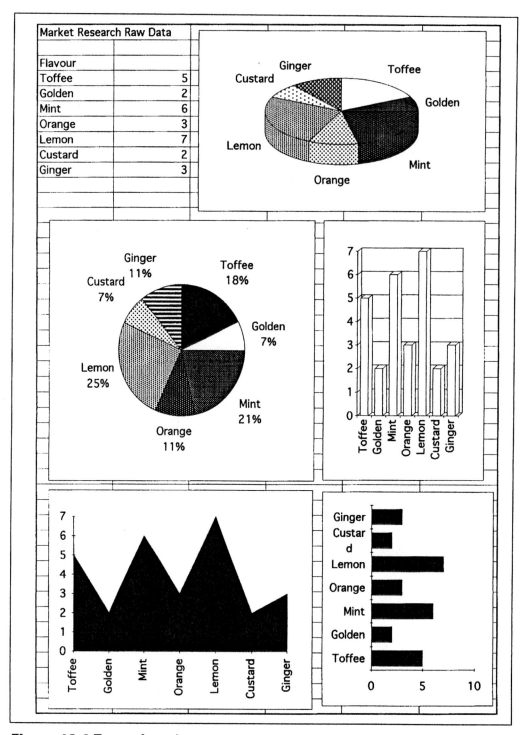

Figure 13.4 Types of graphs

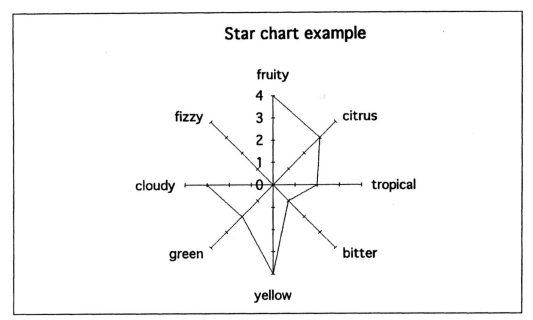

Figure 13.5 Star graph

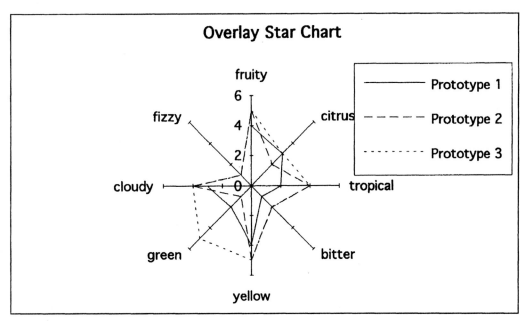

Figure 13.6 Overlay star graph

importance in D&T, using the process of number manipulation as a tool in design work. Modelling is best undertaken using programs such as spreadsheets and nutritional analysis packages, which exploit the areas of costing and nutrient content (see Figures 13.1 and 13.2 for examples).

Financial considerations can sometimes be the main factor affecting the possible creation and launch of a product in industry. At the simplest level, students can model the effects of using different ingredients and amounts against overall costs,

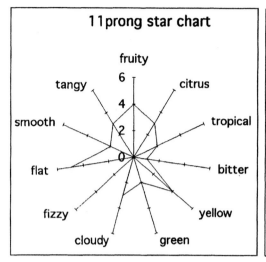

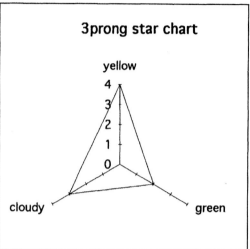

Figure 13.7(a) Eleven prong star   **Figure 13.7(b)** Three prong star

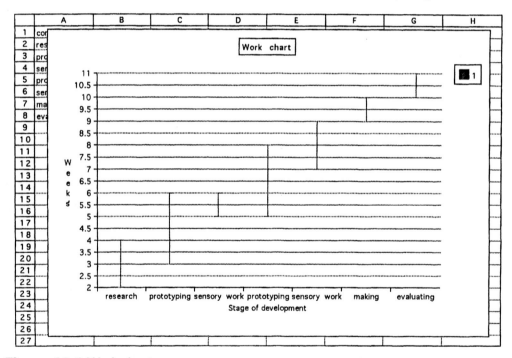

Figure 13.8 Work chart

using the unit cost of the materials. For example, a student may replace some fish with potato to reduce the cost of a fish cake and compare the costs of the samples.

However, even though the financial considerations may have been decided and finalised, proper making of the product using ingredients should then be carried out. The functional properties of the modified combination of ingredients may well have been affected and cause changes in overall consistency and consumer acceptability. Progression can be planned for the more able pupils by adding unit costs of labour and energy to the calculation.

'Rapid prototyping' is another example of using IT to 'model' in the food industry (Moverlay–Brown, 1996). It is a process by which a physical three-dimensional representation of a design is made from Computer Aided Design (CAD) data. This would allow a new biscuit product to be designed, and samples manufactured, at minimal cost in a single working day, so reducing typical development time by up to 70%. Once the rapid prototype is approved, a simple vacuum-formed mould can be made directly from the model for making, for example, samples of chocolate in a day.

Word processors

Word processors which started their life as a copy from a typewriter, are now increasingly sophisticated, powerful applications which can handle photographs, variable fonts, drawings and charts. They may be used in all areas of food technology where reports need to be produced or FPTs written up. The modern word processor, in addition to producing a well-presented piece of writing, may provide some of the following functions:

- *Spell check.* This can be used to check all typed work, or to help students with selected passages or difficult words. It can help pupils with special educational needs improve their overall attainment level in English.
- *Thesaurus.* Writing this chapter has taught me that I rely too heavily on a few hundred words to express myself. To my relief, and to many others, the thesaurus provides immediate access to thousands of other words. I can click on a word in a sentence and the computer will offer an array of alternative suggestions.
- *Grammar check.* Although this is not 100% accurate, this device has improved in the past few years and it can be beneficial to students in helping them understand the basic principles of grammatical rules.
- *Presentation.* Once the text has been typed and the spelling checked, the computer will also allow the user to change the size, style and layout of the writing. However, students all too often overuse these functions, resulting in written text which is hard to read and difficult to understand. For example:

original: Product development: Producing a 'lite' version of a chocolate dessert
overuse: **Product** *development:* Producing *a* 'lite' version of a *chocolate* dessert

It is better to use fewer variations rather than more. It is best to restrict each document to two fonts, and keep variations in sizes to a minimum. The use of underlining is best avoided, and bold and italic should be reserved only for titles, sub-titles and emphasising important words.

Databases

In industry a large retailer, for example, would use a database to store product specifications, so that if a complaint or enquiry is made (for example a consumer has an allergy to peanuts) then the entire product range can be scanned and the 'safe' products listed.

For pupils in schools a database could be used for:

- Compiling a range of successful, and unsuccessful, product specifications.
- Detailed questionnaire results.
- A price database for costing purposes, for example each student is given a homework task of finding out the cost for a selected range of food items.
- A design database containing foods that provide certain functions or have desirable working characteristics, so it can be accessed by students if they need to find out types of ingredient which, for example, aerate. A typical file would have *fields* for each food and look something like this:

ingredient	colour	flavour	bulk	bind	glaze	texture	emulsify	aerate	nutrition
SR Flour	white	bland	yes	yes	no	no	no	yes	starch, calcium

Graphics packages

The scope for the use of graphics packages is wide. For example:

- *Menus.*
- *Ingredient lists.*
- *Nutritional information labels.*
- *Packaging design*, using a 'net' format, which can then be linked to a cutter/plotter to produce a precisely made example of packaging, not using bits of sticky tape and definitely no felt tip pens.
- *Proformas* for focused practical tasks or sensory analysis data collection sheets. For example:
  - hedonic scale (Figure 13.9)
  - star charts (Figure 13.10)
  - viscosity test (Figure 13.11).
- *Visual specifications*. Products in industry, for example the reliable and humble

Sample	Dislike Very Much	Dislike	Neither Like or Dislike	Like	Like Very Much	Appearance	Smell	Taste	Texture

Figure 13.9 Hedonic rating

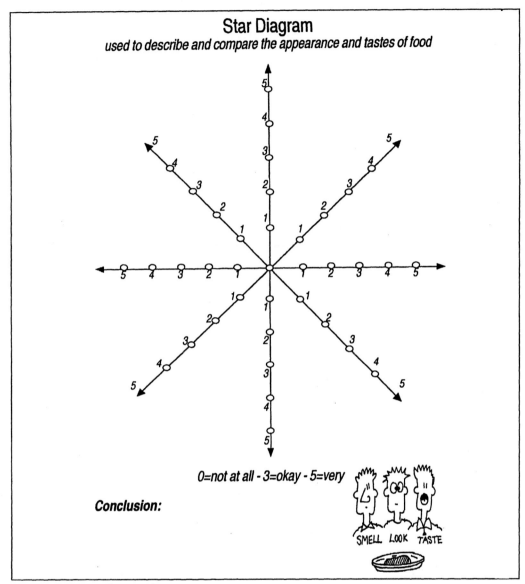

Figure 13.10 Star rating

sandwich, have strict specifications, even to the point of the number of garlic sausage slices and their position on the bread. The easiest way to give this information to an operator on a 'hand made' production line is in the form of a picture. The same is true for fast food chains; for example in producing hamburgers, visual specifications show new employees precisely how many slices of onions, gherkins or cheese to place in a particular product.

Another method is the use of a flat-bed scanner to scan a cross-sections of bakery items so they can be analysed for their aeration and dimension. This could prove useful when looking at the gluten formation in bread samples by comparing the scanned images as in Figure 13.12.

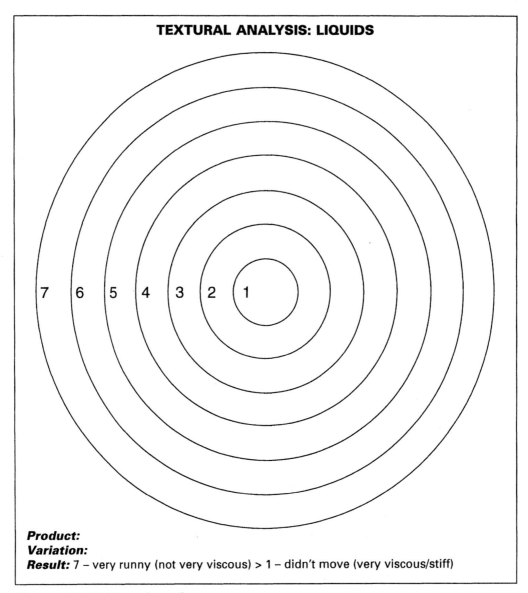

TEXTURAL ANALYSIS: LIQUIDS

7 6 5 4 3 2 1

Product:
Variation:
Result: 7 – very runny (not very viscous) > 1 – didn't move (very viscous/stiff)

Figure 13.11 Viscosity rating

This can be taken a step further, where operators check the quality of a product through visual inspections on automated production lines. At crucial points, large colour photographs may be used to remind operators about acceptable and unacceptable product appearance.

The technology now exists for schools and colleges to carry out the same process. An ion camera, or similar digital camera, can take, a series of electronic photographs of the products under development at different stages. An added bonus is that there are no film processing costs, as the pictures are stored electronically on a disc within the camera and these images can be fed straight into the computer and used for a variety of functions. For example:

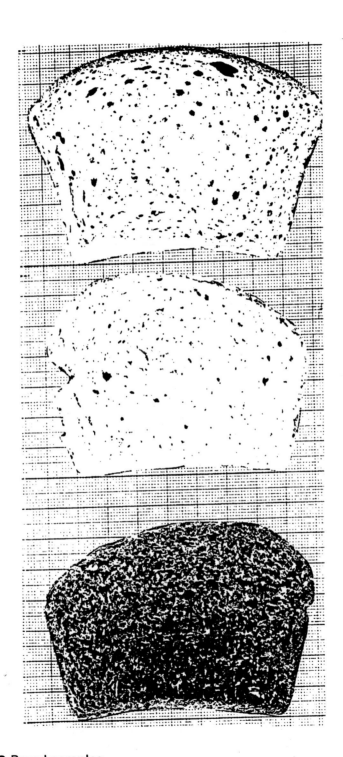

Figure 13.12 Bread samples

- *Visual specifications.*
- *Part of a portfolio/report,* using the 'cut and paste' functions directly into word processors or graphics applications.
- *Creation of specification/product database.*
- *Show control and modification of product prototypes.*
- *Show development stages of product in a visual format.*
- *Creation of a presentation,* using a multimedia authoring program such as 'Hyper studio'.

A simpler method is to use a small cheap camera to produce pictures that can be scanned on to the computer.

Computer-aided manufacture (CAM)

Designing and making a mould for food production can be used as part of a food assignment, though it must be recognised that essentially this is not food technology as it does not directly involve handling food as a material. However, when forming a mould, the IT is being used to ensure a precisely shaped good-quality food product.

If your school or college is lucky enough to have CAD/CAM facilities, you have considerable potential in enhancing food-based design and make assignments. Imagine a pupil sitting at a terminal, plotting his or her mould design, modelling it on the monitor and then using the milling machine to manufacturing the mould. The mould or former may then used to produce a simple, accurate and good-quality vacuum formed plastic packaging container using food grade plastic. Computer-aided-manufacture has additional potential for enhancing the learning of pupils with learning difficulties, including those who have motor impairment.

Possible plastic and food projects
- cheese making
- biscuit cutters
- lolly mould
- chocolate bar mould
- luxury chocolates
- jelly mould
- Easter egg/Christmas figure – or any other religious/cultural festival
- a die for an extrusion device, for example as an icing tube, sausage maker or mincer

Why is an integrated multi-media approach to food product design important?
- It shows pupils how 'resistant' materials are used in industrial food product development.
- It helps pupils understand there are similar core elements in food product design and other areas of design.
- The approach helps D&T staff work towards a common goal.
- Pupils are able to make realistic products and prototypes.
- Teachers and pupils learn to work as part of a team.

- It increases quality outcomes.
- It teaches about quality control and quality assurance procedures.
- Many products may be batch produced with the same specification.
- It helps work towards a balance between understanding and practical experience when designing and making.

Data logging

A computer can also be used to record and interpret data from a range of different input devices. The most common way of interacting with the computer is through the keyboard or mouse, yet sensors are just as effective and ideal when the manual reading of temperature or pH is cumbersome or tricky. Sensors also allow continual monitoring and the instant display of results, which can be printed out for use later (Baume, 1995).

Examples of the use of data logging in food technology:

- *When designing 'cook chill' products:*
  - reducing the temperature level in a specified time to prevent rapid micro-organisms growth
  - ensuring the 'core' temperature of a product being heated is above 70°C
  - investigating looking at the heat retention of different types of products packaging.
- *Biotechnology:*
  - careful logging of pH in the production of yoghurt or cheese, where pH readings are crucial and part of the products specification
- *Other uses:*
  - recording the temperature of chocolate when it is being 'tempered'
  - recording the rotation of a stirring device
  - using light sensors to count the number of packages or products

IT based tasks that could be included in designing and making assignments

- Using CAD and CAM in the production of a mould to control the shape/size of a food product.
- Use of nutrient modelling in product development focusing on *Health of the Nation* targets.
- Monitoring the pH of a product, e.g. yoghurt or cheese during production.
- Using scanners to analyse the volume and texture of bakery products.
- Using digital camera to producing visual specifications of products.
- Using a DTP program to generating HACCP charts in flow diagrams.
- Using CD-ROMs in research investigations. The range of CDs are increasing, they are very versatile, easy to use, stimulating for pupils and provide ideas, data and photographs.
- Professional portfolios can be produced with the help of a spell check!
- Sensory analysis data can be interpreted and presented in the form of bar graphs or star diagrams.
- The temperature of a production system, e.g. brewing, can be observed and controlled.

- The financial figures for the mass production of a food product can modelled.
- 'Nets', graphical design, ingredient list and bar code for a packaging mock-up can be produced.
- The Internet, or other service provider, can be used to gather research data for interviews/research or sent through E-mail to colleagues.

The future

The computer industry is constantly moving forward. We are going through a new information revolution with electronics, with sophisticated powerful computers constantly changing our lives and the way in which we educate our pupils. It is important that we start to use these new technologies in our teaching, to keep pace with recent and future developments. Here are six 'new' technologies we should become familiar with.

The Internet

A recent 'buzz' word, with everyone expected to be able to 'surf' the net. Partridge (1996) and Seaman (1995) both recently noted the amount of food research on the Internet.

The government has seen the potential for the Internet system as a teaching 'tool' in education and commissioned a paper entitled *Superhighways for Education: The Way Forward* (DfE,1995d). It looks at the potential for superhighway use, and concludes that education should be encouraged to use and further its development. American research (Kenny, 1995) has shown that to achieve maximum learning benefit for pupils the Internet is needed on every machine and network, with access for everyone.

However, there have been concerns expressed about the Internet, as the content is not monitored and little research has been done into its effective use in teaching (Frost, 1995). The issue of unregulated materials available through the Internet has been discussed in other articles, and research indicates that nearly 50% of 'surfers', or users, are looking for pornography (Klein, 1995a, b). Fortunately, computer software developers are now offering software which is able to take protective measures against pupils requesting and downloading inappropriate areas of the Internet (Klein, 1995b).

The National Council of Educational Technology (NCET) has released guidelines for teachers and schools on computer pornography. Their advice is:

- be vigilant and make it clear to pupils that you have systems for tracking computers and files
- let pupils know that unauthorised use of equipment and breaching the rules are punishable
- consider offering different levels of access
- use a combination of software and passwords to help prevent pupils stumbling across undesirable materials
- get the police to deal with any obscene publications or unlawful copying.

However, all these issues should not deter you from making use of the Internet. Some useful addresses are as follows:

Discussion groups:
- rec.food.veg
- rec.food.veg.cooking
- rec.food.recipes
- rec.food.cooking
- sci.med.nutrition
- alt.support.diabetes.kids
- alt.support.diet
- alt.support.food.allergies
- alt.food.fat-free
- misc.health.diabetes

These sites may be useful for research and discussion with other users both nationally or globally. The World Wide Web offers more opportunity in the form of 'on-line' magazines:

- *BALANCE diet/health mag:*   http://hyperlink.com:9000/balance/
- *Vegetarian Pages:*   http://www.veg.org/veg/
- *USA Food and Drug Administration:*   http://vm.csfan.fda.gov
- *International Food Information Council:*   www://ificinfo.health.org
- *Readers Digest:*   http://foods.readersdigest.co.uk
- *MAFF consumer help line:*   consumer@info.maff.gov.uk
- *Schoolnet Resources Manual:*   /pub/schoolnet/.manuals/Resources.txt
- *Recipes:*   /pub/Library/Recreation/big-drink-list /pub/recipes
- *The Recipes Folder*   //english-server.hss.cmu.edu/Recipes.htm/
- *Vegetarian*   http://www-sc.ucssc.indiora.edu/cgi.bin/recipes/other/tms/veg
- *Unilever*   http//www.unilever.com/uniguide/
- *Ragu*   http://www.eat.com

These types of addresses could be could be used at the start of a design and make assignment. For example, to research types of flavours of particular food products, to look at processing techniques or general company information. One web site that gives this type of access is:

    http://www.yahoo.com/Entertainment/

This address gives a choice of different food and drinks areas to explore, including:

- countries and cultures
- food allergies
- herbs and spices
- recipes
- vegetarianism
- snacks and desserts.

For example:

- *Researching ice-cream:*
  http://www.benjerry.com/   information on different products
  http://www.sorbet.com/   information on flavours and company data

- *Researching potato crisps:*
  http://www.shift.com/Shift/sponsors/MVickieinformation on different products
  http://www.padutch.com/html/bickles/bickleshtml information and photographs of production

Time spent by the teacher browsing through the pages can be very worthwhile,
so reducing the time spent by pupils carrying out their research in a more
expensive way through 'on line' sources. A directory can be made to help students,
and very quickly the whole class will be 'surfing the net'.

Video conferencing

This is when students are linked with companies or other schools and colleges
across the world to exchange ideas and carry out research. A digital camera and
modem are required.

Speech recognition

Students, using a microphone, can give verbal commands to the computer. This
could be a useful tool for students with motor impairment. Already, some
advanced computers can handle simple verbal instructions.

An optical character reader (OCR)

This would be useful for the interpretation of languages in schools with a rich
multi-cultural mixture of pupils.

Handwriting recognition

A phrase introduced by Apple Newton, where a computer reads the user's
handwriting and converts it into text, drawings and diagrams.

Virtual reality (VR)

This is already used by some industrialists in the UK. Unilever (Glaskin, 1995) has
been examining its use in factory design and computer-based training. Its assessment
so far is that VR should reduce significantly commissioning and maintenance costs
and improve the company's competitive edge. VR has been used to build a *virtual-
supermarket*, placing products on shelves and allowing judgement of new packaging
designing. Unilever has identified several areas in which VR could be exploited,
including engineering and design, rapid prototyping and virtual experiments. Virtual
factories, with expert systems and databases providing information about chemical
processes, material constraints, production techniques, hazard assessment and cost
are other applications of this growing technology.

The explosion in growth in this area has already lead to 'virtual' software aimed
at the home market. At present most of the software available is for entertainment,
for example games. However, as with the current surge of home education, CD
software titles such as Encarta, VR software and hardware technology are only

around the corner. Imagine a school VR system that would allow students to manufacture their designed products within a 'virtual factory'!

Conclusion

What are the main issues for teachers?

- lack of staff training
- where the computer is placed in the school
- what 'platform' or type of computer is available in the school
- clear understanding of computer terminology
- the 'fright' factor, or the pupils knowing more than the teacher
- to ability to monitor progression in IT capability
- the ability to plan for realistic and positive differentiation in teaching and learning
- knowing the difference between good and bad practice
- understanding and meeting students' expectations of IT
- the status of food technology in D&T
- addressing access in terms of gender and special educational needs.

Main issues:

- The best pieces of computer software available at the present time are the industry standard generic packages, including word processors, spreadsheets and databases. Pupils can learn how to use them effectively in all areas of the school curriculum.
- The choice of purely food programs is far more restricted, and it is important that the software package is checked for potential use and whether it will run on your machine.
- New software will become available as food technology becomes more popular in the school curriculum during the next few years and teachers clearly express their needs. The use of IT in food technology in your school depends on your vision, keenness and willingness for it to develop.
- INSET may not be available, but finding the time at the end of the school day to learning and practising new skills on the computer, for at the very least half an hour, can make all the difference. Experiment with the computer programs yourself: you cannot break them! There is no mysterious jargon or secret handshake to stop or keep you out: skills in IT can be learnt by everyone. It is up to all of us, as teachers, to become aware of and be able to use these developing technologies, to move forward and not be content to take a back seat.
- It is important that the 'cookery' image of food is cast aside, and is replaced with an understanding of industrial practices and principles, including science, food chemistry, nutrition, marketing, research, product development, processing and cost implications. As with the egg whisk, extrusion device or sensory evaluation, the computer is yet another tool to enable competent designers to achieve their desired outcome.
- There is little benefit in including IT for its own sake: it must become a useful, integral element of the designing process, enabling students to fulfil their own potential as food product designers.

Glossary

Attribute analysis: an analysis of different sensory and other aspects/attributes of food products to generate different ideas for developing a food product.

Artificial intelligence: the use of IT to control an automated food production process.

Basic formula: a basic recipe that can be increased/decreased using the same proportions of ingredients to make a larger/smaller quantity mix.

Basic mixing method: the basic stages used during the preparation process regardless of the quantity of ingredients.

CAD (Computer aided design): three-dimensional representations of a design can be generated using graphics/drawing computer software, for example a net for packaging a food product or a nutritional information label.

CAM (Computer aided manufacture): computers can be used in the large-scale production of precisely shaped and sized products, for example biscuits on a production line.

Case studies: describe real examples of food technology in the world outside school. They help students learn about the way companies design and manufacture food products, how these products are marketed and sold and their effects on people and the environment.

Challenges/units: learning activities revolving around a central designing and making assignment – RCA Technology Project term.

Concept development stage: carrying out market research to identify and write an outline food product specification.

Consumer acceptance: measures the degree of liking of individual products using hedonic scales.

COMA (Committee on Medical Aspects of Food Policy): provided dietary and nutritional recommendations.

Databases: produced using computer software. A database can organise and store data, for example the functions, desirable working characteristics or nutritional content of foods or a product specification, which can then be scanned or searched for information. Details of, for example, a food would be stored in one *file* (or card) for each food in the database under the same *field* names (or headings) for each food entered.

Data logging: a computer is used to record and store data from a range of input devices which can then be presented as a graph and interpreted. For example, using a temperature probe, with or without a computer, to check the temperature reached during cooking to ensure a 'cook chill' food is heated to a safe temperature for consumption.

Designing and making assignments/capability tasks/challenges: complete designing and making assignments/projects/briefs where pupils design and make food products focused in different contexts:

- designing and making assignment – National Curriculum D&T term.
- capability tasks – Nuffield D&T Project term.
- designing and making assignment (DMA) – RCA Technology Project.

DRV (Daily Reference Values): nutritional guidelines produced by the Department of Health giving the desirable intakes for particular food materials rather than estimates of individual requirements. They are average values for the population and are consistent with good health.

Electronic nose: an IT-based device used in the food industry which can distinguish any smell or aroma.

EARs (Estimated Average Requirements for energy): nutritional information produced by the Department of Health on the daily average energy requirements for individuals of certain ages.

Focused tasks/resource tasks: short practical activities to help pupils develop and practise food technology knowledge, understanding and skills:

- focused tasks and activities where pupils investigate, disassemble and evaluate familiar products and applications – National Curriculum D&T term.
- Resource Tasks (Key Stage 4 – strategy, communicating, food products, food chemistry, nutrition, food production, food sales, products and applications, health & safety) – Nuffield D&T Project term
- Focused Practical Tasks (FPT) – RCA Technology Project.
- Investigating and evaluating products and their application (P&A) – RCA Technology Project.

Food technology: knowledge and understanding of the properties of foods; includes the ability to select and use the appropriate tools and materials to explore these properties for developing food products.

Food technology capability: demonstrated by using the designing skills, many of which are generic to other materials such as textiles, wood, plastic and metal, with the appropriate knowledge and understanding, and selecting the making skills needed to follow the creative design process to develop food products.

Food product design and development: occurs when pupils select ingredients, modify recipes, combine foods to design food products. Food product design as with product design in any materials, is a process consisting of the following elements:

- the consumer market, consumer awareness, retailing;
- principles of food manufacture, raw materials, recipes, formulas, mixing, process centred;
- nutritional aspects;
- devising product specifications, research development;
- test procedures – sensory, evaluation, consumer acceptability;
- large-scale manufacture, pilot, batch, continuous production, packaging, transport.

GNVQ (General National Vocational Qualification): a City & Guilds school/college based vocational qualification.

Graphics packages: computer software which can be used to represent information pictorially and graphically with diagrams, pictures or charts.

HACCP (Hazard Analysis and Critical Point): a system which identifies and controls, by reducing or eliminating them, specific risks and hazards in a food production process.

Hedonic Test: directly measures the degree of liking or acceptability of a product. A typical 9-point hedonic scale would consist of descriptive words such as 'likes extremely' (9) to 'dislikes extremely' (1). For children, picture scales are more appropriate.

Image analysis: imaging devices, such as microscopes or video cameras and digitised images, can be used to scan, for example the particle size and shape analysis of the air bubble size in aerated chocolate or ice cream in the food industry.

Image boards: a collection of pictures of things people may like, places they may visit and activities they may be involved in.

Internet: the use of a computer to investigate, search for and print out a wide range of information and data both nationally and globally through, for example, the use of the World Wide Web.

Least cost formulation: the amount of ingredients needed to produce a product at the lowest possible cost, retaining desirable eating characteristics and using as a base line the specified organoleptic qualities of a food product.

Lines of interest and design guides: Nuffield Design and Technology terminology. A line of interest provides a starting point or context for pupil assignments and the design guide outlines a particular type of food product that could be made based on the context or starting point.

Market research:

- *Quantitative research* involving a survey of a representative sample population, usually through a numerically coded questionnaire with a limited number of answers.
- *Qualitative research* includes more in-depth and open questioning and is particularly useful for exploring feelings and attitudes. In-depth focus discussion groups provide information on how consumers think about a product in their home and among friends. They provide objective, honest and dispassionate opinions.

Modelling and simulations: the manipulation of information to simulate a process or situation and pose a 'what if?' question.

Nutritional analysis: the use of food tables or a computer database to search, analysis and model the nutritional content of foods.

Product profiling: a visual representation, usually in the form of a star diagram or spider's web plot, of sensory attributes of a food.

Quality assurance: a planned sequence of evaluation procedures in a food manufacturing system to ensure high-quality products for consumer consumption.

Quality control: a procedure which tests an attribute of a food against established standards and criteria to assesses whether the product meets the original specification.

Risk: a possible hazard causing harm or damage.

Risk assessment: thinking through a process, identifying and assessing the possible size, harm and damage of danger points or risks.

Risk control: action taken to ensure the harm or damage is less likely to happen.

RNIs (Reference Nutrient Intake): nutritional information produced by the Department of Health on the daily amounts of a nutrient for almost every individual, even those with high needs.

Sensory appraisal: a subjective testing of a food or 'a scientific discipline used to evoke, measure, analyse and interpret reactions to those characteristics of food and materials as they are perceived by the senses of sight, smell, taste, touch and hearing' (Institute of Food Technology).

Sensory Boards: a set of boards designed to create a small booth for use as a food testing area.

Sensory Tests: the name given to the tests used in sensory analysis/evaluation.

1. *Consumer preference tests* evaluate the acceptability and appeal of a product for the consumer. They may be:
- *Paired comparison/preference tests* where the assessor has a choice of two samples.
- *Hedonic ranking tests* which assess the degree of liking of a product by ranking the products on scale in ascending order of consumer acceptability.

2. *Difference tests* designed to compare two samples to see whether there is any noticeable difference in the sensory characteristics. They may be:
- *Paired comparison tests* where the two samples are presented at the same time for sensory evaluation.
- *Triangle tests* where three samples are presented at the same time, two of which are identical. The assessor is asked to select the sample that is different.
- *Duo–trio* where the first sample presented is the control which is followed by two simultaneous samples, one the same as the control and one that is different. The assessor is asked to select the one that is different.

3. *Grading or quality tests* designed to rank specific sensory properties of similar foods. The foods are ranked on a scale from the 'most to least' according to a particular characteristics, for example crumbleness or sweetness. For example, in a ranking sensory test where a range of different brand raspberry instant whips are tested and put into a rank order from least to most sweet.

Spreadsheet: a grid or chart made up of rows and columns which can model or simulate situations or processes. Spreadsheets contain data (usually numbers) and can record and manipulate data, carry out calculations and produce graphs and charts.

Star diagram: used by the food industry to present sensory analysis data with scores or ratings given for each of the identified attributes of the food product.

Systems and control in food technology: an industrial food production system with inputs (e.g. energy, information, foods), outputs (e.g. energy, information, food products) and feedback (e.g. temperature sensor) to adjust/modify and control each stage of the process.

Virtual reality (VR): using a computer to simulate industrial production to assess factory design, possible physical and chemical reactions, production techniques, potential hazards and production costs.

Video conferencing: a computer link between schools, colleges and institutions to communicate, exchange ideas and carry out research using a digital camera and a modem.

Bibliography

APU (1989) *The Assessment of Performance in Design and Technology*. London: Schools Examination and Assessment Council.

Archer, S. (1995) *Designing with Basic Recipes*, Unpublished observations.

Arnold, M. (1908) *Reports on Elementary Schools, 1852–1883*. London: HMSO.

Atherton, M. (1990) 'Technology and Home Economics....So far so good', *Modus*, **8 (2)**, 50–52.

Attar, D. (1990) *Wasting Girls' Time*. London: Virgo Press.

Baker, B. (1991) 'Home Economics and its Future', *Modus*, **9 (3)**, 84–85.

Baker, K. (1988) 'A word from the master'. *The Times*, 2 September.

Banks, F. (1994) *Teaching Technology*. London: Routledge.

Barlex, D. (1995a) *Nuffield Design and Technology: Student's Book*. Harlow: Longman Group.

Barlex, D. (1995b) *Nuffield Design and Technology: Study Guide*. Harlow: Longman Group.

Barlex, D. (1995c) *Nuffield Design and Technology: Capability Task File*. Harlow: Longman Group.

Barlex, D. (1995d) *Nuffield Design and Technology: Resource Task File*. Harlow: Longman Group.

Barlex, D. (1995e) *Nuffield Design and Technology: Teacher's Guide*. Harlow: Longman Group.

Barlex, D. (1996a) *Nuffield Design and Technology, 14–16 Resources – Food Technology: For the Student*. Harlow: Addison Wesely Longmant.

Barlex, D. (1996b) *Nuffield Design and Technology, 14–16 Resources – Food Technology: For the Teacher*. Harlow: Addison Wesley Longman.

Baume, J. and Gill, D. (1995) 'IT puts the children in charge', *Primary Science Review*, **December 95**.

Bennett, R. (1978) 'What is Home Economics?', *Journal of Consumer Studies and Home Economics*, **2**, 78–84.

Bentley, D. and Watts, M. (1994) *Primary Science and Technology*. Buckingham: Open University Press.

BETT (1996) *Emap Education*. BETT Exhibition Programme, London: BETT.

Black, P. and Harrison, G. (1985) *In Place of Confusion: Technology and Science in the School Curriculum*. London: Nuffield–Chelsea Curriculum Trust.

Black, P. and. Harrison, G. (1990) 'Introduction'. In Murray. R. (ed.) *Managing Design and Technology in the National Curriculum*. Oxford: Heinemann Educational.

Board of Education (1904) *Regulations for Secondary Schools*. London: HMSO.

Board of Education (1919) *Circular 1112: Memoranda on Teaching and*

Organisation of Secondary Schools. London: HMSO.

Board of Education (1926) *The Education of the Adolescent* chaired by Hadow. London: HMSO.

Board of Education (1937) *Handbook of Suggestions for Teachers*. London: HMSO.

Board of Education (1938) *Secondary Education with Special Reference to the Grammar and Technical Schools*, chaired by Spens Report. London: HMSO.

Board of Education (1943) *Curriculum and Examinations in Secondary Schools* chaired by Norwood. London: HMSO.

Brennan, T. (1986) 'Home Economics: A quiet revolution', *Modus*, **4 (6)**, 226–7.

Brown, S. (1985) 'Good Morning Ladies', *Modus*, **3 (8)**, 288–9.

Brown, S. (1988) 'Sticking at it', *Modus* **6 (6)**, 224–5.

Buttle, J. (1982) 'A new way of looking at Home Economics and its place in the grand design', *Housecraft*, **June**, 115.

CBI (1994) *Labour Market Trends*. London: Office of National Statistics.

CCFRA (1995) 'Software products for the baking industry', *Campden and Chorleywood Contact*, **April**.

Cockburn (1991) 'The Gendering of Technology'. In Mackay, H., Young, M. and Benyon, J. (eds) *Understanding Technology*. Lewes: Falmer Press.

Corson, D. (1991) *Education for Work – Background to Policy and Curriculum*. Clevedon Avon: Multilingual Matters.

Cracknell, H. and Kaufmann, R. (1981) *Practical Professional Cookery* (2nd edn.) Basingstoke: Macmillan Education.

Crease, B. (1965) *Careers in Catering and Domestic Science*. London: The Bodley Head.

Daniels, A., Chartles, D. and Davies, A. (1993) 'Data logging in science using notebook computers', *EiS*, **September.**

DATA (1995) *Guidance Materials for Design and Technology – Key Stage 3*. Warwickshire: Design and Technology Association.

Davies, H. (1981) 'An investigation into home economics teachers in the contributory areas of the subject', *The Journal of Consumer Studies and Home Economics*, **5**, 148–55.

Davies, L. (1995) 'Progression in design and technology learning', *Modus*, **13 (2)**, 36–39.

Dearing, R. (1993a) *The National Curriculum and its Assessment: An Interim Report*. London: School Curriculum and Assessment Authority.

Dearing, R. (1993b) *The National Curriculum and its Assessment: Final Report*. London: School Curriculum and Assessment Authority.

DES (1959) *15–18. A Report of the Central Advisory Council for Education (England)*. Chaired by Crowther, London: HMSO.

DES (1963) *Half Our Futures. A Report of the Central Advisory Council for Education (England)*. Chaired by Newsom, London: HMSO.

DES (1975) *Educational Survey No 21, Curricular Differences for Boys and Girls*. London: HMSO.

DES (1978) *Curriculum 11–16*. London: HMSO.

DES (1979) *Aspects of Secondary Education in England*. London: HMSO.

DES (1980a) *Girls and Science, HMI Series: Matters for Discussion*. London: HMSO.

DES (1980b) *A View of the Curriculum*. London: HMSO

DES (1981a) *The Practical Curriculum, Paper 70*. London: Schools Council.

DES (1981b) *The School Curriculum*. London: HMSO.

DES (1985) *Home Economics from 5 to 16 – Curriculum Matters 5*. London: HMSO.

DES (1987) *Craft, Design and Technology from 5 to 16*. London: HMSO.

DES (1989) *Design and Technology for Ages 5 to 16*. London: HMSO.

DES (1989) *Special Educational Needs* (Warnock Report) Cmnd 7212, London: HMSO.

DES (1990) *Technology in the National Curriculum*. London: HMSO.

DES (1992) *Technology Key Stages 1, 2 and 3: A Report by HMI Inspectorate on the First Year 1990–91*. London: HMSO.

DfE (1992) *Technology for Ages 5 to 16. Proposals of the Secretary of State for Education*. London: HMSO.

DfE (1995a) *Design and Technology in the National Curriculum*. London: HMSO.

DfE (1995b) *Design and Technology – Characteristics of Good Practice in Secondary Schools*. London: HMSO.

DfE (1995c) *Information Technology in the National Curriculum*. London: HMSO.

DfE (1995d) *Superhighways for Education: The Way Forward*. London: HMSO.

Dyhouse, C. (1977) 'Good wives and little mothers: Social anxieties and the schoolgirl's curriculum 1890–1920', *Oxford Review of Education*, **3 (1)**, 22.

Edwards, M. (1981) 'A last chance for home economics', *Housecraft*, **December**, 246.

Eggleston, J. (1996) *Teaching Design and Technology* (2nd edn.). Buckingham: Open University Press.

Equal Opportunities Commission (1980) *Do you Provide Equal Educational Opportunities?* Manchester: Equal Opportunities Commission.

Equal Opportunities Commission (1983) *Equal Opportunities in Home Economics*. Manchester: Equal Opportunities Commission.

Farrell, A. (1996) 'What do you think and what do we need?', *Modus*, **14 (2)**, 52–56.

Farrell. A. and Patterson, J. (1993) *Understanding Assessment in Design and Technology*. London: Hodder & Stoughton.

Faulkner, H. and Mansell, S. (1982) *Nuffield Home Economics: The Basic Course*. London: Hutchinson Education.

Faulkner, H., *et al.* (1982) *Nuffield Home Economics – Teachers' Guide to the Basic Course*. London: Hutchinson Education.

Firebaugh, F. (1980) 'Home Economics in Higher Education in the United States: Current Trends', *The Journal of Consumer Studies and Home Economics*, **4**, 159–61.

Fisher, A. (1989) 'Under the skin', *Times Educational Supplement*, **17 November**, 24.

Fisher, R. (1989) *Problem Solving in Primary Schools*, Oxford: Blackwell.

Frost, R (1995) 'Licensed to surf the net', *Times Educational Supplement*, **10 November**.

Frost, R. and Wardle, J. (1995) 'Enhancing science with computers', *EiS*, **January**.

Geen, A., Jenkins, H. and Daniels, C. (1988) *Home Economics: Teaching for the Future*. Cambridge: Hobsons.

Gibbs-Smith, C.H. (1981) *The Great Exhibition of 1851*. London: HMSO.

Glaskin, M. (1995) 'An extra dimension', *Uniview*, 100.

Gordon, P. (1978) 'Tradition and change in the curriculum'. In Lawton, D. (ed.) *Theory and Practice of Curriculum Studies*. London: Routledge and Kegan Paul, pp.121–22.

Hampshire LEA (1994) *Nutrients – Database Program.* Winchester: Hampshire Microtechnology Centre.

HIASS (1993) *Orders into Practice.* Winchester: Hampshire Inspection and Advisory Support.

Hutchinson, G. (1995) 'Strategies for achieving differentiation in D&T teaching and learning', *Modus,* **13 (6),** 164–8.

ILEA (1989) *The Future of Home Economics.* London: ILEA Home Economics Team.

Kenny, J. (1995) 'Open all hours', *Times Educational Supplement,* **3 November**.

Kimbell, R., Stables, K. and Green, R. (1996) *Understanding Practice in Design and Technology.* Buckingham: Open University Press.

Klein, R. (1995a) 'Naughty toys and dirty pictures,' *TES Computers Update,* **20 November**.

Klien, R. (1995b) 'Porn Free', *TES Computers Update,* **20 November**.

Lawson, R. (1993) 'Home economics – articulation of force field diagnosis', *The Home Economist,* **12 (1),** 8.

Mathieson, A. (1979) 'Home economics – The future', *The Journal of Consumer Studies and Home Economics,* **3,** 205–14.

Moverlay-Brown, S. (1996) 'Computerised development of new products', *Food Technology International: Europe,* **1996,** 22–3.

NATHE (1988) *The Place of Home Economics in Technology.* London: National Association of Teachers of Home Economics.

NCC (1990) *Non-Statutory Guidance: Design and Technology.* York: National Curriculum Council.

NCC (1992) *National Curriculum Technology.* York: National Curriculum Council.

NCC (1993) *Technology Programmes of Study and Attainment Targets: Recommendations of the National Curriculum Council.* York: National Curriculum Council.

NCET (1992) *Management of Information Technology and Cross-curricular Issues, Information Sheet.* Coventry: National Council of Educational Technology.

NCET (1994) *Attracting Girls to Information Technology, Information Sheet.* Coventry: National Council of Educational Technology.

Newton, D. (1990) 'Does the home economist have a place in National Curriculum Technology?', *Design and Technology Teaching,* **23 (1),** 23.

Ofsted (1993) *Technology Key Stages 1, 2 and 3: Third Year, 1992–93.* London: HMSO.

Page, M. (1995) 'The Psion Series 3a and Comcard Nutritional analysis card', *SNF Newsletter,* **1 December**.

Partridge, C. (1996) 'Tuck in for a healthy host of taste tips', *The Times,* **24 January**.

Penfold, J. (1988) *Craft, Design and Technology: Past Present and Future.* Stoke-on-Trent: Trentham Books.

Perry, D. (1995) *The Royal College of Arts Schools Technology Project Key Stage 3 Students' book – D&T Challenges for Year 7, Teacher's Resources for Year 7.* London: Hodder & Stoughton.

Perry, D (1996) *The Royal College of Arts Schools Technology Project Key Stage 3 Students' book – D&T Challenges for Year 8, Teacher's Resources for Year 8.* London: Hodder & Stoughton.

Ritchie, R. (1995) *Primary Design and Technology: A Process for Learning.* London: David Fulton.

Ridgwell, J. (1992) 'NATHE survey to investigate the status of Home Economics', *Modus*, **10 (8)**, 241.

Ridgwell, J. (1993) *Tasting and Testing*. London: Ridgewell Press.

Riggs, A. (1992) 'Technology education and gender', *Modus*, **10 (2)**, 44.

Rutland, M. (1984) *Vocational Opportunities Available to Students of Home Economics*. Unpublished B. Ed. Dissertation, University of Wales.

SCAA (1994) *Design and Technology in the National Curriculum – Draft Proposals*. London: School Curriculum and Assessment Authority.

SCAA (1995) *Key Stage 3 Design and Technology – The New Requirements*. London: School Curriculum and Assessment Authority.

SCAA (1996a) *Consistency in Teacher Assessment: Guidance for Schools*. London: School Curriculum and Assessment Authority.

SCAA (1996b) *Key Stage 3 Optional Tests and Tasks Unit 1: Keep it Contain it*. London: School Curriculum and Assessment Authority.

Schools Council (1973) 'Aims and objectives of home economics education'. In *Schools Council Occasional Bulletin*. London: Schools Council.

Science with Technology Project (1994) *Developing Food Products*. Hatfield: ASE Booksales.

Science with Technology Project (1994) *Understanding the Science of Food*. Hatfield: ASE Booksales.

Scott, M. E. (1967) *The History of F.L. Calder College of Domestic Science 1875–1965*. Wetternen (Belgium): Universal Press.

SEAC (1991) *The Assessment of Performance in Design and Technology*. London: Schools Examination and Assessment Council.

SEAC (1993) *Instructions for the Statutory Practical Task and Sample Test Questions: KS3 D&T*. London: DfE.

Seaman, C. (1995) 'Computers in the food industry – new developments', *Nutrition and Food Science*, **Jan/Feb**.

Seaman, C. (1995) 'Food on the internet', *Nutrition and Food Science*, **Nov/Dec**.

(SEC) Secondary Examinations Council (1986) *Home Economics GCSE: A Guide for Teachers*, Milton Keynes: Open University Press.

Shannon, R. (1991) 'Creating a home and food technology laboratory', *Modus*, **9 (8)**, 84.

Sillitoe, H. (1966) *A History of the Teaching of Domestic Subjects*. London: Metheun.

Smith, F. (1923) *The Life and Works of Sir James Kay-Shuttleworth*. London: Murray Press.

Smith, D. and Thomas, L. (1996) 'Women finance 30% of families', *The Sunday Times*, **18 February**.

Smithers, A. and Robinson, P. (1992) *Technology in the National Curriculum – Getting it Right*. London: The Engineering Council.

Steenstra, J. (1995) 'Enhancing design and technology through the use of IT', *Datanews*, **November**.

Stone, D. (1976) *The National; The Story of a Pioneer College*. London: Robert Hale & Co.

TEP (1995) *Post–16 Manufacturing*. London: Middlesex University: Technology Enhancement Programme.

Thorne, E. (1979) 'The two faces of home economics', *The Journal of Consumer Studies*, No **3**, 127.

Thorne, E. (1981) 'The role of home economics in the National Economy', *Housecraft*, **March**, 48.

Townsend, G. (1983) 'Problem solving Essex style', *Modus*, **January**, 25.

Wadsworth, N. (1986) 'This subject suffers sexist images. It's literature and resources are riddled with them', *ILEA Contact*, **December**, 8–9.

Watson, D. M. (1993) *The Impact Summary*. London: Kings College.

Watts, M. (1994) *Problem Solving in Science and Technology*. London: David Fulton.

Whyld, J. (1983) *Sexism in the Secondary Curriculum*. London: Harper and Row.

Whyte, J. (1980) 'Home economics and sex differentiation in the secondary school curriculum', *The Journal of Consumer Studies and Home Economics*, **4**, 347–61.

Wynn, B. (1983) 'Home Economics'. In *Sexism in the Secondary Curriculum*. London: Harper and Row.

Yoxall, A. (1965) *A History of the Teaching of Domestic Economy*. Bath: Cedric Chivers.

Software

'Nutrients' and 'Labeller' (1994) HIASS

Suppliers of sensors and data logging equipment

Commotion, Unit 11, Tannery Road, Kent TN9 1RF. Tel: 01732 773399
Philip Harris, Lynn Lane, Shenstone, Staffs WS14 0EE. Tel: 01543 480077
TTS systems, Unit 4, Park Road, Chesterfield S42 5UY. Tel: 01246 850085

Some useful addresses for software

British Nutrition Foundation. Tel: 0171 404 6504. EatMeter – simple dietary analysis program

Further information

For further information about the work of the Royal College of Art Schools Technology Project please address enquiries to: Schools Technology Project, RCA, Kensington Gore, London SW7 2EU. Tel: 0171 590 4246.

For further information about the books acknowledged in the figure captions, please contact: Hodder & Stoughton Direct Services Bookpoint Ltd., Freepost OF 1488, Abingdon, Oxfordshire)X14 4YY. Tel: 01235 400405.

Index

Printed in the United Kingdom
by Lightning Source UK Ltd.
102667UKS00002B/1-10